GLIMPSES
OF
GLORY
THE REGIMENTAL HISTORY
OF THE
61ST ILLINOIS VOLUNTEERS
WITH REGIMENTAL ROSTER

Drew D. Dukett

Heritage Books, Inc.

Published 1999 by

HERITAGE BOOKS, INC.
1540E Pointer Ridge Place
Bowie, Maryland 20716

1-800-398-7709
www.heritagebooks.com

ISBN 0-7884-1405-4

A Complete Catalog Listing Hundreds of Titles
On History, Genealogy, and Americana
Available Free Upon Request

Table of Contents

Introduction

I consider it an honor and a privilege to detail the chronology of the 61st Illinois Volunteers during this country's most pivotal event in its relatively short history, <u>The American Civil War</u>.

The pages that follow are more than mere dates and places; they also contain the thoughts and emotions of the common, and not so common, soldier. When studying a particular event in history, it is essential to capture these thoughts and emotions to lend perspective to the event. Additionally, capturing these feelings allows one to vicariously experience the events, thereby enhancing the reader's adventure.

This Regimental history is unique in that the battles the 61st fought are viewed from two perspectives. The big picture is first articulated. In other words, the overall objective from General Grant's perspective is stated for a particular theater of operation. Finally, the 61st's role in these operations is expressed.

As the story of the 61st Regiment unfolds, the role of logistics is often noted. Throughout eighteen years of military experience, the author's area of expertise has centered much around the logistics field. Although many arguments focus on tactical aspects, more often than not, the outcome of a battle or campaign is essentially decided by which side possesses the superior logistical network. The overall Union victory undoubtedly supports this statement.

The purpose for writing this book is to demonstrate the significant contribution the

61st made during the conflict. They did not fight in the more famous battles of the Civil War, (except Shiloh). Still the role they played was very important to the overall outcome of the war. It is the author's intent that the reader comes to appreciate the sacrifices these men and their families endured during this crisis in our nation's history.

Acknowledgments

There are many people to recognize relative to this fifteen month project which I have thoroughly enjoyed. I would like to issue a hearty ("Thanks Sweetie") to my wife, Laura, who typed 90% of this book. She also encouraged me in ways she probably does not realize, but they are very much appreciated.

I would like to thank Mrs. Emily Esarey of Gregory Farm, and Mrs. Wanda Ward for proofreading this work and making suggestions. Your efforts in assisting me with this book are immeasurable. Thank you.

A special thanks also goes out to Mr. James Esarey of Gregory Farm. The assistance he provided with local primary and secondary sources proved to be invaluable. He has also assisted me in other ways that are incalculable. Thanks Jim!

I would also like to recognize the Jefferson Barracks Historic Site (St. Louis, MO.) for providing me information on Benton Barracks. The Illinois State Archives was also very helpful in providing me copies of extracts of the Official Record of the Civil War, and selected primary sources.

Linda Evans, (not the actress), of the Chicago Historical Society provided copies of the James Lawrence papers which added to the quality of this work.

The president of the Lawrenceville Historical Society (Mike Neal) deserves recognition for pointing me in the right direction to find biographical information on Lieutenant Colonel Daniel Grass. At times, it seemed like a wild goose chase, but the search ended with success in Coffeyville, Kansas.

A special Thank You goes out to the ladies at the Carrollton Public Library, (Donna Droste, and Jean McGuire). Their assistance with the back issues of the *Carrollton Gazette* was a big help.

I would like also to acknowledge Mr. William Alfeld and the Greene County Historical Society for providing select primary sources that proved to be essential in writing this book.

I would also like to thank the Illinois Army National Guard (in Springfield, Illinois) for all their assistance, particularly Mark Whitlock and the Illinois State Military Museum. Also, Bud Roberts, and Richard Strode, Both proved to be essential in making this project complete.

The United States Military History Institute (Carlisle, Pennsylvania) Mrs. Marilyn Hagerstrand (Waukesha, Wisconsin), and Mr. Steve Hicks (Scottville, Illinois) provided primary source material that proved to be invaluable. Thank you.

Finally, Thanks goes out to my mentor in this project, Dr. Charles White of American Military University. His encouragement and support have been instrumental in the culmination of this book. Thanks.

Illustrations

CHAPTER 1

Call to Arms

Illinois, named after the Illinois Indians, means "tribe of superior men".[1] Nicholas Perrot, a Frenchman, was the first white man to visit the Illinois territory in 1671. His destination was Chicago where M. Talon dispatched him for the purpose of inviting the Indians to a peace convention in Green Bay, Wisconsin.[2]

The first settlement for which there is any authentic proof was Fort St. Louis on the Illinois River in 1682; this fort was soon abandoned. Therefore the oldest permanent settlement in Illinois was at Kaskaskia (which was also the first state capitol). It was located six miles above the Kaskaskia River's confluence with the Mississippi and the Prairie Du Rocher rivers, near Fort de Chartress.[3]

Fort de Chartress was built by the Mississippi Company in 1718. Serving the dual purpose it was the military headquarters of the Commandant for Illinois, and was touted as being "The most impregnable fortress in North America." Additionally, Fort de Chartress served as the center for wealth, culture, and fashion in the West at this time.[4]

The French, who were in control of the Illinois territory during this epoch, experienced positive and meaningful relations with the local Indians. Together, they explored remote rivers, hunted, and became quite good friends. The French introduced Christianity to the Illinois Indians, and on many occasions, they worshiped together. This utopia came to an end in 1765 when the country passed into the hands of the English. The

French settlers, not willing to be subjected to English rule, promptly packed up and left Illinois.[5]

In 1787, an ordnance was passed by the US Congress, thus forming the Northwest Territory, which included the Illinois territory (the Ordnance of 1787). This ordnance had three primary points: the first excluded slavery from the territory forever; the second provided land for public schools, giving one township for a seminary, and every section numbered sixteen in each township; (that is one-thirty-sixth of all lands) for public schools; the third point prohibited the adoption of any constitution or enactment of any laws which would nullify any existing contracts.[6]

On February 3rd, 1809, by an act of the US Congress, the Northwest Territory was broken up. Illinois, which included modern-day Wisconsin, became a county of Indiana. This entire area was populated by 9000 people.[7]

On December 3rd, 1818 Illinois, now separated from the above lands, became the 21st state to join the United States of America.[8] Shadrach Bond served as Illinois' first governor with a salary of $1000.00 per year. When the legislature first convened they drafted a state constitution and adopted, almost verbatim, the territorial code for penalties. For example: whipping, stocks and pillory were used for minor offenses. And for offenses such as arson, rape, and horse stealing, death by hanging was the punishment. The penalties were modified somewhat in 1821, because they were deemed too harsh. [9]

The first state capitol, Kaskaskia, was also adopted in 1818. Later the capitol was moved to Vandalia before Springfield became the current Illinois state capitol in 1839. [10]

The first settlers of what is now known as Greene County, Illinois, originally migrated from the southern states of Kentucky, Tennessee, Virginia, and the Carolinas, with a few New Englanders thrown in as well. There were undoubtedly people who settled in present-day Greene County as early as 1813, but there is no evidence to prove this. John Allen is credited as being the first known settler in Greene County when he moved up from Jersey County to settle in Kane Township. [11] Also, one of the first settlers in Greene County, near the White Hall Township, was Colonel Charles Gregory.[12] He was the authors wife's great-great-great grandfather, and her parents, Jim and Emily Esarey, continue to live on the same farm which was established on January 8th, 1821. Twelve days later on January 20, 1821 Governor Bond signed the document establishing Greene County. At this time Greene County was quite large, geographically speaking, it included all of what are now Jersey, Macoupin, Scott, and Morgan counties. This newly created county was named for the famous Revolutionary War officer, Nathanael Greene.[13]

General Nathanael Greene, known as a good strategist, was considered the second best general in the young Continental Army, second to George Washington. His most well known engagements were in South Carolina and Georgia, conducting a series of hit-and-run harassing operations that attrited the British supplies and personnel to the point when they were ultimately forced to withdraw back to Virginia where their fate awaited them at Yorktown.[14]

With the election of the United States' 16th President, Abraham Lincoln, on November 6, 1860, the southern states feared their institution of slavery was in jeopardy.[15]

Consequently, in December of this same year, South Carolina seceded from the Union of the United States.[16] Other states soon followed and by April of 1861 a civil war was inevitable. This inevitability was sparked by a small Union fort in Charleston Harbor, South Carolina. This fort, called Fort Sumter, needed a resupply of food and other provisions. South Carolina regarded Fort Sumter as a post of foreign power on its territory, and the Confederate government authorized General P.G.T. Beauregard to secure the surrender of the fort. He bombarded the fort for thirty-four hours, inflicted no casualties, but did force the surrender of the garrison that was short of supplies with no hope of replenishment.[17]

On April 14, 1861, President Lincoln initiated a call-up of 75,000 volunteers for three months duty to put down the insurrection. The following day, April 15th, Governor Yates of Illinois called a special session of the state's Congress to enact laws and adopt measures necessary to comply with Lincoln's proclamation.[18] Governor Yates had dictated that Illinois' quota would be six regiments of 780 men. Additionally, Governor Yates dictated that each company would consist of one captain, one first lieutenant, one second lieutenant, four sergeants, four corporals, two musicians, and eighty men.[19]

A regiment would consist of one colonel, one major, one first lieutenant, one command sergeant major, two principal musicians, and ten companies. Each company would elect its own officers, and when several companies meet at the place of rendezvous, they would elect their own regimental officers. No one under the age of 18, or over the age 45, would be accepted for duty. Springfield was the place where the rendezvous would occur when regiments formed. The first six regiments to report to Springfield would be the ones to go, other units would encamp near Springfield and await further instructions.[20]

The folks in Greene County did not immediately get involved in the war effort but by Fall of 1861, it looked like this little insurrection might drag out a little longer than expected. As mentioned previously, Greene County was populated by a large number of Southerners. At the time the Civil War began in 1861, it is estimated that 90 percent of the inhabitants fell into this category with a large majority of them claiming Democratic politics.[21]

President Lincoln and Governor Yates, knowing the political make-up of the Greene County area, made a very smart political move. They appointed Jacob Fry, a Colonel in the Illinois Militia, and charged him with raising a regiment from the Greene County area. [22] Jacob Fry was a lifelong Democrat and was probably the most prominent citizen in the area.

Jacob Fry was born on September 20, 1799, in Fayette County, Kentucky. His father, Barnhardt, had served in the Revolutionary War and was a native of Maryland. Jacob was the youngest of six children and obtained his education in a log cabin.[23] At the age of 20, he moved to Greene County, Illinois and was credited with building the first house in the town of Carrollton, which was and to this day remains the county seat. On May 25th of 1826, Jacob Fry married Miss Emily Turney at Carrollton. Miss Turney was the daughter of the late General James Turney, formerly of

Tennessee. At the first county court ever held in Greene County, Jacob was appointed constable and subsequently became Deputy Sheriff. After holding this position for six years, he became Sheriff of the county. He did such a fine job that he was elected to five consecutive terms.[24]

When the Black Hawk Indian war broke out in 1831, Jacob Fry was appointed a Lieutenant Colonel under Colonel Henry. They moved north to Rock Island where his unit was disbanded and sent home because it was no longer needed. The next year, in 1832, Black Hawk was stirring up trouble again and Jacob Fry was recalled, this time as a full Colonel in command of his own regiment as a part of General Whiteside's Brigade. Again, when they reached Rock Island they were disbanded; but at the request of the Governor, Colonel Fry raised a regiment of disbanded troops for twenty days service to guard the frontier from possible hostile Indians; after twenty days they, too, were disbanded. Colonel Fry was then sent to LaSalle, Illinois where he was elected Colonel of a regiment of new recruits, forming a part of General Henry's Brigade.

While at Mud Lake near the Rock River, the Brigade was joined under General Atkinson's regular troops, which constituted a combined effort in this region. Scouts had reported to General Henry and Colonel Fry that there were Indians in close proximity to their location. They wasted no time moving up to the Rock River where they encountered a handful of marauders. They finally caught up with the Indians at the Wisconsin River and a short battle ensued there in the late afternoon. But, because of the impending darkness, many of the Indians escaped across the river. Word was sent to General

Atkinson of the engagement and he arrived the next morning with the main body of his troops. They pursued the Indians to the mouth of the Bad Ax Creek. This battle ended the Black Hawk War. Colonel Fry then took charge of the Brigade and proceeded to Dixon, Illinois where he was mustered out of the service. Because of acts of heroism and bravery he was promoted Brigadier General, and subsequently to Major General in the Illinois militia.[25]

After the Black Hawk War he was elected by the Illinois State legislature to serve as Canal Commissioner for nine years in Lockport, Illinois where he also served with distinction.[26] In 1850, Jacob headed for California. He remained in Sacramento for three years pursuing a mercantile career and then turning his attentions to mining where he became quite successful. Because of his political experience in relation to being a canal commissioner, he was overwhelmingly elected to the California State Senate. He served one term and returned to Ottawa, Illinois.

His political connections while serving in the California State Senate served him well. By appointment of President James Buchanan, with direct influence of his friend Stephen Douglas, he received an appointment to the responsible position of Collector of Customs at Chicago, Illinois.

The subsequent years leading up to the Civil War found Jacob Fry becoming more and more outspoken in favor of his friend Stephen Douglas and of Democratic politics in general. In 1861, Jacob Fry, 62 years old, was back in Carrollton on his 640-acre farm, satisfied to live the remainder of his life farming, when Governor Yates offered a commission he accepted willingly.[27]   Wasting no time with his new appointment, Colonel Fry drafted a letter to *the Carrollton Gazette* calling for volunteers from Greene, Scott, Jersey, and Calhoun Counties.[28]

The Greene County Fairgrounds located a half-mile east of Carrollton, Illinois was designated the "Camp of Instruction" for Colonel Fry's Regiment.[29]   This location is still the county fairgrounds, which consists of forty acres.   John Reddish was made the commander of Company D under Colonel Fry because, he too, had Black Hawk War experience. Captain Reddish was a kind-hearted man that everyone admired and looked up to but was terrible at company drill and barely literate.[30] From October of 1861 to February of 1862 the regiment spent most of its time drilling and recruiting during these cold winter months.

When a volunteer showed up to enlist the first stop was to see the regimental surgeon to ascertain his physical fitness.[31]   At Camp Carrollton the Surgeon was Leonidas Clemmons. His method of determining fitness involved two or three taps on the chest, and running his hands over the shoulders, back and limbs. If everything looked good and nothing was missing you were declared fit for duty.[32] Immediately following the physical examination, the volunteer was taken to the adjutant's tent where an oath of enlistment was signed and the volunteer sworn in.   Next stop was the quartermaster tent for clothing issue; this consisted of a pair of light blue pants, as well as a similar looking overcoat with a cape, dark blue jacket, heavy shoes and wool socks, a little French-army style hat, a gray wool undershirt and underclothing.   Additionally they were given a knapsack, and were told that they would be issued a haversack, canteen, etc. at a later time. It was also the custom in the regiment to give an enlistment bonus, a two-day furlough upon signing up.[33]

As of November 30, 1861, Illinois was doing quite well in providing soldiers for the Union Army. Eighty-five thousand had volunteered including Colonel U.S. Grant, who was appointed Regimental Commander of the 21st Illinois Volunteers.[34] The initial call for volunteers was so overwhelming in Illinois that Colonel Grant commented "There were so many more volunteers than had been called for that the question whom to accept was quite embarrassing for the governor."[35]

Camp Carrollton was surrounded by a seven to eight foot timber plank fence with one entrance and exit located on the north side primarily to keep the soldiers in camp. No enlisted man was permitted outside without a pass signed by his captain and approved by Colonel Fry. Drilling was conducted inside the camp, but for skirmish drill the men were allowed outside so as to have plenty of room to maneuver.[36]

The barracks for the men were crudely thrown together and consisted of lumber covered with clapboard and straw. Each barracks housed a company with two rows of bunkbeds inside them. Leander Stillwell commented in the quarters of Company D, "They were abodes of comfort and luxury compared to what we frequently had later"[37]

The 61st spent a good deal of its time drilling. The "bible" utilized for training was *Hardee's Infantry Tactics*. It was generally accepted that *Hardee's Tactics* were fairly easy to understand; the main points being promptness, care, and close attention. While at Camp Carrollton, the volunteers were drilled in the school of "the Company", "the Soldier", and skirmish drill, with dress parade at sunset. It should be noted that the 61st did not receive their muskets until they arrived at Benton Barracks, Missouri.[38]

While at Camp Carrollton the meals generally consisted of bread, coffee, fresh meat at some meals and salt meat at others, Yankee beans, rice, onions, Irish and sweet potatoes, with stewed dried apples on occasion for supper. The salt meat, as a rule, was pickled pork and fat side meat which was also known as "sow belly". When the 61st was in the field, a usual meal consisted of coffee, sow belly, Yankee beans, and hard tack (basically a hard cracker); there was, of course, occasional forage providing fruits and berries. Food was always a problem in one fashion or another, not only for the 61st, but for the entire Army overall. Many of these young soldiers did not know how to prepare food properly and generally had no concept of hygiene, "the death of many a poor boy, especially during our first two or three months in the field, is chargeable to the bad cooking of his food." [39]

Many soldiers looked forward to and enjoyed the time between taps (after dress parade) and lights out. It was considered "the jolliest time of the day". The troops would engage in what was known as "prairie dogging" This entailed visiting other barracks and singing all sorts of patriotic songs that were popular· at the time. One such song that appeared during this period was "The Happy Land of Canaan" in commemoration of the January 19,1862 Union victory at the Battle of Mill

Springs, Kentucky, where Confederate General Felix Zollicoffer was killed.

> Old Zolly's gone,
> and Secesh will have to
>   mourn,
> For they thought he would
>   do to depend on;
> But he made his last stand
>   on
> The rolling Cumberland,
> And was sent to the happy
>   land of Canaan."[40]

The health of the soldiers was very good during these winter months. There were only a few cases of measles and the usual assortment of colds. A good many of the men were back-woodsmen and farmers and were quite familiar with home remedies for colds. For example, boiling the bark of a hickory tree made hickory bark tea. It was green in color and intensely bitter, about a quart served hot at bedtime usually did the trick.[41]

On February 16, 1862 General Grant achieved a glorious victory at Fort Donelson which elated the men of the 61st. But, they also feared what their fate may be, "...could the war end, and that we would see no actual service, and never even fire a shot?" They thought they might be discharged and sent home to hear war stories from other veterans who had gone off to fight. Little did they know at this time, that they would have many opportunities to "fire a shot" in the months and years to follow.[42]

The day had finally come. The boys from Camp Carrollton received their marching orders. They were to depart February 27, 1862 for Alton, Illinois and there, be transported via river to St. Louis, Missouri. (Benton Barracks). Colonel Fry, the Regimental Commander, in a letter to Governor Yates on the day preceding their departure from Camp Carrollton (February 26, 1862) expressed several concerns. In his letter he stated that he was at an "extreme" disadvantage because the regiment had not yet been assigned the 61st designation (this happens at Benton Barracks). With typical Army bureaucracy, no supplies could be obtained from the US Quartermaster without a unit designation.[43]

A second concern Colonel Fry had was that a Captain Wilson was supposed to come to Camp Carrollton to muster the regiment into service and as of that late date he had not appeared.

The biggest concern Colonel Fry had was his regiment's strength; he only had three full companies and the rest were incomplete. Ten companies were needed to form a regiment and Colonel Fry knew that a regiment normally does not receive its numerical designation prior to being a full regiment. Colonel Fry's fear was that the regiment would be broken up and used as fillers in other regiments. Therefore he finished his letter to Governor Yates, by pleading him to intercede on the regiment's behalf to ensure that it would not be split up.[44]

At 10:00 A.M. on February 27, 1862 the regiment formed up and started marching south for Alton. Leading the way was (A) company a.k.a. the "Woodson Guards" (The majority of the boys were from the township of Woodson). Just two weeks earlier Captain Simon Ohr (the commander) was presented a "beautiful" company flag, hand made by the ladies of Woodson and presented to Captain Ohr by D.M. Woodson himself.[45]

The reporter for the *Carrollton Gazette* commented that "It was the most amazing military spectacle ever witnessed in these parts." Hundreds of people from all over the county turned out to send them off with cheers, pats on the back, and other patriotic displays. All along the route to Jerseyville people came out and cheered the boys enthusiastically. Approximately halfway between Carrollton and Jerseyville was the township of Kane, where Colonel Fry's home was located. Having sent word home a couple days prior, Colonel Fry instructed his family to prepare a meal for the boys as they would be passing very near his farm. Although it is not known exactly what was served, the entire regiment was fed by Colonel Fry's family and they departed at 2:30 p.m. for Jerseyville.[46]

The regiment arrived at Jerseyville just about sunset. Word had gone out that Colonel Fry's regiment was "leaving for the front" and all of the country folks came to town to see the spectacle.[47] The regiment was met at the outskirts of town by a delegation of citizens and a light detachment of artillery commanded by a Major Sanford. The Jerseyville band also escorted the regiment into town. The unit was marched to the front of the National Hotel where they were welcomed by the chairmen of the Reception Committee, Dr. Buffington. Naturally, this welcome speech did not occur until both the regimental band, and the Jerseyville Band finished their assortment of patriotic tunes.

The regiment, now totaling about 700 men, were quartered overnight by the hospitality of the people of Jerseyville. They were housed in the Courthouse, Clandennin's Hall, the Baptist Church, and Morean's Warehouse.[48]

The next morning (Friday, February 28,1862) at 8:00 AM the regiment was formed on Main Street and, with three cheers of "Hip Hip Hooray!" from the regiment in gratitude to the citizens of Jersyville, then departed for Alton. Before the regiment could get out of town they were met by an army of wagons totaling 127. The country folks had come from miles around and insisted that they would transport the entire regiment to Alton, Illinois. Their invitations were accepted "with pleasure". It was reported that this wagon train stretched out over a mile and a half.[49]

A few miles north of Alton the regiment would pass a popular school for girls called the *Monticello Female Seminary*.
The girls had heard that Colonel Fry's boys would be passing by, so when the men arrived, there were "a hundred or more girls with red, white, and blue ribbons in their hair, and on their persons as well. They waved white handkerchiefs at the boys and looked their 'sweetest'." The boys reciprocated with vociferous Hoorays! and hat-waving until they were out of sight of the Seminary.[50]

The regiment had arrived at Alton just about sundown where they were immediately placed on board their transportation to St. Louis, the side wheel steamboat, "City of Alton". Guards were promptly stationed to prevent the men from leaving the boat. In typical Army fashion someone had failed to coordinate the rations for the evening meal, there were none. The officers pooled what money they could and went out on the economy and purchased provisions. Supper that evening consisted of a barrel of oyster crackers washed down with as much river water as one could drink.[51]

The regiment arrived the next morning at St. Louis where they debarked and marched out to Benton Barracks. At the time, the barracks were clear out of town on the north side, past the suburbs. The remnants of Benton Barracks are no longer there today, but it was located on land that is now downtown St. Louis. As early as August 21, 1861 troops from Illinois, Iowa, Indiana, and Ohio began arriving at St. Louis for training.

Benton Barracks was named after the late Senator Thomas Hart Benton, who also acquired some fame from his Mexican War contributions. General Fremont was the commanding general of the St. Louis area, and was Benton's son-in-law. The barracks, located on 150 acres, were constructed in five east-west rows, each 740 feet long and 40 feet wide. Warehouses, stables, and headquarters were there as well.[52]

The first commander was Colonel B.L.E. Bonneville, he was subsequently followed by General Samuel R. Curtis on September 18, 1861. In order to maintain control of the area, General Curtis was given authority over Benton Barracks, and all other facilities, civilian or military, within a one mile radius. Curtis required all the civilians within this radius to move out. All but one person, James Horne Tooke, complied. In an encounter with Tooke (a self-proclaimed atheist), General Curtis solved the problem and appointed Tooke, Chaplain of Benton Barracks. He became known as "Parson Tooke" and accepted his role agreeably.[53]

The next commander of Benton Barracks was William T. Sherman, beginning on December 23, 1861. He had been placed under the command of

General Henry W. Halleck, Commander of the Department of Missouri. Sherman was sent to Missouri because he was considered unfit for duty in the East, where he had had a nervous breakdown of sorts. He was commander less than two months before he was ordered back to combat duty under General Halleck.[54]

In June of 1862, the War Department ended the practice of allowing paroled Union soldiers to go home on furlough and required them to go to one of three parole camps, based upon the geography of their units. Soldiers from Illinois, Iowa, Minnesota, Missouri, and Wisconsin were to report to Jefferson Barracks. This site proved unsuitable and consequently, Benton Barracks was chosen as the site for the camp of paroled Union prisoners. The paroled soldiers were generally dissatisfied, some even refusing to pull guard duty for their own safety on the grounds that bearing arms violated the conditions of their parole. [55]

Benton Barracks also witnessed the first black soldiers to be mustered into service in December of 1863. They were initially designated the first, second, and third Missouri Infantry (Colored). Within a few months they became known as the 62nd, 65th, and 67th regiments U.S.C.T. (United States Colored Troops), in a general reorganization of the black troops. For these soldiers, Benton Barracks was much more than a military encampment. The Christian Commission organized schools to teach the blacks how to read and write. These simple skills had previously been denied by law to slaves. In September of 1865, after the war, the 150 acres that Benton Barracks sat upon was returned to its owner, Colonel John O'Fallon.[56]

While at Benton Barracks the regiment from Greene County finally received its designation as "the 61st Illinois Infantry", which surely made Colonel Fry happy. It rained almost non-stop during the regiment's four-week stay at Benton Barracks. The drill grounds became "oceans of mud". Due to these conditions little time was spent drilling, allowing monotony and boredom to set in.[57]

It was at Benton Barracks that the 61st received their weapons. They were issued the Austrian Rifle Musket, (it was common for Western troops to be issued foreign-made muskets). The 61st used these until June of 1863 when they exchanged them for the Model 1863 Springfield Rifled Musket. The 61st used the Springfield rifle until they were mustered out in September of 1865. The general reaction among the men was that it was a very efficient weapon and much lighter than the Austrian version. Therefore, it received overwhelming approval.[58]

When the 61st left Camp Carrollton locals noticed two of the companies did not possess a flag (Companies B and G). The townspeople immediately started soliciting donations to raise the money estimated to be $40.00 per flag. The $80.00 was raised and sent off to the 61st quartermaster, First Lieutenant Vedder, at Benton Barracks for the purchase of the two flags. The two company commanders (Captain Mann, and Captain Nulton) were extremely grateful and acknowledged their apprecieation in a letter that was published in the local paper, the *Carrollton Gazette*. [59]

It was at Benton Barracks that mustering the 61st into service was completed. There was one small glitch though; the 61st was one company (Company K) short of the ten required to be a full regiment. It would not be until March of 1865 that the 61st would get its full complement of men. Because of this technicality, Colonel Fry was only commissioned a Lieutenant Colonel. The 61st also witnessed five deaths at Benton Barracks due to disease. In the months and years to follow, death from disease would claim many lives, as it did in other regiments of both Union and Confederate Soldiers.

March 22nd, 1862 was a fateful day for the 61st Illinois Infantry. Headquarters Department of the Mississippi issued Special Order 31. This order stated that the 61st would proceed immediately to Major General Grant at Savannah, Tennessee.[60] No one in the 61st would know at the time that their final destination would be reached on March 31st, 1862, at an unheard of place called "Pittsburg Landing", but forever to be remembered as "Shiloh".

Chapter 2

Shiloh

The Battle of Shiloh would prove to be a defining moment for the boys of the 61st Illinois. They had yet to see the "Elephant", but would finally now get their chance. The 61st was immediately placed in General B.M. Prentiss' Division, which subsequently became known as the "Raw Division".[61] Within General Prentiss' line, the 61st occupied the almost extreme left flank.[62]

To give a brief overview of the order of battle on the morning of April 6, 1862, we find General W.T. Sherman's Division securing the right flank of the Union line. In the middle and slightly to the rear is the division of General McClernand. And to his left is Prentiss' Division. The extreme left of the Union line consisted of one of Sherman's small brigades commanded by General Stuart. There were two divisions held in reserve. The first was General Hurlbut's Division located to the rear of Prentiss. General W.H.L. Wallace, who was located at a great distance to the rear of Sherman, formed the second reserve division.[63]

During the 61st's seven-day transport from St. Louis to Pittsburg Landing the soldiers had to eat hard tack, raw fat, and drank river water until they reached their destination. Upon arriving at Pittsburg Landing the unit was quartered in Sibley tents (small conical shaped white tents that housed up to 12 soldiers). Many of the men where extremely happy to be on dry land again, and looked forward to cooked meals. [64]

The 61st was used to eating its meals in mess hall fashion whereby a couple of soldiers prepared the meal for the entire company. The men would now have to get used to preparing meals for just the members of their tent (up to 12 people). Each man would take his turn at preparing the food.[65]

The men did not know much about baking or cooking in those days so it goes without saying that whatever food was edible, was very poor in taste and quality. As a consequence of this; improperly cooked food (especially sow belly, pork), the change in climate and water, and the neglect of proper sanitation measures in the camps, diarrhea became epidemic. Everyone suffered from it the first six weeks, the only difference being the severity one suffered.[66] The only relief a soldier could get came at the hands of the sutlers (merchants who followed the various armies with wagons full of goods to sell to the soldiers). In one day sutlers made five hundred dollars selling blackberry syrup to the soldiers to alleviate their diarrhea.[67] This first major battle of the Civil War would be a prelude to many more to follow, one of the most relevant being the losses due to disease. Leander Stillwell comments that "This loss to the Union armies in Tennessee in the spring of 62 by disease would undoubtedly surpass the casualties of the great battle".[68]

The fateful morning of April 6, 1862 was a beautiful spring day; not a cloud in the sky. The camp was bustling with activities such as breakfast and preparing for the 9:00 AM inspection. Then, out of nowhere a loud "pum" was heard off to the right in the direction of Shiloh church. Then there were several more loud "pums" in succession, and everyone rose to their feet and wondered what that noise was.[69]

It wasn't long before the first dull ominous growl of massive musket fire was heard to the southwest of their position. The Battle of Shiloh was on. It took a few seconds for it to sink in that the new soldiers of the 61st were actually in a battle, and when it did the men went into quick action to strap on cartridge belts and start loading weapons. Despite the obvious confusion that ensued, the companies were formed and the regiment was formed in line. Colonel Fry gave the order to "load at will" despite the fact the men had already taken the initiative to do so, then Colonel Fry told the boys "Gentleman, remember your state, and do your duty today like brave men".[70]

The 61st advanced forward across a small field to the edge of a tree line, which brought the unit on line with the unit on their right flank. The roaring of musket fire got louder and louder as the Rebels advanced, and off in the near distance the sight of gunpowder could now be seen. Within five minutes the Rebels had advanced to within firing range of the 61st, and the men wasted no time in letting the Confederates know that *they* were a force to be reckoned with. After firing two to three volleys, the 61st was ordered to fall back across the field at the edge of the wood line near their tents. Basically, they had to fall back because the middle of the line was being pushed back and the 61st was in danger of being flanked.[71]

They held this position for about an hour and ten minutes, and were again instructed to fall back. Again, the enemy had broken through to the right of the 61st. The first time the unit fell back it was a fairly well organized retreat executed with admirable professionalism; but the second one was not so orderly. This time enemy troops could be seen

21

breaching the line. When the order came to fall back again, a general panic set in and the entire unit ran helter-skelter to the rear. They had run about a half-mile when they came upon General Hurlbut's reserve division forming a second line. The 61st took up a position on this line.[72]

During the next few hours, from approximately 9:00 AM to noon, there was a lull in the fighting primarily due to the fact that the Rebels had stopped their advance when they overran the Union encampments. The reason the Confederates stopped was to eat the food that was cooking over the fires because they had consumed almost all of their rations before they even left Corinth, Mississippi five days before the battle.

It was during this lull at approximately 10:00 AM that the 61st was detached from General Prentiss' division to General Hurlbut's division to support an artillery battery that was still engaged. It was at this time that many members of the 61st witnessed General Grant checking the line and assessing the situation. Leander Stillwell commented that "Grant rode through the storm with perfect indifference, seemingly paying no more attention to the missiles than if they had been paper wads."[73]

The 61st remained here in support of the artillery battery until approximately 2:00 PM, at which time they were ordered up to the left of General Hurlbut's line to relieve a regiment that had been engaged the entire day. The men of the 61st saw many Union soldiers of this regiment who were shot to death holding this line. They had stayed on this line until all cartridges were expended. They were then relieved by another regiment. The 61st, however

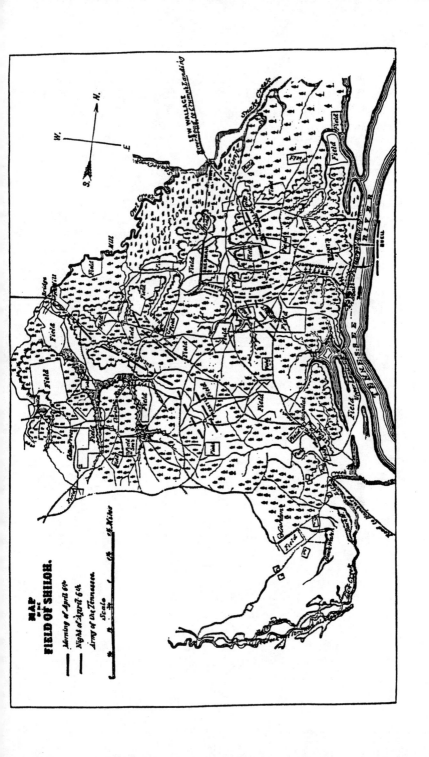

had drawn more ammunition and returned to guarding the artillery battery. The battle raged on unceasingly all afternoon, from all directions, the roar of musket and cannon fire was deafening.[74]

At approximately 5:00 PM everything became ominously quiet, then the order was given once again to fall back. The 61st did not get far when they started receiving musket fire all up and down the line from their former position, again a general panic ensued among all the regiments in this sector and they crowded the road leading back to Pittsburg Landing.[75]

When they arrived near Pittsburg Landing they found General Hurlbut's last line of defense. They quickly joined ranks with this line along the road leading down to the landing. McClernand had fallen back and was on Hurlbut's right flank, and Sherman was on McClernand's right flank forming the final line of defense for the Union.[76]

At this stage of the battle the men of the 61st were tired and or demoralized from the day's protracted events. To make matters worse, it was discovered that General Prentiss and a significant number of his division (2200) were captured. Just when matters seemed to be at their worst, martial music could be heard coming from the vicinity of the landing. A band was playing a tune called "Dixie Land". And a column of men were seen marching up from the landing. It was obvious these men had not been in the fight because their faces were not covered with powder smoke and they were wearing haversacks. They just looked too neat! It was soon discovered that this was the 36th Indiana, the advance guard of General Buell's army.[77]

The original plan was for Grant and Buell to meet at Pittsburg Landing to join forces for an assault on Corinth, Mississippi, located about thirty miles south of Pittsburg Landing. The Confederate Army, under the command of General Albert Sidney Johnston, had to attack Grant by surprise before Buell arrived thereby maximizing the Confederates' hopes of victory. The plan was a good one, and may have succeeded with a victory for the Rebels on the first day had it not been for Albert Sidney Johnston's death on this fateful afternoon. Next in command was General P.G.T. Beauregard, the hero of Fort Sumter, who failed to organize a coordinated attack with the daylight remaining. Although attacks were made in piecemeal fashion, all were repulsed by Union forces, inflicting heavy casualties to the Rebels. The opportunity had been lost. The thought of one soldier can best sum up the exultation that was felt upon the arrival of Buell's advance guard.

> "In all my obscure military career, never to me was the sight of reinforcing legions so precious and so welcome as on that Sunday evening when the rays of descending sun were flashed back from the bayonets of Buell's advance column as it deployed on the bluffs of Pittsburg Landing."[78]

With the arrival of Buell's army that evening, the Union mounted a counter-offensive the next morning (Monday, April 7, 1862) and drove the Rebels from the battlefield thereby claiming a Union victory, which was sorely needed at this point in the war. (The Union Army in the East had yet to achieve any significant victories.)

The 61st saw no action on Monday; they were held in reserve and never called into battle.[79] In the aftermath of the battle, the green troops of the 61st got to see first-hand the carnage of this famous engagement. For many of the boys it was an eye-opening experience to see the battlefield covered with literally thousands of dead, mangled bodies. One word used to describe the scene was "horrifying".[80]

One of the most memorable sights was the dead that littered the "Peach orchard". (The Confederates had attacked across this large field several times during the first day.) There were so many dead Confederates in this orchard that a man could walk from one end to the other across the corpses and never touch the ground.[81]

In less dramatic terms CPT Lawrence (I Company Commander) described the scene as "The gallant dead are stretched over five miles, and the wounded are almost without number". He further lamented that on the first day when their positions were over run, he lost all of his possessions including paper, stamps, and trunk blankets.[82]

News began spreading throughout the entire country about the events at Pittsburg Landing. It was rumored in the *Carrollton Gazette* that the 61st was captured along with General Prentiss and that half of the unit lay dead.[83] Obviously, a full accounting of the battle had not reached Greene County yet. If it had, the folks would have realized that the 61st was detached to General Hurlbut's division prior to Prentiss' capture.

When supposed-eyewitness accounts started appearing in the papers, another error was made by the *Chicago Tribune*. The *Tribune* specifically mentioned the 61st and three other regiments as being cut to pieces at the initial onslaught and in full retreat; that thousands of troops had taken refuge at the bank of the landing and were utterly demoralized and refused to fight.[84]

These reports were pure nonsense. For example, in General Prentiss' official report, his comments were quite the opposite of what the Tribune reported, "Col. Fry, of the 61st Illinois, with an undrilled regiment fresh in the service, kept his men well forward under every assault until the third line was formed, when he became detached and fought under General Hurlbut."[85]

In the April 26th, 1862, edition of the *Carrollton Gazette* the true accounting of the battle was printed in reference to the 61st being detached to Hurlbut's Division prior to Prentiss's capture. This news obviously relieved many of the folks back home.[86]

Two weeks later, in the May 10th edition of the *Carrollton Gazette*, it was reported that both the *Chicago Tribune* and the *St. Louis Republican* had been besmirching the reputation of the 61st. Further eyewitness accounts attested to the fact that the 61st fought "gallantly"; in fact they were the only regiment that held their positions on the first day. They did not retreat until General Prentiss, himself, ordered Colonel Fry *three times* to fall back; the colonel still did not until it became evident that they were flanked.[87]

Overall, the boys of the 61st fought well for their first battle of the Civil War. During this engagement the regiment suffered 75 casualties, 12 killed, 45 wounded, and 18 missing.[88] Comparatively speaking, the 61st

received rather light losses, which speaks well of the discipline of the regiment. Additionally, they were not in the fight on Monday the 7th which surely played a role in the low casualty rate as well. The Battle of Shiloh was the largest battle of the Civil War up to this point. There were approximately 23,000 casualties combined (North and South) and was one of the hardest fought battles of the entire war. Sherman had remarked in his memoirs that, "The battle of Shiloh, or Pittsburg Landing, was one of the most fiercely contested of the war."[89] Grant also commented in his memoirs that "Shiloh was the severest battle fought in the West during the war, and but few in the East equaled it for hard, determined fighting."[90]

The Battle of Shiloh was a significant victory for a few reasons. First, it affirmed the use of the river networks to move both men and material fairly long distances in the shortest amount of time. Second, it was a much-needed victory for President Lincoln and the Eastern theater because to this point, not much good news had come out of the Eastern theater. Finally, Grant said it best, "The result of the Union victory that gave the men who achieved it great confidence in themselves ever after."[91] Remember, almost all the soldiers and officers had never been in battle before. This victory instilled a confidence that allowed the Union troops to remain on the offensive in the West the remainder of the war.

Chapter 3

"Disappointed" in Mississippi

Within a few days following the glorious victory at Shiloh, the 61st, along with the entire Union Army, now under the command of General H.W. Halleck, followed the Rebels south and set in for the siege at Corinth, Mississippi. As of April 28, 1862, the 61st continued under the direction of acting commander Major Simon P. Ohr. This change was brought about due to the deteriorating health of its commander, Colonel Jacob Fry. During the siege at Corinth, the 61st was moved around quite a bit for the first few weeks until the middle of May, 1862, when they were settled on a point at Owl Creek to the right rear of the main army. Their duty was to guard from a possible attack from this direction. Additionally, as is common with siege warfare, a great deal of time was spent throwing up breast works (logs and earth piled about breast high) and standing picket.[92]

At this point the overwhelming majority of the regiment were still suffering from diarrhea. To make matters worse, outbreaks of malaria and other "Camp Diseases" started to surface too. Morale was at an all-time low during this routinely boring siege. Homesickness was starting to get to some of the men due to the wretched conditions they had to endure.[93]

Despite the unpleasant conditions, there were a couple of positive things in the regiment's favor. While at Owl Creek the men ate extremely well. There was an abundance of beef, pork, ham, and eggs. Also the weather during the early summer was quite pleasant.[94]

The Army Medical Authorities developed what they believed to be, not only the preventative medication, but also the cure for malaria; this treatment became very popular with the boys. It consisted of a gill (5 ounces of whiskey) mixed with some quinine given to each man before breakfast. Morale at least temporarily improved.[95] The siege ended on May 30th, 1862 when the Confederates evacuated the town, and the Union troops moved in unopposed that evening.[96]

On June 6th, under a general reorganization, the 61st, along with the other regiments in the Owl Creek area were transferred to Bethel, Tennessee, a small station on the Mobile and Ohio Railroad located some twenty-five miles to the northwest. A majority of the men were still quite ill. This resulted in stragglers by the score. In fact, when the 61st arrived at Bethel that evening, Company D had only four soldiers to stack arms when they arrived.[97]

The brigade to which the 61st was assigned was given orders to move to Jackson, Tennessee, on June 16th, 1862. This was a town also located on the Mobile and Ohio Railroad approximately 35-40 miles northwest of Bethel. It is noteworthy to mention that this is the point when soldiers started abandoning the cumbersome knapsack for the lighter and more convenient "blanket roll" system. A soldier would fold in the blankets, an extra shirt, and a few other light articles, roll the blanket tight, double it over and tie the two ends together. Then throw the blanket over one shoulder. With the tied ends under the opposite arm the arrangement was complete.[98]

The 61st arrived in Jackson on the evening of June 17th, and settled into camp on the outskirts of town. The regiments quickly got back in the routine of conducting drills; this is something that the units had not had much time for since Shiloh. No sooner did the 61st start their routine of daily drills when an order came down that required immediate execution. The tents were struck and loaded onto the wagon; knapsacks or bed rolls were also made ready. Major Ohr gave the order to "fall in" (Colonel Fry was still too ill to lead the unit) and the men stood in formation awaiting for what was to come next.[99]

It was quickly realized that this was not any minor affair, the entire division at Jackson under the command of General McClernand was told to be ready to load the trains at Jackson. After waiting all day for "the word", it never came. The entire division was told to stay put and continue with what they were doing prior to this somewhat puzzling alert. No one at the time really understood what was going on, and why such a big fuss had been raised over nothing.[100]

It was not learned until years after the war. What happened was General McClernand's division almost became a part of General McClellan's Peninsula Campaign in Virginia. In a dispatch from E.M. Stanton (Secretary of War) to General Halleck, (who at this time, 28 June 1862, was still in charge of the Western Armies) the directive was given to move 25,000 men by the quickest means possible (rail) to Richmond, Virginia, via Baltimore and Washington D.C. The reason is given that McClellan had suffered a "serious" reverse before Richmond the previous day.[101]

Consequently, Halleck sent McClernand a dispatch which stated that he was to collect all of his infantry regiments, and transport them by rail to Columbus, Kentucky, then on to Washington.[102] But that same day, June 30th, President Lincoln personally sent General Halleck an order summarily revoking the order given by Stanton. Obviously the 61st never became a part of the Army of the Potomac which was just fine with the boys of the 61st, because there was not much confidence in the leadership of the Army of the Potomac until, of course, General Grant took charge.[103]

The regiment stayed at Jackson, Tennessee, until July 17th, 1862, when the Brigade that the 61st was a member of under the command of General L.F. Ross was detached to Bolivar, Tennessee, a town about twenty-eight miles to the southwest of Jackson, which was located on the Mississippi Central Railroad. The 61st arrived at Bolivar the next day without incident.[104] A few days after their arrival at Bolivar, scouts had reported that a significant Cavalry force under the command of General Frank Armstrong had moved up from the south. The scouts indicated these forces were planning to conduct guerilla-type operations in the vicinity of Bolivar.[105] This situation caught the eye of General Grant who subsequently reinforced Bolivar from units at Corinth and Jackson. Grant was now the Western Army Commander which took effect on July 17, 1862 when General Halleck departed for Washington to become the General of all Armies.[106]

During this time period of July, August, and part of September, the 61st was kept on their toes, not necessarily by large scale battles, but by a great deal of guerilla activity in its area. A look at the big picture reveals that both the North and South during this period were strategically moving their forces into place and establishing lines of communication for the anticipated clashes.

During the early summer months the commanders were fairly liberal in granting furloughs to the soldiers since there was not much happening. By July, this practice was all but eliminated due to the abuse of this furlough privilege by the soldiers of the 61st.[107]

Desertion was starting to become a problem throughout the entire Army from this point of the war to the end. The problem was not unique to the North because the South experienced the same level if not more desertions than the North. Relative to the 61st an ad appeared in the *Carrollton Gazette* placing a reward of five dollars on three men who deserted from Company A. This money was made available via the federal government because of the ever increasing problem. All indications are that this program did not experience much success. The 61st desertion rate was extremely low; from all accounts there were only a handful of men who deserted during the war.[108]

Advertisements placed by the Greene County Benevolent Society, started running in every edition of the *Gazette* until the end of the war These ads solicited donations of food for destitute families of soldiers who had gone off to war.[109] Unfortunately, this was a common theme throughout the nation; the bread-winner was off to war, leaving the wives and children with next to nothing. Generally, an enlisted soldier made thirteen dollars a month and would try to send as much as he could home. Even if a soldier managed to send home eight or nine dollars for his family, it often was not enough for a family to live on. Another problem that was frequently encountered was the infrequency of pay because of fighting or being on the march. In fact the 61st was not paid from July, 1862 until January 31st, 1863 and then only received two month's pay.[110] This did not help the families back home. Needless to say, benevolent societies in general provided a valuable service during the Civil War.

The 61st, along with the rest of the brigade, departed Bolivar, Tennessee on September 16th and traveled via railroad to Corinth, Mississippi. Subsequently on the 19th, they marched eight miles east in the vicinity of Burnsville, Mississippi, to form a line of battle facing South. It was learned that just two miles away occupying the town of Iuka, Mississippi, was Confederate General Sterling Price with a force of 8000 men.[111]

The 61st was now placed in General E.O.C. Ord's Division, which was formed up about two miles North of Iuka and ready for battle. General Grant instructed Ord that General Rosecrans was maneuvering himself South of Iuka and would attack from the South while Ord would attack from the North in a coordinated effort. Also, Grant told Ord that it would be midday before Rosecrans was ready to attack. He further instructed Ord that he should attack when he hears the gunfire and cannonade coming from Rosecrans' guns.[112]

Although appearing to be a solid plan, the hopes of a fairly certain victory, were quickly laid to rest. This battle is one of those battles in which "Murphy's Law" was in full vigor (anything that could go wrong, would). First, Rosecrans attacked as planned from the south about 2 p.m. and was heavily engaged with Price, but no sign of Ord! In fact, Ord never did attack at all! Well, as it so happened, the wind on this particular day was extremely strong and blowing from the North, in other words away from Ord, who claimed that he never heard Rosecrans' guns, his signal to attack.[113]

When the fighting had ended that evening both Rosecrans and Price had taken significant casualties during the few hours they were engaged. Rosecrans suffered 790 killed and wounded, and Price suffered 700 killed and wounded. At this point Rosecrans made a tactical error. During the night he reorganized his units in order to continue the battle in the morning, but in the process left open one route of escape, the Fulton Road, Price took advantage of this oversight the next morning and slipped right past Rosecrans. Actually, Price wanted to stay and fight it out but was talked out of it by his subordinate commanders, primarily due to the death of General Little (one of Price's Division commanders) during the day's battle. It was feared that his field experience and leadership would be sorely missed and morale was extremely low due to this loss.[114]

That next morning Rosecrans and Ord moved into Iuka to find only that it had been abandoned. Word was sent to Grant that Iuka had been taken and that Price had escaped. Grant proceeded immediately to Iuka (he was only a few miles away at Burnsville). He arrived to find that Rosecrans had not even initiated a pursuit of Price even by cavalry. Grant ordered him to take his command and give pursuit. Rosecrans did for a few miles then went into camp. Grant further commented that he was "disappointed" in the results of the Battle of Iuka.[115]

In the author's opinion it seems incomprehensible that Ord never heard Rosecrans' guns during this fierce fighting

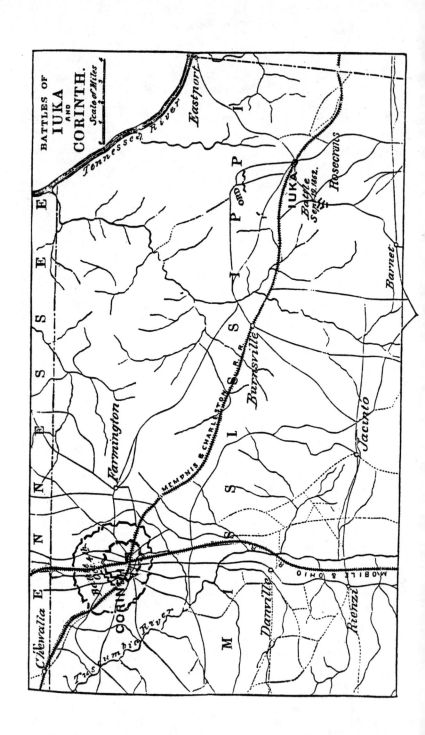

despite the fact that the wind was blowing in the opposite direction! It is difficult to believe that Ord being only two miles to the north did not have some means of intelligence either on the outskirts, of town or even in it. This would seem quite prudent given the tactical situation combined with the known wind direction.

As previously stated, the 61st was assigned to Ord's division to the North, and as an obvious consequence never fired a shot at the Battle of Iuka. They were not even a part of the occupation force on the following morning (September 20th); on this occasion they were left at their current location in reserve. As mentioned, word was sent to Grant that Iuka had been occupied and he proceeded there immediately.[116]

To get from Burnsville to Iuka Grant would have had to pass near the 61st's location. It just so happened that Leander Stillwell had received permission from his company commander to go off into the nearby woods to pick muscadine grapes. He was on his way back to the regiment when he heard the thundering hooves of horses. He ran out to the road just in time to catch a glimpse of General Grant riding at the head of a column of cavalry.[117] Stillwell commented that, "He(Grant) was looking downward as he rode by, and seemed immersed in thought."[118] Stillwell was curious about what troops these were so he asked one of the troops near the rear. The young troop answered, "Company A Fourth Illinois Cavalry, General Grant's Escort."[119] That evening the 61st was drawn back into Burnsville and bivouacked at the "Harrison Hotel". Despite the fact that the hotel had been stripped of all furnishings, the boys enjoyed spending the night somewhere with a roof over their heads.

The next day, (September 21st), they formed up and marched back to Corinth, Mississippi.[120] The 61st reached Corinth that same evening and bivouacked for a couple of days. On the morning of the 24th they marched down to the railhead and loaded boxcars bound North for Jackson, Tennessee. They arrived about noon, transferred trains and moved back to Bolivar, Tennessee. Subsequent trains brought more troops from Corinth to Bolivar because Grant feared that Bolivar or Corinth would be assailed soon. He was hinging on Bolivar.[121]

The 61st arrived at Bolivar that same afternoon and reoccupied their old camp. Then work was done fortifying breastworks for what was believed to be an impending battle. Within a few days Grant had surmised that the attack would now more likely come at Corinth instead of Bolivar. So once again, all troops except the 61st and two other regiments were left to man the garrison at Bolivar. Needless to say, the 61st did not get to participate in the battle of Corinth or the subsequent Battle of Hatchie Bridge. The boys of the 61st felt "mortified" that they had been excluded from both of these battles.[122]

The battle of Corinth was a significant victory for the North. It also was a bloody one, especially for General Van Dorn's Confederates who suffered 1,423 dead, and 2225 taken prisoner, while the Union's losses were 315 killed and 1812 wounded. General Rosecrans again made a mistake here similar to the one he made at Iuka. He failed to give pursuit to a badly wounded foe. The effects of Rosecrans inability to follow Grant's orders were almost disastrous. General Ord was approaching from the south to the aid of Rosecrans when he met the head of Van Dorn's retreating Rebels at Hatchie Bridge. Fortunately, Ord held this bridge and avoided being routed by Van Dorn. The Rebels backtracked to the North, crossed another bridge and escaped.[123]

General Grant summed up the Battle of Corinth as follows:

> "This battle was recognized by me as being a decided victory, though not so complete as I had hoped for, nor nearly so complete as I now think was within easy grasp of the commanding officer at Corinth (Rosecrans). Since the war it is known that the result, as it was, was a crushing blow to the enemy, and felt by him much more than it was appreciated at the North. The Battle relieved me from any further anxiety for safety of the territory within my jurisdiction, and soon after receiving reinforcements I suggested to the General-In-Chief (Halleck) a forward movement against Vicksburg".[124]

The 61st remained at Bolivar, Tennessee, until mid-December. Their duties at this garrison were primarily guarding the railroad tracks and junctions in that particular vicinity. The regiment was also tasked from time to time with foraging duty. This consisted of taking wagons to the nearby farms and plantations and commandeering the supplies (food) necessary to supplement the garrison's needs. During these early stages of the war, only corn was taken and compensation provided to the owners, but later in the war, this policy changed.[i] It was also during this garrison duty at Bolivar that Captain Ihrie, the Commander of C Company, died (Sept. 9, 1862) of what was termed as "Brain Fever".[126]

It also became apparent during this time that some close fighting may be called for and the 61st really didn't possess any training with bayonets. In an ominously humorous letter to his wife Sarah in Chicago, Captain James Lawrence (I Company Commander) asked her to find a copy of J.C. Kelton's book on bayonet drill. To add incentive to her search Captain Lawrence suggested that she would probably not only be saving his life, but also the lives of every man in his company.[127]

Chapter 4

Merry Christmas To You Too,
General Forrest!

It was eluded to the fact that after the Battle of Shiloh, back in April 1862, that Major Simon P. Ohr became the acting regimental commander due to the age and frail condition of its commander, Colonel Fry. For some reason, Colonel Fry never rejoined the 61st for the remainder of his service, which ended with his resignation on May 14, 1863.[128]

The details are sketchy, but during the fall of 1862, while the 61st was at Bolivar, Colonel Fry was given a brigade command at Trenton, Mississippi on October 10, 1862.[129] Colonel Fry remained here until December 10th upon which time Trenton was attacked by Confederate General Nathan Bedford Forrest. Forrest's Cavalry numbered 6000 men, which was an overwhelming force compared to the small garrison brigade Colonel Fry commanded. Also, prior to Forrest's arrival, Colonel Fry transferred all the healthy men, leaving only the sick, wounded, and Colonel Fry.[130]

Colonel Fry erected barricades with cotton bales and whatever else was available. Every man present who could stand and fire a weapon was placed on line and ordered to fight. The attempt was very short and quite futile, but noble; a white flag of truce was waved and the battle ended as quickly as it started. Forrest immediately paroled Colonel Fry who subsequently reported to Benton Barracks, now a parole camp (POW camp).[131]

During this stage of the war, if you were paroled by the enemy, you were on your honor to report to a parole encampment. For Illinois

41

troops, it was Benton Barracks, Missouri. Upon Colonel Fry's arrival he was placed in command of all paroled soldiers, and served in this capacity until he was exchanged. He soon tendered his resignation on May 14, 1863 and sat the rest of the war out in Greene County, Illinois.[132]

Unfortunately for Major Ohr, he was only an acting commander until the time in which Colonel Fry resigned. Then he was officially designated the regimental commander.

Major Simon P. Ohr, prior to the war and living in Carrollton, Illinois, served as the first editor of the Carrollton Press. This paper emerged as a voice of the Free Soil or Republican Party, which espoused views contrary to the administration in Washington in 1857-1858.[133]

Major Ohr was known as a man of ability, and upon the breaking out of the rebellion, being willing to endorse the principles he advocated, even with his life; he entered the service of the general government and made a gallant soldier.[134]

On December 18th, 1862, the 61st (at Bolivar, Tennessee), now numbering 242 men, received orders to proceed immediately via rail to Jackson, Tennessee.[135] The majority of the men figured they were just out for scout duty and would return by nightfall. They were wrong. They had arrived at Jackson just before sundown and were promptly marched two miles east of town and bivouacked at Salem Cemetery for the night. No one had brought any blankets, or anything to keep warm. It was believed they were within a half-mile of a Confederate force so no fires were permitted. They tried to keep warm by huddling in groups and walking around, but to no real relief. They even tried to sleep on the ground by gathering in as tight as possible, but this did not work either. Sergeant Stillwell summed up this long arduous night, "How we suffered with the cold, I shall never forget the night of December 18, 1862."[136]

Morning took forever to come, but it finally did; permission was given to build a small fire to cook breakfast. No one had to give the order twice, hot coffee was promptly made. Bacon cooked on a stick over the fire, and hard tack was consumed very quickly. This helped to thaw the boys out somewhat. As soon as breakfast was over the regiment was placed in line in the cemetery behind the fence, and facing out towards the road.[137]

There was one other regiment in this vicinity with the 61st; it was the 43rd Illinois commanded by Colonel A. Engelmann who served as the Brigade Commander as well. They were located in the woods across the road from the cemetery facing the same general direction as the 61st.[138]

The boys of the 61st did not have to wait very long for trouble to find them. Proceeding down the road in the direction of their firing line was a column of Confederate cavalry. There were four columns progressing at a walk, and initially the depth could not be determined. The word immediately went out not to fire until given the command. When the command was given, they are to fire by file, beginning on the right. This essentially meant that only two men in the front and rear rank would fire together and so on down the line. The result of this maneuver is to maintain continuous fire; in the hope that by the time the left end of the line had fired, the right would be re-loaded and ready to fire again.[139] When the column had reached musket range Major Ohr stood up and shouted "AT-TEN-SHUN, BAT-TAL-YUN! FIRE BY FILE! READY! -- COMMENCE FIRING!" A few seconds later the 43rd opened up as well. The Confederate column was taken completely by surprise. The slaughter lasted only a few minutes, but the effects were devastating. Several dead and wounded horses as well as men lay in the road, and the rest retreated in the direction they came from. A handful of the Rebels dismounted and began to fight, but when they saw how outnumbered they were, they promptly surrendered.[140]

The 61st and the 43rd Illinois were now waiting for a counter attack. It was generally thought that when the Southerners regrouped they would be seeking revenge. Instead of a cavalry assault, which was expected, an artillery barrage commenced within sight, but out of musket range. There were only two pieces of artillery, and they did little damage. This cannonade continued for about two hours, with the 61st suffering a few minor injuries and only one death when a soldier of Company G was decapitated (a shell exploded near him).[141]

Colonel Engelmann was getting concerned at this point that this ineffective artillery display may be a diversion so that the Rebel cavalry could possibly move around on a flank and attempt to roll up the line, or even get into the rear of the regiments and cut them off from Jackson. The order was given to retire to Jackson. On the way back they met reinforcements. The whole command joined forces and advanced back to Salem Cemetery, and to the positions occupied by the Rebels, but the Johnies had disappeared.[142]

In Colonel Engelmann's official report he indeed had cause for concern of being flanked or cut off. He states that the enemy cavalry was harassing both his flanks, and subsequently he sent to Jackson for reinforcements, and detached two companies from the 43rd Illinois to a position several hundred yards to the rear to watch the back door. He further remarked that Major Ohr of the 61st Illinois was "valuable" in this operation, and that, " I cannot speak too highly of the coolness and bravery of the officers and men of the 43rd and 61st regiments." He further states that while only two men were killed (One from the 61st and one from the 43rd), his command had killed sixty in the cavalry ambush and taken three prisoners.[143]

The next couple days were spent patrolling for the Rebels, but to no avail. The men, still without blankets and supplies, were reasonably comfortable at night primarily due to an unseasonable warm front that moved into the area. On December 21st, the 61st marched back to Jackson to discover they had engaged a part of General Nathan Bedford Forrest's Cavalry. Unfortunately, Forrest got the last laugh when it was learned that his main force had swung completely around the flank of Jackson and Lexington undetected, destroying railroad tracks while also burning bridges north of Jackson all the way to the Kentucky border.[144]

It is imperative at this point to give a short background history on Nathan Bedford Forrest and the significant impact he had in, not only the Civil War, but also his contributions to modern warfare.

Forrest wreaked much havoc in the Western theater by employing a logistical raiding strategy. In other words, more often than not, instead of attacking another force in a defensive position, he would maximize the use of his mobility (cavalry) and strike deep into

Union territory to destroy supply depots, railroad tracks, bridges, trestles, etc. This guerilla tactic of hit-and-run worked extremely well for the Rebels because the Union forces had to spare many men to guard these facilities which in turn, decreased the number of soldiers that could be used offensively. Additionally these constant interruptions in the flow of supplies (food, ammunition, etc.) had a profound effect on morale; it also delayed the offensive timetable in the West.[145]

Nathan Bedford Forrest, one of the most colorful and controversial generals of the war, was born in Tennessee in 1821. He had barely six months of formal education when he was 13. When he was 16, his father, a blacksmith died, leaving Forrest, on his own to earn a living. After he served a brief tour with the militia down in Texas, he returned to Mississippi to go into the livestock and livery stable business with his uncle. All was going reasonably well for Forrest when a long-standing feud came to a head between his uncle and the Matlock family.[146]

In the public square in Hernando, Mississippi, three Matlocks and a friend of theirs ambushed Forrest and his uncle. Forrest's uncle was immediately killed and, in the gunfight that ensued, Forrest killed one Matlock and wounded the other participants. After his uncle's death, and up until the outbreak of the Civil War, Forrest left his business and became a slave trader from which he made a great deal of money.[147]

At the outbreak of the Civil War, Nathan Bedford Forrest enlisted as a private in a Tennessee regiment. But Governor Harris, who favored Forrest, got him a discharge so he could recruit his own battalion of cavalry. He fought at Fort Donelson against Grant and escaped with his entire command in the middle of the night prior to Fort Donelson's surrender the following day. He again fought at Shiloh where he was severely wounded.[148] Forrest, who stood six feet two inches (tall for those days) had blue-gray eyes, steel gray hair, and a black chin beard. While his men practically idolized him, it is said they feared *him* more than the *enemy* because of his terrible temper and use of extreme profanity. Despite those facts, he did not drink liquor, smoke, or chew tobacco.[149]

Forrest had no military education whatsoever, but he seemed to possess a natural genius for tactics and logistics. His ferocity in battle soon became "proverbial", and by war's end he had been wounded four times, had twenty-nine horses shot from underneath him, and had killed thirty enemy soldiers in personal combat. After the war, Forrest was questioned about how, on one occasion, he was able to capture an *entire* brigade (including the general) and hundreds of thousands of dollars worth of supplies. He replied, "I just took a short-cut and got there first with the most men." His formula for success would serve as the blueprint or genesis of modern warfare in the 20th century.[150]

Thanks to Nathan Bedford Forrest, Christmas of 1862 was not very pleasant for the 61st. They were camped just outside Jackson, Tennessee on a muddy hill. It was an overcast and "gloomy" day. As previously mentioned, General Forrest had cut their communications to the north and, to add insult to injury, Confederate General Van Dorn, just five days earlier, had captured the stores at Holly Springs, Mississippi. Over a million dollars' worth of food and supplies went up in smoke.[151] As a result, the 61st's rations, which were already meager, were cut. The Christmas meal consisted of a half-ration of coffee and one-quarter rations of hardtack and bacon. Items such as beans, rice, and peas had been exhausted and would be sorely missed until communications could be restored.[152]

As to be expected, the men were passing the time on this day by exchanging stories of what Christmas Day was like back home. Naturally, they discussed what fine meals were prepared for this occasion. It was enough to make one "crazy", commented Sergeant Stillwell. A good friend of his (John Richey) proposed a solution to their problem. He suggested to Sergeant Stillwell that they go out of camp to forage for a square meal, Sergeant Stillwell remarked, "that it didn't take much persuading," and they were soon off.[153]

They had not gone very far, about one-half mile, when they came upon a two-story house which had slave cabins in the rear. The plan was to sneak around the main house and see if they could bum a meal from the slaves. Before they could get around the house the Lady of the House came out to ask in a pleasant tone what they wanted. They were initially too embarrassed to tell the truth, but she kept prodding in her gregarious manner until they came clean. She promptly invited them in and had her servants prepare their meal.[154] This woman made both the men feel like generals. They ate at the main dining table complete with white linens and china. They were served fried beefsteak "that was as tender as chicken", bread and butter, stewed dried apples, cucumber pickles, two or more kinds of preserves, coffee with sugar and cream, and New Orleans golden syrup. For dessert, a stewed dried apple pie, and custard.[155]

The two boys engaged in conversation for a couple hours, and were warmed by the roaring fire and fine hospitality for which they were immeasurably grateful. The attractive woman, who in their estimation was in her mid-30's, remarked that she could not stand to see young boys hungry and did what she could to bring temporary relief. She further commented that many soldiers had eaten a meal at this dining table, both Union and Confederate. She never let on as to which side her sympathies fell, and they did not ask. They were just grateful for her hospitality and likened her to an "angel".[156]

On December 29th, three companies were detached to Carroll Station about eight miles north of Jackson. The rest of the regiment was sent back to Bolivar. There had been a detachment of about one hundred men from the 106th Illinois placed there to guard the railroad; but thanks to Nathan Bedford Forrest, the entire detachment had been captured. When the three companies of the 61st arrived, there was no one to welcome them. They stayed and guarded Carroll Station until relieved by a detachment of the 62nd Illinois on January 27, 1863. Upon being relieved, the 61st detachment rejoined the rest of its regiment back at Bolivar, Tennessee, where they resumed their duty of guarding the railroad from Bolivar north to Toone's station. The 61st remained guarding the railroad until May of 1863.[157]

On April 20th, 1863, Major S.P. Ohr entered into a contract with Dr. Clinton Armstrong to provide medical services for the 61st Illinois. This contract which was simply written in a narrative letter format basically stated that Dr. Armstrong would be paid the sum of $125 per month for services rendered. The contract further declared that it would continue until determined by Dr. Armstrong, the commanding officer, or the Surgeon General that the contract should be ended.[158]

Major Ohr was probably very happy to receive Dr. Armstrong because the regiment was already one surgeon short due to Dr. Clemmons' resignation back on August 31, 1862.[159] It's not very clear how Dr. Armstrong ended up with the 61st other than he was from Carrollton, Illinois, where the unit came from. What is clear is that Dr. Armstrong's enlistment was made possible by a letter from Secretary of War Stanton to Illinois Governor Yates on April 30, 1862, that authorized Governor Yates to appoint two additional surgeons for each Illinois regiment.[160]

A few weeks later, on May 17th, 1862, special order No. 94 was issued from Allan Fuller's office (The Adjutant General of Illinois) appointing Dr. Armstrong a surgeon in the Illinois Volunteers. He subsequently was ordered to report to the State Medical Board for assignment to an Illinois regiment in the field.[161] Dr. Armstrong's whereabouts between March 17th, 1862 and April 20th, 1863 are unknown. He probably served in some capacity on the medical board because of the probable influx in enlistment due to Secretary Stanton's letter. This of course is only a hypothesis.

Chapter 5

Victory at Vicksburg

Throughout the winter months of 1863, General Grant made various attempts to attack the seemingly impregnable defenses at Vicksburg, Mississippi. It was virtually protected on three sides by a combination of the Mississippi River and swamplands. General Grant tried four schemes to avoid a frontal assault; one even included dredging a canal. All were finally abandoned in what culminated on May 19th, and 22nd, in failed direct assaults.[162]

Grant, at this point, realized that Vicksburg would have to be taken by siege. In order to do this he was going to need strong reinforcements. They were sent to him from various places throughout the Western Theater. On May 31st, 1863, the 61st boarded the trains at Bolivar, Tennessee, never to see it again during the remainder of the war.[163] The entire division, of which the 61st was a part under the command of General Nathan Kimball, set out for Vicksburg. The same day (May 31st) they arrived at Memphis, Tennessee, where they bivouacked overnight on a sandbar. The next evening (June 1st) the boys boarded the side-wheel steamer "Luminary" and embarked with other transports, south towards Vicksburg.[164]

Sergeant Stillwell remembers quite well the last time the regiment rode a steamer; it was fourteen months ago on their way to Shiloh. He remarked that the regiment had dramatically changed since that time. The regiment back then was "loud, boastful, and confident." Now they were "more quiet, and grave in their demeanor." They had come to realize that war was a bloody and serious business, and the uncertainty of one's own fate weighed heavily upon one's mind.[165]

On June 3rd, the 61st reached the mouth of the Yazoo River where they promptly turned and started following this route. Near the mouth of the Chickasaw Bayou the fleet stopped for the night so the men could have a chance to bivouac on solid ground and have an opportunity to walk and stretch their legs. The next morning they re-embarked and continued down the Yazoo River.[166]

The following day, June 4, 1863, the steamers arrived at the river town of Satartia. There the entire fleet debarked and marched out to the highlands in back of the town. The boys from Illinois were now quite a long way from home. They were beginning to see unusual vegetation and wildlife. The light and fluffy Spanish moss, that seemed to hang from virtually every tree, was grayish-white in color and looked quite ghostly on a moonlit night. There were also black squirrels, and birds called "chuck-wills-widow" because of the resemblance of those words to the notes it warbled when it sang.[167]

This same afternoon (June 4th, 1863) the division marched toward the town of Mechanicsburg, which was only a few miles away. The advance elements of the division encountered some Confederate cavalry and a skirmish unfolded that ended relatively quickly. The 61st was not engaged. The 61st did participate in the burning of this town and in the process captured about forty Rebels.[168] In fact the 61st "laid waste" to the entire country between Mechanicsburg and Haines Bluff, burning houses, barns, cotton, and anything else that was in their path.[169]

Bright and early on June 6th the 61st, along with the rest of the division, fell in and marched southwest toward Vicksburg. The route they took was through the heart of the Yazoo River Valley with its stifling heat this time of year. The corn was already higher than their heads and the so-called roads were very narrow which did not allow for much air movement. Combined with the dust being kicked up this journey was an arduous one.[170]

Several men died on this march from heat stroke, although none from the 61st. This phenomenon could be due in part to the fact that most of the boys that comprised the 61st were country folks and were familiar with backwoods methods of staying cool. For example, saturating hickory leaves with water and placing the leaves in the cap was said to keep one's head cool.[171]

On the evening of June 7th, they arrived at Haines Bluff, which is on the Yazoo River approximately twelve miles north of Vicksburg. The Confederates had heavily fortified it, but gave it up without a fight due to Grant's tactical maneuvering. While the Confederates indeed were driven out, the mosquitoes were not, and they defended their territory with vigor.[172]

On the 16th of June, the 61st departed Haines Bluff and marched two miles south to Snyder's Bluff where they once again established camp. The duties here were the same as at Haines Bluff: picket duty, and constructing breastworks and fortifications.[173]

Six days later, on June 22nd, General Grant received "positive information" from scouts that Confederate General Joseph Johnston had crossed the Big Black River somewhere Northeast of Vicksburg for the purpose of

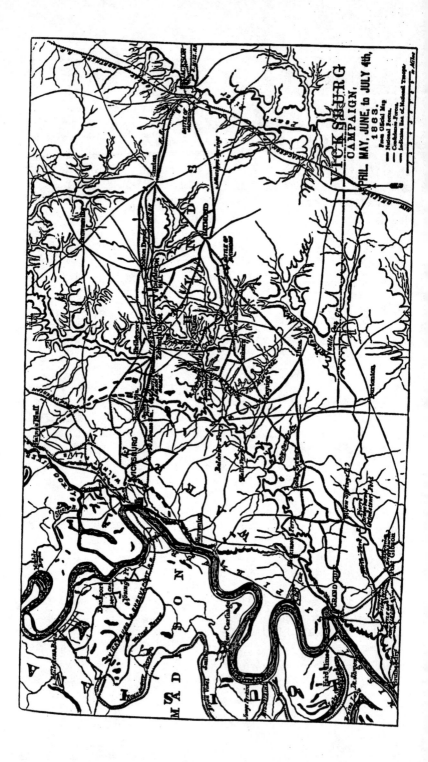

attacking Grant's besieging army at Vicksburg from the rear. Grant subsequently placed General Sherman in charge of establishing a line of defense from Haines Bluff on the Yazoo to the Big Black River in a southeasterly direction. Grant dedicated one half of his entire army to this line of defense, the other half was obviously dedicated to the siege at Vicksburg.[174]

The 61st was on this line. Great measures where taken to fortify this line for what was thought to be a major battle that was inevitable. This country was perfect for defensive purposes. It was covered with high ridges and sharp narrow summits. Brush and trees were cleared away and placed far to the front so as to form obstacles for an advancing army.[175]

General Grant was extremely happy with the defensive line established by Sherman. He felt confident that any attack by Johnston would be futile. As it turned out Johnston never did attack and "wisely" so Grant commented. Grant's final remark on this impenetrable line was "I would have rejoiced at the opportunity of defending ourselves against an attack by Johnston."[176]

The men of the 61st ate quite well during the siege of Vicksburg. Corn was already ripe enough to eat during this time of the year in Mississippi, and it made a splendid supplement to the standard army ration. The favorite method of cooking was to roast it in the shuck. This was accomplished by caking the shuck with mud and covering it with hot coals; when the shuck was burned down to its last layer, it was generally done. There was no butter available, but the corn was said to taste "delicious" anyway.[177]

Blackberries were also plentiful, especially in this region with numerous ridges and peaks, which hosted an ample supply of wild berries. They were also quite large and juicy and could be eaten right off the vine or prepared any number of ways.[178]

As was the case at Shiloh, so it was at Vicksburg with the return of diarrhea and malaria. Several deaths in the 61st were attributed to these factors primarily because of moving, once again, into a new environment with poor water sources. Eventually, the entire force was to drink water only from the Yazoo River and then only after it had been boiled. Many men obviously did not adhere to this advice and suffered the consequences.[179] The sickness of the soldiers becomes quite serious while in Mississippi. A month later the regiment was transferred to Arkansas; in one company alone, half the soldiers including the commander would have to be sent to a convalescent camp in Helena, Arkansas.[180]

On the Fourth of July, the canon fire that had been kept up virtually nonstop since they entered the Vicksburg area, suddenly stopped. It was initially thought that General Grant declared a holiday and gave the artillerymen a rest. Later that day it was learned that Pemberton had surrendered Vicksburg to Grant. This victory was received as a matter of fact without much excitement because the outcome was never really in question, only the timing.[181]

Grant wasted no time. He immediately ordered Sherman to set out towards Jackson, Mississippi, and engage Johnston. Sherman elected to leave a division behind on this particular mission, and once again it was the division that included the 61st.[182]

Johnston had received word that Pemberton surrendered and promptly went into "full retreat" back to Jackson, Mississippi. The weather was still "fearfully hot" and water was scarce too, which made pursuit of Johnston all that much more arduous. To make matters worse, Johnston was implementing a pseudo-biological warfare tactic. On the route of retreat, whenever he came across a pond or likely water source, the Rebels would drive sheep, cattle, or hogs (a few) into the water, then shoot the animals, leaving the rotting carcass in the reservoirs thereby contaminating them.[183]

Sherman finally caught up with Johnston on July 11th at Jackson, Mississippi, where Johnston's troops were behind strong defenses. Sherman's army besieged Jackson until the 17th when Johnston slipped away. Sherman wanted to pursue Johnston but decided against it because of the extreme heat. He commented that, "Pursuit in that hot weather would have been fatal to my command."[184]

The 61st, for their part, stayed at Snyder's Bluff until the 12th of July when they marched Southeast to Messingers Ford on the Black River. What was unique about this two-day march is that the majority of it was conducted at night to avoid possible heat casualties. Five days later, on the 17th, they moved a few miles south to the railroad crossing, and bivouacked on the west side of the Big Black River.[185]

While temporarily stationed on the Big Black, the 61st had the opportunity to see thousands of Confederate soldiers that Grant had paroled from Vicksburg. For the most part, they were following the railroad track east. The paroled soldiers looked "emaciated, depressed, and disconsolate." Grant gave strict orders not to insult or taunt these men in any way; this order was obeyed.[186]

On the 22nd of July 1863, the 61st along with the entire division marched back to Snyder's Bluff. Subsequently, on the 29th the regiment received orders to march to the landing on the Yazoo River and board the steamer "Sultana" where they would be transported north to Arkansas. An interesting side note about the "Sultana"; on April 25, 1865 she fell victim to what was described as the largest maritime tragedy of the Civil War. With 1900 Union soldiers on board, almost all paroled prisoners on their way home, a boiler explosion killed many and the speed at which the steamer sank was responsible for many more deaths. Out of 1900 soldiers, 1100 perished.[187]

The 61st arrived at Helena, Arkansas on July 31st, debarked and went to camp near the Mississippi approximately two miles south of town; the commander in charge of all Union forces in Arkansas was General Frederick Steele. The purpose of the 61st (and its division) was to reinforce General Steele's army in order to push Confederate General Sterling Price out of Little Rock and subsequently out of the state.[188]

Chapter 6

"We planted the Stars and Stripes on the capital of the state before the setting of the sun".

On the 13th of August the regiment left Helena, Arkansas, heading out in pursuit of General Price. They reached Devall's Bluff on August 26th. These two weeks of marching had consisted of uneventful, monotonous marching with no sign of any Rebel activity. At the conclusion of a few days' rest and reorganization, General Steel's Army departed Devall's Bluff on September 1, 1863 to advance on Little Rock, a distance of about fifty miles.[189]

By September 9th, the stage was set for Union forces, under General Steele, to drive out the Confederate forces under General Price the following morning. The town of Little Rock was on the west side of the Arkansas River, and the Union forces were attacking from the east. General Price had constructed strong breastworks a short distance east of town and east of the Arkansas River, which commanded the main road leading into Little Rock. The right side of these works was secured by the river and on the left an impassable swamp.[190]

General Steele came up with a brilliant plan of attack to take Little Rock. His reconnaissance revealed a "chink in the armor" in relation to the Confederate defenses. Price had 7749 soldiers present for duty, and 6500 of these were in the breastworks east of town; The remainder, about 1250, were south of the town to halt what Price believed to be an unlikely crossing of the river by the Union forces. Price failed to do two basic things; first he failed to conduct his own reconnaissance, and second he did not use his common sense. It was September, and after a long, hot summer, the river was quite low and fordable in many places.[191]

General Steele took full advantage of this glaring mistake by Price and dispatched Brigadier General Davidson and his six thousand calvary trained as dragoons (calvarymen who are also trained to fight as dismounted infantry) to cross the Arkansas River south of Little Rock and get to the rear of Price. In a coordinated effort, General Steele would demonstrate against the breastworks east of town with his 4500 infantry, thereby negating any reinforcements being taken from this position.[192]

General Steele's plan was executed superbly; by 5:00 p.m. that same afternoon General Price had evacuated Little Rock with two brigades under Colonel Lewis Merrill in a halfhearted pursuit. General Price made his escape to Arkadelphia and Merrill returned to Little Rock two days later. The casualties for the Battle of Little Rock were fairly light, primarily due to Price's timely departure. The Union forces suffered 137 killed, wounded, and missing, while the Confederates suffered numbers totaling sixty-four.[193]

The 61st obviously was part of General Steel's demonstration east of Little Rock. They suffered no casualties during this engagement unless you count some shaking nerves of some fresh recruits who had not been under fire before.[194] In any event, that afternoon (September 10th, 1863) "We planted the Stars and Stripes on the capitol of the state before the setting of the sun.", Captain Lawrence commented in a letter to his wife.[195]

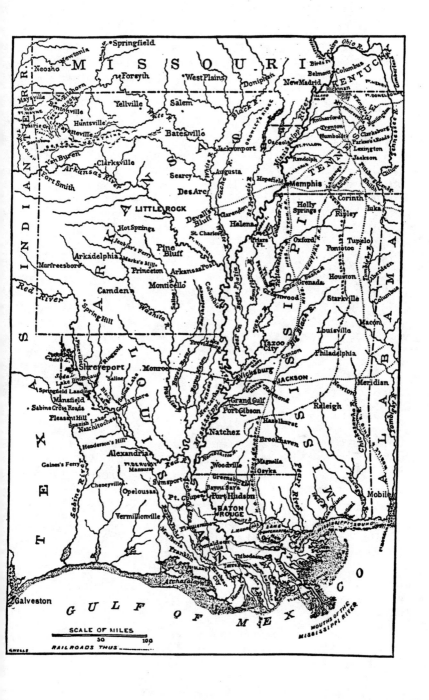

The day after the capture of Little Rock, the 61st went into camp just east of Little Rock near the east bank of the Arkansas River in a grove of trees known at this time as "Huntersville".[196]

The only point of interest about Huntersville is that it was the end of the only railroad in the State of Arkansas during this epoch. It extended from Devall's Bluff on the White River to Little Rock (Huntersville) and served as the only line of communication for Union forces at Little Rock. This fifty-mile stretch of track no doubt made the trek for troops traveling to and from the city much faster and easier.[197]

During their stay at Huntersville, the boys lived quite well on food locally confiscated. In addition to the typical Army ration, plenty of sheep in the surrounding area made for many fine meals with some variation of mutton. Additionally, corn, cornmeal, and yellow sweet potatoes (yams) were plentiful too, which, all things considered, made the 61st's stay at Little Rock relatively pleasant.[198]

The 61st moved over to the west side of the river in mid-October and there, went into winter quarters where they would spend the next six months. There were plenty of trees in this region for constructing log cabins. There was also ample wood to use as fuel too. Every cabin was equipped with an old-fashioned fireplace and a "rock" or "stick" chimney. The winter of 1863-64 was a particularly cold one, with significant snowfalls and bitter cold temperatures, even as far south as Little Rock, Arkansas.[199]

During these long winter months, hostilities practically dropped off to almost nothing because of the severe cold weather. However, there were a couple of memorable events that took place during this period. On January 8, 1864 the entire command stationed at Little Rock was called out with their arms, and put into a formation to witness the hanging of a Confederate spy. Obviously, General Steele wanted to impress upon everyone, both military, and civilian, the severity of punishment that would be exacted for such treachery.[200]

This hanging was very memorable for two reasons; first no one in the regiment had witnessed a hanging before now. Second, the hanging was "wretchedly bungled". It was usually the practice during a hanging to drop a man from a gallows thereby snapping his neck and killing him instantly. This did not happen for some reason, and the spy effectively strangled to death at the end of the rope. This was described as a "repulsive" sight, so much so, that a man in the front rank fainted and fell flat on his face, and others were sickened by the spectacle.[201] Captain Lawrence (I Company Commander) described this event as "chilling", but necessary because the spy was caught red handed with maps of the fort, which detailed gun emplacements, etc.[202]

It was also in January of 1864 that the 61st was presented the "veteranizing project". Soldiers of the regiment were offered sundry enticements to enlist for three more years. The one that got the most interest was a 30-day furlough for every man who re-enlisted. It was not initially certain if enough soldiers in the regiment would reenlist to keep the regimental designation. Acting Commander Daniel Grass gave one of the most eloquent, patriotic speeches the boys had ever heard. Subsequently, enough re-enlisted to maintain the regiment's current designation to the end of the war.[203]

In General Steele's official report as of January 31, 1864 he wrote that, out of an aggregate of 30,687 soldiers, 21,908 are present for duty in his 7th Corps. Additionally in a minor reorganization, the 61st becomes part of the 3rd Brigade of General Carr's 2nd Division.[204]

2LT Thomas H. Dayton CO. G 61st IL INF.
Photo courtesy of Mr. Steve Hicks,
Scottville, Illinois

SGT Charles A. Ayers CO. A 61st IL INF.
Photo courtesy of Mr. Steve Hicks,
Scottville, Illinois

E. E. Hall

1LT Edward E. Hall CO. I 61st IL INF.
Photo courtesy of Mr. Steve Hicks,
Scottville, Illinois

PVT Richard Pruitt CO. A 61st IL INF.
Photo courtesy of Mrs. Marylin Hagerstrand,
Waukesha, Wisconsin

1LT Thomas J. Warren CO. D 61st IL INF.
Photo courtesy of Mr. Steve Hicks,
Scottville, Illinois

SGT Charles Jewel CO. A 61st IL INF.
Photo courtesy of Mr. Steve Hicks,
Scottville, Illinois

CPT John McCoy CO. K 61st IL INF.
Photo courtesy of Mr. Steve Hicks,
Scottville, Illinois

Chapter 7

(Arkansas) Where is the enemy?

In the spring of 1864 (April) the military authorities decided to take an offensive initiative. The decision was made to conduct operations in Louisiana with the objective of taking Shreveport. Generally the plan was for General N.P. Banks to proceed north from New Orleans with his Army while General Steele would move south with his Army from Little Rock Arkansas, ultimately converging at Shreveport, Louisiana.[205]

Once again the soldiers of the 61st were "mortified" to find out that they would not be going on this mission.[206] They were informed by special order No. 8, issued from 7th Army headquarters, Little Rock, that they (the 61st) and the 3rd Minnesota would stay behind and pull provost duty at Little Rock.[207]

The attack on Shreveport, which would come to be known as the "Red River Campaign", was a dismal failure. Both Banks and Grant opposed this campaign for various reasons, but Halleck had ordered it and the order was obeyed. Grant's final thoughts on the expedition were, "I had opposed the movement strenuously but acquiesced because it was the order of my superior at the time."[208]

While Banks was busy being defeated, General Steele had begun his march south from Little Rock the latter part of March. Steele was successful at driving Price out of Arkedelphia, Camden, and Washington by means of skillful maneuvering and well-chosen fights as he advanced. Unfortunately, in the midst of this successful campaign, General Steele received word of Banks' defeat on April 8th, 1864, in Louisiana. He further learned that Price would now be reinforced with eight thousand infantry and complement of artillery from General Kirby Smith, and that the Confederates were planning an offensive movement (against Steele).[209]

General Steele did not feel he could defeat Price's combined army, so he decided to fall back into his defenses at Little Rock. No sooner had Steele began his retrograde, when he was attacked by Price and Smith's combined force. General Steele's force fought a retreating battle for several days until, pressed hard by the Rebel Army, they reached Jenkins Ferry on the Saline River. The swollen condition of the stream and the almost impassable swamp on the opposite side held up Steele's force until he could get all of his supply trains across on a makeshift pontoon bridge. While trying to accomplish this task, the entire combined Confederate Army attacked. The theory was that the Union forces, with the swollen river to their backs, had no escape route. This, by and large, was true and on April 30th 1864, the battle of Jenkins Ferry took place. The Confederates, to their surprise were so badly beaten in this battle that they made no further effort to pursue Steele's army across the river back to Little Rock.[210]

While General Steele was conducting his retrograde operation, both regiments and a small detachment of cavalry stationed at Little Rock (61st IL, 3rd MN, and 8th MO CAV) departed via rail to Devall's Bluff on April 19th. The next morning they were placed on the Steamboat, "James Raymond", and proceeded eighty miles up the White River to Augusta, Arkansas. They arrived on the 21st, immediately debarked, marched approximately a mile east of the town and formed a line of battle along the edge of the woods overlooking an open field.[211]

After waiting a short while for something to happen, skirmishers were ordered to cross the field and enter the woods on the far side. It was quite tense for awhile, expecting any second to hear the cracking of musket fire, but none was heard. It was soon discovered that there had been enemy cavalry encamped in these woods; 1000 in strength under the command of General McRae, however upon learning of a Union force in this vicinity, they retired.[212]

The expedition spent the next few days trying to find the Rebels, but all they found were a few Confederate stragglers who were promptly taken prisoner by the cavalry. Subsequently, on April 24th they boarded the steamboat at Augusta to make their way back to Little Rock the same day.[213]

Colonel Christopher Andrews, the 3rd Minnesota commander and the overall expedition commander conveyed these sentiments in his official report of April 24th. He describes that, of the eight prisoners captured, one was a regimental commander of the 9th MO INF, and another a dispatch carrier for General Price with his papers. Additionally, Colonel Andrews enlisted seventy-five "able-bodied" colored recruits, sixty head of serviceable horses and mules, and $2000 worth of cotton. Colonel Andrews finally commends Major S.P. Ohr and the soldiers of the 61st IL for "efficient service" during this expedition.[214]

In another reorganization after General Steele's return, the 61st IL found themselves in General West's 2nd Division and assigned to the First Brigade. Additionally, on May 11th,

12th 1864, the regiment had an aggregate strength of 420 men.[215]

On May 6, 1864, with the cold winter months behind them now, the troops moved out of their cozy cabins and back to Huntersville where they were earlier the previous winter.[216] By virtue of special order No. 4, District of Little Rock, upon their arrival back in Huntersville, along with another regiment and some cavalry, Major Ohr (61st commander) was placed in command of this encampment and all Regimental Commanders were to report directly to him. Essentially, the Huntersville area was made a subordinate command for two reasons. First, it's geographic location outside Little Rock and opposite the Arkansas River necessitated this decision. Second, the mission of this encampment was: to guard the one-and-only railhead coming into Little Rock, and to guard the main entrance to the city of Little Rock itself.[217]

On May 19th the 61st received orders to board the trains and deploy twenty-eight miles east to Hicks Station. The force that departed from Little Rock consisted of the 61st, 54th, 106th, Illinois Infantry Regiments and the 12th Michigan (Infantry Regiment), a battery of artillery and a few detachments of cavalry. General West was the Division Commander in charge. The force arrived on the same day and bivouacked until the 22nd, then promptly moved another eighteen miles further east to Austin.

The weather was quite hot for this time of year already. Heat casualties were beginning to rise as the troops marched into the afternoon hours. In fact, when the 61st arrived at Austin, not a single commissioned officer in D Company had completed the eighteen-mile trek.[218]

The soldiers made several forced marches over the next few days, the purpose of which was to find the Confederate Cavalry under the command of General J.O. Shelby, who was supposedly operating in this region. Intelligence had summarized that he was in this region to disrupt the railroad somewhere between Devall's Bluff and Little Rock. On May 25th they arrived and bivouacked at Springfield, Arkansas, and stayed to rest until the 28th.[219]

While at Springfield, the boys of the 61st began foraging for food (pigs, chickens, etc.) to supplement the standard army rations. About two miles outside of Springfield, a few of the foragers from the 61st came across the 10th Illinois Cavalry who had commandeered a fully operational still. They had apparently run the proprietor off and taken charge of the operation. The 61st foragers went back and told the rest of boys about the still and a plan to relieve the cavrymen of the still was immediately discussed.[220]

They came up with a plan that entailed a small compliment of soldiers, and a very big sergeant. They claimed to be Provost Guards and arrested the cavalrymen for being in possession of whiskey. The "Provost Marshal's" made several threats in relation to what could happen to the horsemen. When they had them thoroughly scared, the "Marshal's" let them off the hook by making them promise to be good and immediately return to their own camp. A couple of the boys in the 61st were quite familiar with moonshining and wasted no time at working the still to capacity day and night while they were at Springfield. News spread like wildfire among the enlisted men of this still outside town and many took part in the libations offered.[221]

At 4:00 A.M. on May 28th, the task force began a four-day forced march back to camp Huntersville arriving on the 31st. This expedition covered some 190 miles roundtrip and not a single Confederate soldier was encountered. Some soldiers did get the opportunity to experience their first scorpion and tarantula bites that were indeed very painful. But, when amply treated with an application of well-moistened chewing tobacco, the poison would become neutralized.[222]

On June 20, 1864 the 61st left Huntersville (Little Rock) for the last time, they would not return here again for the remainder of the war. They moved via rail to Hicks Station. On the 24th the 61st received marching orders to move to Devall's Bluff and board the steamboat "Kentucky", to be transported to Clarendon on the White River just below Devall's Bluff. Intelligence had discovered that Confederate General Shelby was there with his cavalry. Additionally, he had commandeered a Union ironclad (steel plated gunboat) and was enforcing a blockade at Clarendon. It was imperative to remove this blockade because the White River was the only line of communication for all Union forces north of Clarendon to and including Little Rock.[223]

The task force, which was to assail Clarendon, Arkansas, consisted of 2000 infantry and 2000 cavalry with five days' rations. General E.A. Carr was commanding.[224] The expedition had an accompaniment of gunboats that escorted the soldiers down river. They reached Clarendon on the morning of the 26th where the gunboats wasted no time starting to shell the town. There was no return fire from the town, so it was ascertained that the Rebels were not in there. The transports quickly landed and put the soldiers ashore where they immediately formed a line of battle and moved out. The enemy under the command of General Shelby was found in force about two miles northeast of Clarendon where some skirmishing and artillery had begun. The 61st was held in reserve and "did not get to pull a trigger."[225]

Shelby did not hang around long before he decided to retreat. The prospect of cavalrymen fighting the infantry, supported with a strong contingent of artillery, was obviously unpalatable. The Northerners tried to pursue Shelby but the infantry could not pursue the much quicker cavalry. Although the Union Cavalry did nip at their heels for awhile, they could not get them to engage in a decisive confrontation.[226]

The route upon which the 61st pursued followed an old corduroy road. In many places the logs were completely rotted away leaving large mud-filled gaps at various places. To avoid getting wet and muddy shoes and socks, the boys took them off and had a fun time laughing and joking as they splashed barefooted through the soppy warm mud.[227]

The morning of June 28th, the expedition headed back to Clarendon. There was a problem however, the five days rations that they were supposed to get, never arrived. Luckily on this day the commissary sergeant found a lone steer and butchered it for the entire regiment. It wasn't much but everyone got a morsel, and that was all they had to eat until they returned to Clarendon on the following day, June 29th. As soon as the boys reached Clarendon they received a "square" meal that was much appreciated by all.[228]

Soon afterwards it was noticed that fires were breaking out almost simultaneously all over town. And not long after that the entire town lay in ashes. The town had been abandoned. It was believed that these empty houses along the river afforded excellent cover for the Confederates to harass Union supply ships headed up river. Consequently, the town was ordered to be burned. That evening, the 61st boarded the steamer, "Lillie Martin" and transported back to Devall's Bluff. There they went into camp near the river for a much-needed rest.[229]

The 61st remained encamped here on the river at Devall's Bluff until August 14, 1864, upon which time they were paid six months back pay and their veteran bounty. They also received good news; the 30-day furlough for the veternized soldiers had finally been approved. On this date they started home! The recruits and non-veterans left behind had not earned the leave time. The veterans expected that they would return after their furlough and the regiment would once again be together. As we will see later, the veterans never returned to Arkansas for the remainder of the war.[230]

The 61st's 220 veterans were not the only veterans who received their furlough at this time. Several other regiments' expiration of term of service had arrived. These included 100 soldiers from the second Indiana battery, 360 soldiers from the 1st Iowa Cavalry, 267 soldiers from the 62nd Illinois, 200 soldiers from the 3rd Minnesota, 120 from the 5th Kansas Cavalry, and the 1st Indiana Cavalry term would expire a week later.[231]

The boys of the 61st boarded the steamers and headed down the White River to the Mississippi River and then disembarked at Cairo, Illinois. Unfortunately, this trip took ten days due to the Mississippi River water level being so low. On three occasions the steamboat ran aground on sandbars and had to be pulled off by another steamer. Once all the men had to be put ashore to march two or three miles along the bank because the river was so low.[232]

The troops loaded onto rail cars at Cairo and arrived at Springfield, Illinois, on August 24th. Fortunately, their thirty-day furlough didn't include the ten-day travel time, so for the most part, the boys didn't mind the long trek. When the regiment arrived at Springfield, Illinois, they stored their weapons and accoutrements in a public building for safe keeping and then everyone dispersed to their respective homes.[233]

There was a fine welcome home for the boys of the 61st. They had been off to war for two and a half years. There was some sort of party going on all the time they were home. There were big picnics, oyster suppers and speeches by politicians throughout the entire time just to show how much their local residents appreciated them.[234]

Unfortunately, a sobering event occurred while home on furlough; the regimental commander Major Simon P. Ohr died at his home in Carrollton on September 14th, 1864. He died of an apparent bronchial infection, the cause of which was probably harsh field living or exposure to Army camp life. In any event, army life had worn him to the point of being susceptible to any serious illness.[235]

With the untimely death of Simon Ohr, Daniel Grass was next in the chain of command to take charge of the regiment. He was born in Rockport, Indiana on September 21, 1824. When he was two, his family moved to Illinois where he grew up in a little village about eight miles from Vincennes, Indiana. He studied law under Preceptor Aaron Shaw at Lawrenceville, Illinois, and was subsequently appointed to the Illinois Bar sometime prior to the Civil War. Colonel Grass married a widow with three children. She unfortunately died in 1860. Additionally, the one child that was procreated from this union died at three years of age.[236]

After the war, he returned to Illinois and practiced law. While in Illinois, Colonel Grass was instrumental, along with General B.F. Stephenson, in the organization of the G.A.R. (Grand Army of the Republic) which was, of course, a Civil War Veterans' organization. Colonel Grass served as the Adjutant General of this organization under General Stephenson.[237]

In 1870, Daniel Grass moved to Kansas. In 1876, he was elected to the Kansas State Senate and served one term. At the conclusion of his term as Senator, Colonel Grass moved to Independence, Kansas where he practiced law until 1892. He moved to Coffeyville, Kansas where he practiced law until the day he was struck by a train while crossing the tracks on December 18th, 1894. He died a few days later on the 21st from the injuries he sustained.[238]

Chapter 8

"God's Country"

The regiment rendezvoused at Springfield, Illinois on Sept. 26th and left the next day on the trains bound for St. Louis. They were temporarily housed at the Hickory Street Barracks within the city. A panic started to take hold in St. Louis when it was learned their old adversary and nemesis, General Price and General Shelby had joined forces and had been spotted eighty-five miles south of St. Louis at Pilot's Knob.[239]

On September 28th while at the Hickory Street Barracks, the furloughed veterans received Special Order No. 269 from Headquarters Department of the Missouri, Major General Rosecrans Commanding. This order detailed one company from the 61st to act as sharpshooters on the steamer "Bart Able". They were issued ten days rations and 200 rounds of ammunition per man.[240]

Subsequently, Special Order No. 270 was issued which effectively sent the remainder of the 61st (Companies B,D, and G-excluding the non-veterans and recruits still in Arkansas) to Chester, Illinois, on the Mississippi River at the mouth of the Kaskaskia River.[241] The purpose of their presence was to guard the ferry crossing, on the Mississippi River, so they could repel a Confederate raid in this vicinity if the need arose. Generally, the duty at Chester was quite easy. There was plenty of food, little duty, fair autumn weather, and large vacant warehouses in which the regiment resided.[242]

It may be noted at this time that Major General Rosecrans was now commanding at St. Louis. If you will recall, in the battles of Iuka, and Corinth, Mississippi he blundered; but was still held in fairly high esteem by General Grant. After another major blunder in the battle that ultimately became known as the Battle of Chattanooga, Tennessee, (where he was commander of the Army of the Cumberland), he was transferred to Missouri where he could not do any more damage.

Meanwhile the one lone company from the 61st (E Company) was still steaming up and down the Mississippi aboard the "Bart Able" looking for the enemy. Rumors were heard of Rebels here and there but when checked out, nothing materialized. The only incident of interest on this excursion was the steamer's running aground on "Crawford's Bar" due to the low water level of the river.[243]

While E Company was trying to get off the sandbar, the rest of the regiment was still down in Chester, Illinois, enjoying their ferry-guarding duty. The First Sergeant of Company G, Pressley T. Rice got the idea that since they were in "God's Country" (Illinois), they should have soft bread to eat. He got together with First Sergeant Stillwell of Company D and both agreed. So, they proceeded into town to the local mill to buy two barrels of flour, hopefully on credit because they were too strapped for cash.[244]

First Sergeants Rice and Stillwell, after a short jaunt, arrived at H.C. Cole & Co. where they made their proposal to the proprietor. The man looked at the two soldiers with "narrowed eyes" as if to convey a message of contempt and distrust. He reluctantly agreed to the price of seven dollars for two barrels of flour, figuring that if he didn't, the Union boys would take it anyway. Obviously the boys of the 61st, or at least these two companies were extremely happy to have soft bread during their stay at Chester. Unfortunately, because of the infrequency of the paymaster, it would be six months before they could settle the bill with the mill. However, after H.C. Cole & Co. received its seven dollar payment, the milling company responded with a short letter thanking the military for payment. The business also wrote that the generally fair and honest dealings experienced with the Union Army were appreciated.[245]

On October 3, 1864, special order No. 206, from Headquarters St. Louis District was issued. This order effectively reunited Company E (on the steamer, "Bart Able") with the rest of the regiment at Cheltenham, Missouri, although, it would be the 14th before the bulk of the regiment at Chester could load the steamer "A. Jacobs" and move to St. Louis.[246]

On October 18th, Special Order 219 was issued sending the 61st, 250 strong, to Mexico, Missouri, along with a few other regiments including a cavalry detachment.[247] Their mission was to find an "irregular" Confederate cavalry of 500 men under the command of Colonel McDaniel. Orders were to either destroy them in battle or drive them out of the area. McDaniel had apparently been operating in this area for some time and had earned a reputation of being "predatory and uncivilized" in his warfare.[248]

The next nine days were spent chasing McDaniel from town to town with only the Union cavalry engaging in some minor skirmishing. McDaniel would not stop and fight, and being cavalry, they would always get away just ahead of the infantry. So effective was their pursuit of McDaniel that on October 27th he crossed the Missouri River and joined General Price, and they subsequently left the state.[249]

This excursion was obviously reminiscent of the Arkansas expeditions, but with one or two significant differences. The weather could not have been better. They were enjoying a beautiful Missouri Indian summer and fruits and vegetables were more than abundant along their routes of pursuit. Almost all farms by this time had been abandoned because of the so-called Confederate raiding parties and other guerilla activities; so the Union troops didn't feel guilty for taking such supplies. Besides, if *they* hadn't taken the food, the enemy would have.[250]

On October 29th the expedition loaded railcars at Allen, Missouri, to head back to St. Louis. About halfway back to St. Louis at approximately midnight, near Montgomery City, the train stopped and the men were pulled off the train. It was believed that there were some Confederate Cavalry a few miles away at Danville, Missouri. The boys were given strict orders to be quiet on the march so as to give surprise when they came upon Danville. They arrived just before dawn and once again found no enemy in town. Although they did find out that two weeks earlier Bill Anderson (a.k.a. "Bloody" Bill Anderson) and his gang had been through the town and murdered five or six unarmed civilians including a ten year old boy.[251]

Having found nothing at Danville the 61st marched back to the train, boarded and continued on the journey to St. Louis. Upon arrival, the 61st was ordered to familiar stomping grounds, Benton Barracks. In fact they took up the same quarters they had used almost three years ago. Apparently the barracks were in a state of disrepair and showed signs of transient wear and tear.[252]

The boys would be here only a few days until November 5th, 1864, when Special Order No. 306 was issued from Headquarters Department of the Missouri. This effectively ordered the 61st to Springfield, Illinois.[253] On this day they boarded the steamer "David Tatum" and made their way up to Alton where they boarded trains for Springfield, Illinois. Initially the boys of the 61st did not know why they had been ordered to Springfield, but it was made clear very shortly as to the reason why. The Presidential elections were to be held on November 8th. Illinois was only one of a few states that had not passed legislation allowing soldiers to vote in the field. The cause of this inconvenience was political. The Illinois legislature (since 1862) was Democratic, and in general did not look favorably on this action.[254]

The boys no sooner got situated on the train at Alton when they were told to collect all their gear, get off the train and "fall in". They were immediately informed that their orders had been countermanded by telegraphic dispatch. They were to proceed immediately back to St. Louis.[255] Needless to say there was much disappointment and anger at this news; almost everyone had been looking forward to a few days furlough back home.[256]

The next morning, November 6th, the 61st got back on the steamer "David Tatum" and steamed down to St. Louis where they spent the night. The next morning the men boarded the steamer "Jennie Brown" headed for "Dixieland" once again. First Sergeant Leander Stillwell best describes the sentiment most of the men had come to expect at this point of the war.

> "By this time we had become philosophical and indifferent in regard to the ups and downs of our careers. If we had been ordered some night to be ready the next morning to start to California or Maine, the order would have been treated with absolute composure, and after a few careless or sarcastic remarks, we would have turned over and been asleep again in about a minute." [257]

The 61st's intermediate destination along with General A.J. Smith's division and an assortment of other regiments and batteries, was Paducah, Kentucky.[258] The final destination of this large force was Nashville and Murfreesboro, Tennessee. All were to become a part of General George H. Thomas' Army of the Cumberland. It was believed (and rightly so) that Confederate General John Bell Hood and General Nathan Bedford Forrest were heading north out of Georgia to invade Tennessee. In anticipation of this occurrence all available troops were being sent to join Thomas' Army.

On Election Day November 8th while the troops were in route to Paducah, a heavy fog set in and the steamer had to pull off and tie up the entire day. To pass the time the officers held a mock presidential election. Almost all the officers were Democrats and supported General McClellan for President. They were very confident the majority of the regiment felt the same way. To the befuddlement of many, President Lincoln won by 16 votes; which clearly demonstrated that among the enlisted men, political opinions had changed over the course of the war. An overwhelming majority of the regiment had been Democratic early in the war.[259]

On the 11th of November, the 61st arrived at Paducah where they debarked and went into camp for almost two weeks. Subsequently, on the 24th, the regiment boarded the steamer, "Rosa D.", proceeded up the Ohio, and then down the Cumberland to Nashville. They arrived late on the 27th, debarking the next morning for Murfreesboro, Tennessee. They boarded trains and were transported to Murfreesboro, about thirty miles southeast of Nashville, where they went into camp at Fort Rosecrans.[260] Upon joining the Army of the Cumberland, the 61st Illinois was assigned to the 20th Army Corps, 4th Division, Major General Robert Milroy, commanding under the auspices of Special Order 325, Headquarters Department of the Cumberland.[261] December 4th, 1864, was a pleasant and warm day in Murfreesboro, Tennessee, reminiscent of the Indian summer days back in October. About the middle of the afternoon, without warning, a loud "boom" was heard very close by. In fact the smoke from the cannon could be seen rising through the trees. The order was immediately given to "fall in". The 61st Illinois, along with the 8th Minnesota, 174th Ohio, and a section of the 13th New York Artillery marched out of Fort Rosecrans toward the cannon fire.[262]

The spot of trouble was only four miles away where Confederate artillery was trying to destroy a railroad blockhouse. The 13th Indiana Cavalry had arrived prior to the 61st and were skirmishing with the Rebels. The 61st moved forward in line to the right of the railroad pike. The Minnesota regiment formed on their right, and the Ohio Regiment formed on their left. Additionally, the New York Artillery took a position on the high ground and started exchanging artillery fire.[263]

The order came down to Lieutenant Colonel Grass to deploy the 61st as skirmishers, and advance toward the enemy. They proceeded ahead, cautiously crossing Overall's Creek (for which this battle is named), when Confederate skirmishers started shooting at them. The boys pressed on, as the hour of the day was late and darkness was almost upon them. The Rebel skirmishers were driven back to their main line where they held the high ground near the edge of the woods. The 61st took cover and starting firing into this line. The enemy returned fire, but most of the balls went over the heads of the 61st. By this time of evening it was dark, but the boys of the 61st still maintained their rate of fire by aiming at the muzzle flashes from the Rebel muskets. Additionally, the artillery duel continued as cannonballs could be heard screaming and exploding overhead.[264]

The Battle of Overall's Creek ended when the 174th Ohio, situated to the left of the 61st, slipped around to the Confederates' right flank and delivered a "destructive volley" which forced the Rebels to retire. A short pursuit ensued, but in the darkness, nothing came of it. The men were soon gathered together where they recrossed Overall's Creek and proceeded to build large campfires out of rails to make the enemy think they were bivouacking there for the night. But, they didn't! They marched back to Murfreesboro, and arrived about midnight.[265]

At the Battle of Overall's Creek, the 61st performed admirably once again. For their efforts they captured forty-five prisoners and suffered fifteen casualties, both dead and wounded.[266]

Over the next two days, December 5th-6th, 1864, the Rebels made numerous demonstrations to the west of the fort just out of musket range. The defenses at Fort Rosecrans were quite excellent. It was felt that an attack would be repulsed with heavy losses to the attackers if one were to come. Just to be on the safe side, the regiment was up at 4:00 AM to man the trenches behind the breastworks in the event of a dawn attack.[267]

The 61st performed most admirably during this engagement; in fact, in General Milroy's official account of this battle he echoes this sentiment, "The 61st being also a veteran regiment and being much reduced by long and hard service well sustained their reputations as veterans".[268]

Chapter 9

The Thrill of Victory and the Agony of Defeat

Early in the morning on December 7th, 1864 the 61st Illinois, along with six other regiments (174th, 177th, 178th and 181st Ohio, and the 8th Minnesota), headed out of Fort Rosecrans. There was also a detachment of cavalry from the 12th Indiana and 5th Tennessee, and one battery of the 13th New York Artillery. This Union force consisted of 3325 men under the command of General Milroy.[269]

The force marched northwest out of Murfreesboro to find General Forrest and attempted to engage the elusive Rebels. They had not gotten very far before Union cavalry came upon Confederate Vedetts (mounted sentinels). Contrary to previous battles where the 61st was either left to guard the fort or left in the rear to be a reserve, they were put out front as skirmishers and were in the thick of battle. The 61st, along with the Tennessee Cavalry, drove back these Rebel outposts until noon when they came upon the main defensive line of the Confederates on the Wilkinson Pike. This defensive line was hastily constructed breastworks made of logs, rails, and dirt, but nonetheless effective.[270]

Before the 61st could get into musket range the enemy artillery opened up on them; this temporarily halted the advance. General Milroy and his staff rode up to the 61st's position to assess the situation. The General pulled out his field glasses, looked the Confederates' positions over for about five minutes, then made his decision. The order was given to fall in, and they began to withdraw.

It was immediately assumed that the general thought that the Confederates were too strong defensively and they would fight them some other day. Shortly after retiring from the sight of the enemy the 61st began a slow left wheel maneuver.[271]

General Milroy had ascertained that a frontal assault would be futile, but he did notice that the enemy's flanks were exposed. Consequently, he ordered the 61st to withdraw so the Rebels could see and, when out of sight, swing around to their left flank and attack. By this time, the entire force had moved over to the enemy's left flank and once again the 61st was placed as skirmishers in front of the advancing first line.[272]

The 61st had proceeded to a point where they came upon an open cotton field. The enemy had quickly brought up a couple of pieces of artillery and were shelling the advancing 61st, but to no avail, primarily due to the inaccuracy and limited range of the artillery. Near the artillery, a Confederate officer was observing from his iron-gray horse. Although he was mostly out of musket range, it did not stop the soldiers from taking a few pot shots at him. In any event, he rode off probably, when he heard bullets passing in his direction. After this battle (The Battle of Wilkinson's Pike) it was learned, from a captured soldier, that the Confederate officer on the horse was none other than General Nathan Bedford Forrest who had ridden up to the front to assess the situation.[273]

The boys of the 61st continued their advance across the cotton field withstanding skirmish fire and artillery when they came upon the high ground of the field. There they could see the reformed main line of the Confederates at the edge of the field. The skirmishers (the 61st) immediately fell back into the main line and starting pouring musket fire into the Rebel line. After a few volleys the order was given to charge! The whole line began to advance, but shortly after forward movement began, the 174th Ohio, a green regiment who was on the 61st's left, stopped. It was plain to see the fear and shaky self-confidence in these boys' faces. If they stopped, the 61st would have to stop too. And they did.[274]

At this stage the musket fire and artillery were deafening. From the looks on the faces of the 174th Ohio, it would be only seconds before they would fall to pieces and run. Just at that moment General Milroy rode to the front of this Ohio regiment with his hat in his right hand, waving it in the air, and encouraged the Ohio boys to carry on. The whole time he was out in front (which was not long), the Confederates were letting loose with their Rebel yells trying to unseat the old general; but they failed. The general's leadership was *tremendously* inspiring. The entire Union line went forward, in a fury, right over the Confederate works and won the day![275]

The Confederates retired in a hurry, at least the ones that could retire. Approximately 200 were taken prisoner plus two 12-pound Napoleon canons, and the colors of the 29th Georgia. A short pursuit took place for about a half-mile and more prisoners were taken. Because of darkness and completely exhausted ammunition levels in a couple of regiments, the pursuit was called off and the troops moved back into Fort Rosecrans.[276]

At this stage of the war (December 1864), it was obvious, by the condition of the Rebel prisoners, that the logistical network of the south was almost non-existent. The only food these Rebel soldiers had was raw shelled corn in the haversacks. Many had, apparently, not had shoes for quite some time because their feet were black and the skin was wrinkled and "corrugated" much like the skin of an alligator.[277]

General Milroy's report contained glowing remarks of all the regiments under his command at the Battle of Wilkinson's Pike. The casualties were remarkably low as well, 167 wounded, twenty-one killed. From these numbers the 61st suffered one killed and fourteen wounded. As for the enemy, their casualties were estimated at 100 killed and wounded.[278]

After a few days rest on the afternoon of December 12th, 1864, the 61st was ordered to provide escort on a train bound for Stevenson, Alabama to procure 10,000 rations of hard tack to replenish the nearly exhausted supply.[279] The 61st, with a combined strength of 150 men, along with 40 engineers of the 1st Michigan made this trek together, primarily due to likely enemy contact as well as the possibility of sabotaged railroad tracks.[280]

The engineers came in quite handy, not more than ten miles out of Murfreesboro, the train started coming upon places where the tracks had been torn up and culverts destroyed. The engineers fixed the track as they went along with the 61st pulling security while they worked. With excellent forethought a flat car had been brought along that carried all the necessary tools and supplies to fix breaks whenever they were encountered. Once the train reached about thirty-five miles distance from Murfreesboro, the track was unfettered on into Stevenson, Alabama, where they arrived around 10:00 AM the next morning (Dec. 13th). [281]

The train was subsequently loaded with the 10,000 rations. On the morning of the 14th, the group started back to Murfreesboro, Tennessee, along with thirty dismounted cavalrymen, of the 12th Indiana, they picked up. The return trip progressed quite slowly due to the steep ascending grade of the eastern slope· of the Cumberland Mountains and because of the icy drizzly rain the night before. Nevertheless, steady progress was maintained and eventually they made it over the mountain intact.[282]

All was going routinely well until dusk when the train reached Bell Buckle, thirty-two miles from Murfreesboro. There was a Confederate Vedette near the tracks here, and pot shots were taken at the train as it passed. Naturally, everyone was wondering how much further they could go before they would find the tracks torn up. The train pressed on into the night, cautiously moving forward so as not to derail should the track be damaged.[283]

The hour was now approximately 2:00 AM and the train had just passed through Christiana, fifteen miles from Murfreesboro when they encountered a substantial Confederate Calvary force and the railroad tracks badly torn up. The 61st was immediately ordered off the train to form a line in front of the train on both sides of the track and advance.[284] Also at this time a messenger was dispatched to Murfreesboro to bring up reinforcements in the event the Rebel force was too great.[285]

The 61st hadn't advanced very far when they came upon a line of mounted cavalry on either side of the track obviously awaiting a victim. But not on this day! When the cavalry line fired into the 61st, almost all misfired. All that was heard was the popping of caps all along their line.[286] The boys of the 61st

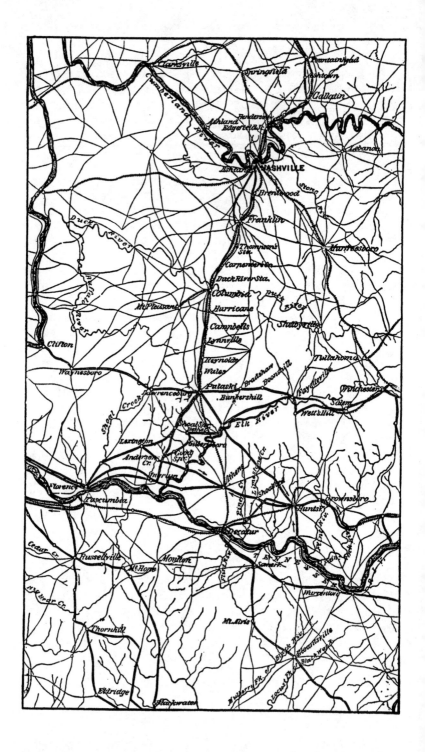

immediately returned the favor but, with one big difference, no misfires. A murderous thunder was launched at the cavalrymen they were repulsed with "considerable loss" and the rest retreated.[287] Over the next seven miles the 61st advanced on foot skirmishing the entire distance with the Confederates who were trying to impede their advance.[288]

At six miles out from Murfreesboro with still no signs of reinforcements yet, the Union soldiers came upon the worst break in the tracks yet. This break was so severe that it was estimated that it would take several hours to repair.[289] The engineers went right to work and for the moment there was no sign of the enemy, but that didn't last long, of course.[290]

Heavy musket fire started to rain into the 61st from the tree-covered ridge to their left front. They instantly began returning fire. This exchange continued for some time when it was discovered that a second force had maneuvered behind the train slightly out of musket range and were in the process of tearing up the track, obviously to prevent any attempt on the 61st's part to escape. At the same time a third force opened fire on the train from the right from across the stream. Part of the 61st was shifted to meet this threat. Now, because of the overwhelming firepower, the engineers had to stop work to pick up their weapons and fight too.[291]

The 61st, being virtually surrounded during the overnight hours and engaging in the heaviest fighting of their careers, saw the sunrise that morning on a very bleak landscape. They were surrounded indeed. When the Rebels got a good look at the relatively small force that had held them off through the night, they launched an immediate assault. Much to the

Rebels' dismay, the 61st hurled a furious volley that eventually sent the Confederates reeling with heavy losses.[292]

Still recovering from the sting of the 61st the Southerners brought up two cannons and began shelling the train with grape and canister (artillery munitions). At this point, Lieutenant Colonel Grass had to decide whether to protect the train and its cargo, or abandon it. The decision was quickly made to abandon the cargo for two reasons; first, the engine was being pummeled with artillery and would soon be rendered inoperable; second, and most importantly, their ammunition was nearly exhausted. Thus, the decision was made. With the few remaining shots each man possessed and completely surrounded by three thousand rebels, they would punch their way out.[293]

The only logical route of escape was straight-ahead six miles towards Murfreesboro. All the soldiers on the train ran as fast as they could towards Murfreesboro, and in pretty good order. They fought a running battle for two and a half miles and repulsed two assaults by the Rebels.[294] For those who had made it this distance, there was a block house where a small garrison of troops were waiting for the train. They were the reinforcements sent out from Murfreesboro. Unfortunately, only about half the regiment made it this far, the others were either captured or killed.[295] During this engagement, the 61st suffered five killed, 32 wounded (some severely) and eighty captured including the regimental commander Lieutenant Colonel Grass.[296]

What was left of the 61st, along with the reinforcements sent out from Murfreesboro, were quickly organized and marched back toward the train with hopes of recapturing it and assisting their comrades. No opposition was encountered. Yet by the time they arrived back at the train the Rebels had already disappeared and the train was ablaze.[297]

Most of the boys had not eaten since they left Stevenson, Alabama, and those that did have some food had left it on the train when they abandoned it. They did, however, remember that one of the cars was loaded with pickled pork. As the train was burning, they grabbed fence rails or whatever they could get their hands on and began pulling out the barrels that contained the pork. The meat was pretty charred on the outside, but the inside was just fine, so the boys enjoyed a fine pork dinner before marching back to Murfreesboro.[298]

The next day December 16th, 1864, General Rousseau the commander at Murfreesboro received a letter from General Nathan Bedford Forrest. In this letter Forrest proposed an exchange of prisoners, rank for rank, and man for man. Additionally he requested that a Mrs. David Spence be allowed safe passage through Union lines to come over to see her husband who was very ill, and a soldier under Forrest's command.[299]

General Rousseau agreed to these terms with a few stipulations: first, he wanted prisoners belonging to the 61st Illinois and the Michigan engineers exchanged first, then the prisoners of the 115th Ohio, who were captured between Murfreesboro and Nashville. General Rousseau continued that he would like to see the civilian railroad employees released who were captured in an earlier engagement, and that all Union soldiers have their personal property and equipment returned to them prior to the exchange.[300]

Apparently most of the boys made it back to Murfreesboro within a few days by one means or another, including Lieutenant Colonel Grass. Those who were not exchanged, escaped anyway as a result of Hood's defeat at the Battle of Nashville, Tennessee, ironically on the same day as the train incident (December 15th).[301]

Chapter 10

War's End and Demobilization

With John Bell Hood's retreat from Tennessee, the Union forces underwent a reorganization in order to maximize their available resources. The 61st Illinois, while in Murfreesboro, was placed under the command of Brigadier General Horatio Van Cleve (First Brigade). Major General Milroy was the division commander, and he reported directly to General Rousseau, who was in turn the "District of Tennessee" commander. The commander of all Tennessee forces was General George H. Thomas, "Department of the Cumberland".[302]

Now that things had settled down, the 61st moved out of Fort Rosecrans into the open area at the edge of Murfreesboro. They began immediately constructing winter quarters just as they had done a year before in Little Rock, Arkansas. They built the same basic log style cabin, but not with pine as before. Cedar was plentiful around Murfreesboro and very fragrant to burn as well.[303]

The railroad tracks were badly torn up in the middle Tennessee area, (thanks to Nathan Bedford Forrest). This resulted in a lack of rations for the troops in this area. So, with the abundance of corn in the fields and water powered mills north of town, General Rousseau ordered out foraging parties to make corn meal. For the next few weeks the soldiers subsisted on "ash cake". Ash cake was made of corn meal, water, grease, and salt made into a dough. The meal dough was wrapped with dampened paper, or wet cloth, put in the fire and covered with hot ashes and coals. And in a short time the soldiers would have "ash cake".[304]

On January 21st, 1865, orders were issued to Headquarters Department of Arkansas from General Grant that the non-veterans and recruits of the 61st Illinois that were still in Arkansas would rejoin their regiment at Murfreesboro, Tennessee.[305] On February 4th they arrived and once again the regiment was complete. The boys were quite excited to see each other again, and many hours were spent swapping stories of their adventures and misadventures over the past few months.

As mentioned, the regiment was whole once again with the exception of a few whom were not exchanged due to the December 15th train incident. One such unlucky prisoner was George L. Barton. In a letter written from his father to Captain Stuart, the (F) company commander, Mr. Barton inquires as to the fate of his son, George, because he has not received a letter from him for some time now. Additionally, he had heard a rumor that his son had fallen overboard on their way to Murfreesboro and drowned. In response, Captain Stuart informed the father that his son in fact did fall overboard during the journey in the Cumberland river enroute to Nashville, but he did not drown. He actually caught up with the regiment at Nashville after he had been given up for dead. Captain Stuart concluded his letter by stating that his son George was a "brave man" and a "good pluck" but unfortunately he had been captured on December 15th, during the train incident.[306]

The winter of 1864 came and went with no significant developments in the west; for practical purposes the war was all but over. On March 21st, 1865, the 61st was moved to

Franklin, Tennessee, site of the famous battle that recently took place on November 30th,1864. In fact the 61st was the only regiment at Franklin and was responsible for the entire region, until September when they mustered out of service.[307]

In a final reorganization, the 61st became an unassigned regiment within General Rousseau's District of Tennessee, 4th Division, 20th Army Corps.[308] Many regiments were put into the unassigned category for the final phase of the war.

Soon after the move to Franklin, there was also a change of command for the 61st. Lieutenant Colonel Grass had decided to resign his commission effective on May 15th, 1865. Therefore, the final commander of the 61st Illinois would be Major Jerome B. Nulton.[309]

Jerome Nulton was born in Washington County, Ohio in 1835. He was the youngest of eleven children when the family emigrated from Ohio to Greene County, Illinois in 1843. Jerome Nulton was a farmer in Greene County when the war broke out in 1861, and he subsequently sold everything he had and accepted a Captain's commission in the 61st Illinois from Governor Yates. He was given command of Company G. He was the only company commander who received a promotion due to gallantry displayed on the field of battle. He was promoted to the rank of Major as a direct result of his leadership displayed at the Battle of Little Rock.[310]

After the war, Colonel Nulton returned to Greene County, Illinois, where he received an appointment as the Deputy Revenue Assessor, in which capacity he served two years. He then went into the grain transaction business, which was the largest in the county during this epoch. In 1871, Jerome married Miss Henrietta

Sieverling. Two children came of this union. In 1872, Colonel Nulton was elected to the Illinois House of Representatives, representing the 39th District where he served one term. In 1875, he went back to his grain business in Greene County where he lived the remainder of his life.[311]

News arrived by telegraph on April 9th, 1865 that General Robert E. Lee had surrendered at Appomattox and the war was over. The feelings among the soldiers were one of "heartfelt relief and satisfaction" that indeed this long conflict would be drawing to a close, and they would soon be going home. But jubilation was soon turned to sorrow and mourning on April 14th when President Lincoln was assassinated (Lincoln subsequently died the next day). Everyone seemed "dazed and stunned" to hear the news. After subsequent reports were received that this terrible news was true, the boys of the 61st reluctantly had to accept it. The citizens of Franklin, Tennessee, locked their doors and stayed inside in fear that they might become victims of some sort of retaliation for the President's death. Had the citizens displayed any sign of joy over Lincoln's death the town would have been burned to the ground.[312]

In June, soldiers of the 83rd, 98th and 123rd Illinois regiments were transferred to the 61st, and for the first time, the 61st was a complete regiment with approximately 900 soldiers. Subsequently Major Nulton on July 11th was promoted to the rank of full colonel, the one and only full Colonel of the 61st during the war. [313]

The summer months of 1865 were like a picnic for the 61st. With the war over, there was no picket duty or railroads to guard, just occasional company drills to occupy the boys' time until they were ordered home. Finally, on September 4, 1865 the 61st was ordered to Nashville, Tennessee, to be mustered out of service. Due to some unforeseen delays they arrived in Nashville on September 8th and then climbed aboard the railcars bound for Springfield, Illinois, where final payment and discharge certificates were issued.[314]

On September 10th the train crossed the Ohio River at Louisville, Kentucky, on a long ferryboat. The train had to be ferried in sections because of its length, but it did not take long. Once again they were on their way, destined for Indianapolis, Indiana, This was a Sunday morning. Many ladies were all dressed up in their Sunday best headed for church. Naturally the fine Indiana folks waved and cheered the 61st as they rolled through these small towns, and the boys of the 61st reciprocated in like manner.[315]

The train arrived in Indianapolis about noon when they were marched to a nearby soldiers' home, where they were provided with a splendid dinner (noon) meal; they were subsequently placed back on the train, the next stop was Springfield, Illinois. They arrived at Springfield the next day, September 11, 1865. The 61st was promptly marched a few miles northeast of town to Camp Butler where they went into camp (Camp Butler is still there today. It is now a National Cemetery). It was quite frustrating, but the troops had to wait at Camp Butler for over two weeks to receive their final payment and discharge. Nevertheless, that day finally arrived. On September 27, 1865, the 61st Illinois Volunteers fell in for the last time. The roll of each company was called in alphabetical order. One by one the soldiers proceeded to the paymaster tent for final payment and his discharge certificate. A soldier walked into the tent; a civilian walked out. And so concludes the story of the 61st Illinois Infantry Regiment where on this date, September 27, 1865, they broke ranks forever. [316]

The End

---

[1] *New Standard Encyclopedia,* 1986 ed., s.v. "Illinois."

[2] Continental Historical Company, *History of Illinois: Greene and Jersey Counties,* (Roodhouse, Illinois: The Daily Eye Book Printing House), 21.

[3] Ibid., 22.

[4] Ibid., 23.

[5] Ibid.

[6] Ibid., 27.

[7] Ibid.

[8] *New Standard Encyclopedia,* 1986 ed., s.v. "Illinois."

[9] Continental Historical Company, *History of Illinois: Greene and Jersey Counties,* (Roodhouse, Illinois: The Daily Eye Book Printing House), 28.

[10] Ibid.

[11] Ibid., 567.

[12] Ibid., 571.

[13] Ibid., 579.

[14] *New Standard Encyclopedia,* 1986 ed., s.v. "Nathanael Greene."

[15] R.Ernest Dupuy and Trevor N. Dupuy, *The Harper Encyclopedia of Military History: From 3500 B.C. to the Present,* 4th ed., (HarperCollins*Publishers*, 1993), 951.

[16] Archer Jones, *Civil War Command and Strategy: The Process of Victory and Defeat,* (New York: The Free Press, 1992), 1.

[17] Ibid., 2.

[18] *Carrollton* (Illinois) *Gazette,* April 20, 1861.

[19] Ibid.

[20] Ibid.

[21] Leander Stillwell, *The Story of a Common Soldier of Army Life in the Civil War 1861-1865,* Second Edition (Franklin Hudson Publishing Co., 1920), 10.

[22] Ibid., 11.

[23] *History of Greene County, Illinois,* (Chicago: Donnelly, Gassette and Loyd, Publishers, 1897), 752.

[24] Ibid., 753.

[25] Ibid.

[26] Ibid.

[26] Ibid.

[28] *Carrollton* (Illinois) *Gazette,* October 19, 1861.

[29] Leander Stillwell, *The Story of a Common Soldier of Army Life in the Civil War 1861-1865,* Second Edition (Franklin Hudson Publishing Co., 1920), 11.

[30] Ibid., 12.

[31] Ibid., 14.

[32] Ibid., 15.

[33] Ibid.

---

[34] Ulysses S. Grant, *Personal Memoirs of U.S. Grant* (New York: The Great Commanders, 1994), 104.

[34] Ibid., 99

[36] Leander Stillwell, *The Story of a Common Soldier of Army Life in the Civil War 1861-1865,* Second Edition (Franklin Hudson Publishing Co., 1920), 16.

[37] Ibid.

[38] Ibid., 18.

[39] Ibid.

[40] Ibid., 19.

[41] Ibid.

[42] Ibid., 21.

[43] Colonel Jacob Fry, Carrollton, Illinois [to Governor Yates, Springfield, Illinois], February 26, 1862, Illinois State Archives, Springfield, Illinois.

[44] Ibid.

[45] *Carrollton* (Illinois) *Gazette,* February 22, 1862.

[46] Ibid., March 1, 1862.

[47] Leander Stillwell, *The Story of a Common Soldier of Army Life in the Civil War 1861-1865,* Second Edition (Franklin Hudson Publishing Co., 1920), 23.

[48] *Carrollton* (Illinois) *Gazette,* March 8, 1862.

[49] Ibid.

[50] Leander Stillwell, *The Story of a Common Soldier of Army Life in the Civil War 1861-1865,* Second Edition (Franklin Hudson Publishing Co., 1920), 23.

[51] Ibid., 25.

[52] William Winter, *The Civil War in St. Louis: A Tour,* (St. Louis: Missouri Historical Society Press, 1994), 73.

[53] Ibid.

[54] Ibid.

[55] Ibid.

[56] Ibid., 74.

[57] Leander Stillwell, *The Story of a Common Soldier of Army Life in the Civil War 1861-1865,* Second Edition (Franklin Hudson Publishing Co., 1920), 27.

[58] Ibid., 28.

[59] *Carrollton* (Illinois) *Gazette,* April 5, 1862.

[60] *OR*, Ser. 1, Vol. 52, pt. 1, 228.

[61] *Battles and Leaders of the Civil War,* Vol. 1, (New York: The Century Co. 1887), 469.

[62] Leander Stillwell, *The Story of a Common Soldier of Army Life in the Civil War 1861-1865,* Second Edition (Franklin Hudson Publishing Co., 1920), 40.

[63] *Battles and Leaders of the Civil War,* Vol. 1, (New York: The Century Co. 1887), 470-471.

[64] Leander Stillwell, *The Story of a Common Soldier of Army Life in the Civil War 1861-1865,* Second Edition (Franklin Hudson Publishing Co., 1920), 34.

[65] Ibid., 35.

[66] Ibid., 36.

[67] Edgar Embley, camped near Monterey, Mississippi [to brother, W.F. Embley, Jerseyville, Illinois], May 10,

1862, US Army Military History Institute, Carlisle Barracks, Carlisle, Pennsylvania.

[68] Leander Stillwell, *The Story of a Common Soldier of Army Life in the Civil War 1861-1865,* Second Edition (Franklin Hudson Publishing Co., 1920), 37.

[69] Ibid., 42.

[70] Ibid., 44.

[71] Ibid., 45.

[72] Ibid., 46.

[73] Ibid., 48.

[74] Ibid.

[75] Ibid., 49.

[76] Ibid., 51.

[77] Ibid., 52.

[78] Ibid.

[79] Ibid., 53.

[80] Ibid., 63.

[81] Ibid., 64.

[82] Captain James Lawrence, Pittsburg Landing [to wife, Sarah Lawrence, Chicago, Illinois], April 8, 1862, Chicago Historical Society, Chicago, Illinois.

[83] *Carrollton* (Illinois) *Gazette,* April 19, 1862.

[84] *Chicago* (Illinois) *Tribune,* April 13, 1862.

[85] *OR,* Ser. 1, Vol. 10, 279.

[86] *Carrollton* (Illinois) *Gazette,* April 26, 1862.

[87] Ibid., May 10, 1862.

[88] *OR,* Ser. 1, Vol. 10, 104.

[89] William T. Sherman, *Memoirs of General William T. Sherman* (New York:Da Capo Press, Inc., 1984), 247.

[90] Ulysses S. Grant, *Personal Memoirs of U.S. Grant* (New York: The Great Commanders, 1994), 163.

[91] Ibid.

[92] Leander Stillwell, *The Story of a Common Soldier of Army Life in the Civil War 1861-1865,* Second Edition (Franklin Hudson Publishing Co., 1920), 69.

[93] Ibid., 70.

[94] Captain James Lawrence, Bethel, Tennessee [to wife, Sarah Lawrence, Chicago, Illinois], June 10,1862, Chicago Historical Society, Chicago, Illinois.

[95] Leander Stillwell, *The Story of a Common Soldier of Army Life in the Civil War 1861-1865,* Second Edition (Franklin Hudson Publishing Co., 1920), 75.

[96] Ibid., 77.

[97] Ibid., 78.

[98] Ibid., 82.

[99] Ibid., 85.

[100] Ibid., 86.

[101] *OR,* Ser. 1, Vol. 16, pt.2, 69-70.

[102] Ibid., 76.

[103] Leander Stillwell, *The Story of a Common Soldier of Army Life in the Civil War 1861-1865,* Second Edition (Franklin Hudson Publishing Co., 1920), 87.

---

[104] Ibid., 90.

[105] Ibid., 92.

[106] Ulysses S. Grant, *Personal Memoirs of U.S. Grant* (New York: The Great Commanders, 1994), 183.

[107] Captain James Lawrence, Jackson, Tennessee [to wife, Sarah Lawrence, Chicago, Illinois], July 5,1862, Chicago Historical Society, Chicago, Illinois.

[108] *Carrollton* (Illinois) *Gazette,* Aug. 30, 1862.

[109] Ibid.

[110] Captain James Lawrence, Bolivar, Tennessee [to wife, Sarah Lawrence, Chicago, Illinois], January 31,1863, Chicago Historical Society, Chicago, Illinois.

[111] Leander Stillwell, *The Story of a Common Soldier of Army Life in the Civil War 1861-1865,* Second Edition (Franklin Hudson Publishing Co., 1920), 98.

[112] *Battles and Leaders of the Civil War,* Vol. 2, (New York: The Century Co. 1887), 732.

[113] Ibid.

[114] Ibid., 733.

[115] Ulysses S. Grant, *Personal Memoirs of U.S. Grant* (New York: The Great Commanders, 1994), 191.

[116] Leander Stillwell, *The Story of a Common Soldier of Army Life in the Civil War 1861-1865,* Second Edition (Franklin Hudson Publishing Co., 1920), 100.

[117] Ibid., 101.

[118] Ibid.

[119] Ibid.

[120] Ibid., 102.

[121] Ibid., 103.

[122] Ibid., 106.

[123] Ulysses S. Grant, *Personal Memoirs of U.S. Grant* (New York: The Great Commanders, 1994), 193.

[124] Ibid., 194.

[125] Leander Stillwell, *The Story of a Common Soldier of Army Life in the Civil War 1861-1865,* Second Edition (Franklin Hudson Publishing Co., 1920), 107.

[126] *Carrollton* (Illinois) *Gazette,* Sept. 27, 1862.

[127] Captain James Lawrence, Bolivar, Tennessee [to wife, Sarah Lawrence, Chicago, Illinois], October 15,1862, Chicago Historical Society, Chicago, Illinois.

[128] Adjutant General's Report (Illinois), (1900), vol. 4, 203.

[129] Ibid., 235.

[130] *Carrollton* (Illinois) *Gazette,* Dec. 27, 1862.

[131] Ibid., Jan. 3, 1863.

[132] Ibid., Jan. 10, 1863.

[133] Continental Historical Company, *History of Illinois: Greene and Jersey Counties,* (Roodhouse, Illinois: The Daily Eye Book Printing House), 743.

[134] Ibid., 744.

[135] *OR,* Ser. 1, Vol. 27, 482.

[136] Leander Stillwell, *The Story of a Common Soldier of Army Life in the Civil War 1861-1865,* Second Edition (Franklin Hudson Publishing Co., 1920), 114.

---

[137] Ibid., 115.

[138] *OR,* Ser. 1, Vol. 27, 482.

[139] Leander Stillwell, *The Story of a Common Soldier of Army Life in the Civil War 1861-1865,* Second Edition (Franklin Hudson Publishing Co., 1920), 117.

[140] Ibid.

[141] Ibid., 118.

[142] Ibid., 119.

[143] Ibid., 120.

[144] Archer Jones, *Civil War Command and Strategy: the Process of Victory and Defeat,* (New York: The Free Press, 1992), 144.

[145] Steven E. Woodworth, *Jefferson Davis and His Generals: The Failure of Confederate Command in the West,* (University Press of Kansas, 1990), 131.

[146] Ibid., 132.

[147] Ibid.

[148] Ibid.

[149] Ibid.

[150] Ibid.

[151] Leander Stillwell, *The Story of a Common Soldier of Army Life in the Civil War 1861-1865,* Second Edition (Franklin Hudson Publishing Co., 1920), 121.

[152] Ibid., 124.

[153] Ibid., 125.

[154] Ibid., 126.

[155] Ibid., 127.

[156] Ibid., 128.

[157] Ibid., 132.

[158] Major Simon P. Ohr, Bolivar, Tennessee [contract for medical services provided by Dr. Clinton Armstrong, Bolivar Tennessee], April 20, 1863, Greene County (Illinois) Historical Society.

[159] Adjutant General's Report (Illinois), (1900), vol. 4, 203.

[160] Edwin M. Stanton (Secretary of War), Washington D.C. [to Governor Yates, Springfield, Illinois], April 30, 1862, Greene County (Illinois) Historical Society.

[161] Allen Fuller (Adjutant General State of Illinois), Springfield, Illinois [special order No. 94], May 17, 1862, Greene County (Illinois) Historical Society.

[162] Ulysses S. Grant, *Personal Memoirs of U.S. Grant* (New York: The Great Commanders, 1994), 210.

[163] Leander Stillwell, *The Story of a Common Soldier of Army Life in the Civil War 1861-1865,* Second Edition (Franklin Hudson Publishing Co., 1920), 133.

[164] Ibid., 135

[165] Ibid.

[166] Ibid., 136.

[167] Ibid., 137.

[168] Ibid.

[169] Captain James Lawrence, Haines Bluff, Mississippi [to wife, Sarah Lawrence, Chicago, Illinois], June 10, 1863, Chicago Historical Society, Chicago, Illinois.

[170] Leander Stillwell, *The Story of a Common Soldier of Army Life in the Civil War 1861-1865,* Second Edition (Franklin Hudson Publishing Co., 1920), 137.

---

[171] Ibid., 138.

[172] Ibid.

[173] Ibid., 139.

[174] Ulysses S. Grant, *Personal Memoirs of U.S. Grant* (New York: The Great Commanders, 1994), 262.

[175] Leander Stillwell, *The Story of a Common Soldier of Army Life in the Civil War 1861-1865,* Second Edition (Franklin Hudson Publishing Co., 1920), 139.

[176] Ulysses S. Grant, *Personal Memoirs of U.S. Grant* (New York: The Great Commanders, 1994), 262.

[177] Leander Stillwell, *The Story of a Common Soldier of Army Life in the Civil War 1861-1865,* Second Edition (Franklin Hudson Publishing Co., 1920), 141.

[178] Ibid., 142.

[179] Ibid.

[180] Captain James Lawrence, Helena, Arkansas [to wife, Sarah Lawrence, Chicago, Illinois], August 20,1863, Chicago Historical Society, Chicago, Illinois.

[181] Leander Stillwell, *The Story of a Common Soldier of Army Life in the Civil War 1861-1865,* Second Edition (Franklin Hudson Publishing Co., 1920), 143.

[182] Ibid., 144.

[183] William T. Sherman, *Memoirs of General William T. Sherman* (New York: Da Capo Press, Inc., 1984), 331.

[184] Ibid., 332.

[185] Leander Stillwell, *The Story of a Common Soldier of Army Life in the Civil War 1861-1865,* Second Edition (Franklin Hudson Publishing Co., 1920), 144.

[186] Ibid., 146.

[187] Ibid., 149.

[188] Ibid., 150.

[189] Ibid., 158.

[190] Ibid., 160.

[191] *Battles and Leaders of the Civil War,* Vol. 3, (New York: The Century Co. 1887), 457.

[192] Ibid.

[193] Ibid.

[194] Leander Stillwell, *The Story of a Common Soldier of Army Life in the Civil War 1861-1865,* Second Edition (Franklin Hudson Publishing Co., 1920), 161.

[195] Captain James Lawrence, Little Rock, Arkansas [to wife, Sarah Lawrence, Chicago, Illinois], September 26, 1863, Chicago Historical Society, Chicago, Illinois.

[196] Leander Stillwell, *The Story of a Common Soldier of Army Life in the Civil War 1861-1865,* Second Edition (Franklin Hudson Publishing Co., 1920), 162.

[197] Ibid.

[198] Ibid., 163.

[199] Ibid., 182.

[200] Ibid., 183.

[201] Ibid.

[202] Captain James Lawrence, Little Rock, Arkansas [to wife, Sarah Lawrence, Chicago, Illinois], February 13, 1864, Chicago Historical Society, Chicago, Illinois.

[203] Leander Stillwell, *The Story of a Common Soldier of Army Life in the Civil War 1861-1865,* Second Edition (Franklin Hudson Publishing Co., 1920), 185.

[204] *OR,* Ser. 1, Vol. 34, pt. 2, 200-201.

[205] Leander Stillwell, *The Story of a Common Soldier of Army Life in the Civil War 1861-1865,* Second Edition (Franklin Hudson Publishing Co., 1920), 190.

[206] Ibid.

[207] *OR,* Ser. 1, Vol. 10, 104.

[208] Ulysses S. Grant, *Personal Memoirs of U.S. Grant* (New York: The Great Commanders, 1994), 350.

[209] *Battles and Leaders of the Civil War,* Vol. 4, (New York: The Century Co. 1887), 375.

[210] Ibid.

[211] Leander Stillwell, *The Story of a Common Soldier of Army Life in the Civil War 1861-1865,* Second Edition (Franklin Hudson Publishing Co., 1920), 192.

[212] Ibid., 193

[213] Ibid.

[214] *OR,* Ser. 1, Vol. 34, 898.

[215] *OR,* Ser. 1, Vol. 41, pt. 3, 561.

[216] Leander Stillwell, *The Story of a Common Soldier of Army Life in the Civil War 1861-1865,* Second Edition (Franklin Hudson Publishing Co., 1920), 193.

[217] *OR,* Ser. 1, Vol. 41, pt. 3, 638.

[218] Leander Stillwell, *The Story of a Common Soldier of Army Life in the Civil War 1861-1865,* Second Edition (Franklin Hudson Publishing Co., 1920), 194.

[219] Ibid., 196.

[220] Ibid., 198.

[221] Ibid.

[222] Ibid., 201.

[223] Ibid., 204.

[224] *OR,* Ser. 1, Vol. 34, pt. 4, 534.

[225] Leander Stillwell, *The Story of a Common Soldier of Army Life in the Civil War 1861-1865,* Second Edition (Franklin Hudson Publishing Co., 1920), 203.

[226] Ibid., 204.

[227] Ibid.

[228] Ibid., 205.

[229] Ibid., 206.

[230] Ibid., 216.

[231] *OR,* Ser. 1, Vol. 41, pt. 2, 702.

[232] Leander Stillwell, *The Story of a Common Soldier of Army Life in the Civil War 1861-1865,* Second Edition (Franklin Hudson Publishing Co., 1920), 219.

[233] Ibid., 220.

[234] *Carrollton* (Illinois) *Gazette*, Sept. 10, 1864.

[235] Leander Stillwell, *The Story of a Common Soldier of Army Life in the Civil War 1861-1865,* Second Edition (Franklin Hudson Publishing Co., 1920), 221.

[236] *Coffeyville* (Kansas) *Journal,* Dec. 21, 1894.

[237] Ibid.

---

[238] Ibid.

[239] Leander Stillwell, *The Story of a Common Soldier of Army Life in the Civil War 1861–1865,* Second Edition (Franklin Hudson Publishing Co., 1920), 221.

[240] *OR,* Ser. 1, Vol. 41, pt. 3, 442.

[241] Ibid., 479.

[242] Leander Stillwell, *The Story of a Common Soldier of Army Life in the Civil War 1861–1865,* Second Edition (Franklin Hudson Publishing Co., 1920), 222.

[243] *OR,* Ser. 1, Vol. 41, pt. 3, 561.

[244] Leander Stillwell, *The Story of a Common Soldier of Army Life in the Civil War 1861–1865,* Second Edition (Franklin Hudson Publishing Co., 1920), 222.

[245] Ibid., 224.

[246] *OR,* Ser. 1, Vol. 41, pt. 3, 584.

[247] *OR,* Ser. 1, Vol. 41, pt. 4, 78.

[248] Leander Stillwell, *The Story of a Common Soldier of Army Life in the Civil War 1861–1865,* Second Edition (Franklin Hudson Publishing Co., 1920), 225.

[249] Ibid., 226.

[250] Ibid., 227.

[251] Ibid.

[252] Ibid., 228.

[253] *OR,* Ser. 1, Vol. 41, pt. 4, 431.

[254] Leander Stillwell, *The Story of a Common Soldier of Army Life in the Civil War 1861–1865,* Second Edition (Franklin Hudson Publishing Co., 1920), 228.

[255] *OR,* Ser. 1, Vol. 41, pt. 4, 439.

[256] Leander Stillwell, *The Story of a Common Soldier of Army Life in the Civil War 1861-1865,* Second Edition (Franklin Hudson Publishing Co., 1920), 229.

[257] Ibid.

[258] *OR,* Ser. 1, Vol. 39, 684.

[259] Leander Stillwell, *The Story of a Common Soldier of Army Life in the Civil War 1861-1865,* Second Edition (Franklin Hudson Publishing Co., 1920), 230.

[260] Ibid., 230-232.

[261] *OR,* Ser. 1, Vol. 45, pt. 1, 1084.

[262] Leander Stillwell, *The Story of a Common Soldier of Army Life in the Civil War 1861-1865,* Second Edition (Franklin Hudson Publishing Co., 1920), 233.

[263] Ibid., 234.

[264] Ibid., 236.

[265] Ibid.

[266] *Carrollton* (Illinois) *Gazette,* Jan. 7, 1865.

[267] Leander Stillwell, *The Story of a Common Soldier of Army Life in the Civil War 1861-1865,* Second Edition (Franklin Hudson Publishing Co., 1920), 237.

[268] *OR,* Ser. 1, Vol. 45, pt. 1, 616.

[269] Ibid., 617.

[270] Leander Stillwell, *The Story of a Common Soldier of Army Life in the Civil War 1861-1865,* Second Edition (Franklin Hudson Publishing Co., 1920), 238.

[271] Ibid., 239.

[272] Ibid.

[273] Ibid., 240.

[274] Ibid., 243.

[275] Ibid., 244.

[276] *OR,* Ser. 1, Vol. 45, pt. 1, 618.

[277] Leander Stillwell, *The Story of a Common Soldier of Army Life in the Civil War 1861-1865,* Second Edition (Franklin Hudson Publishing Co., 1920), 245.

[278] *OR,* Ser. 1, Vol. 45, pt. 1, 620.

[279] *Carrollton* (Illinois) *Gazette,* Jan. 7, 1865.

[280] *OR,* Ser. 1, Vol. 45, pt. 1, 620.

[281] Leander Stillwell, *The Story of a Common Soldier of Army Life in the Civil War 1861-1865,* Second Edition (Franklin Hudson Publishing Co., 1920), 247.

[282] Ibid., 248.

[283] Ibid.

[284] Ibid.

[285] *OR,* Ser. 1, Vol. 45, pt. 1, 621.

[286] Leander Stillwell, *The Story of a Common Soldier of Army Life in the Civil War 1861-1865,* Second Edition (Franklin Hudson Publishing Co., 1920), 249.

[287] *Carrollton* (Illinois) *Gazette,* Jan. 7, 1865.

[288] *OR,* Ser. 1, Vol. 45, pt. 1, 621.

[289] *Carrollton* (Illinois) *Gazette,* Jan. 7, 1865.

[290] Leander Stillwell, *The Story of a Common Soldier of Army Life in the Civil War 1861-1865,* Second Edition (Franklin Hudson Publishing Co., 1920), 249.

---

[291] Ibid.

[292] *Carrollton* (Illinois) *Gazette,* Jan. 7, 1865.

[293] Leander Stillwell, *The Story of a Common Soldier of Army Life in the Civil War 1861–1865,* Second Edition (Franklin Hudson Publishing Co., 1920), 253.

[294] Ibid.

[295] *Carrollton* (Illinois) *Gazette,* Jan. 7, 1865.

[296] Ibid.

[297] Leander Stillwell, *The Story of a Common Soldier of Army Life in the Civil War 1861–1865,* Second Edition (Franklin Hudson Publishing Co., 1920), 253.

[298] Ibid., 256.

[299] *OR,* Ser. 2, Vol. 7, 1233.

[300] Ibid., 1234.

[301] Leander Stillwell, *The Story of a Common Soldier of Army Life in the Civil War 1861–1865,* Second Edition (Franklin Hudson Publishing Co., 1920), 257.

[302] *OR,* Ser. 1, Vol. 45, pt. 2, 455,459.

[303] Leander Stillwell, *The Story of a Common Soldier of Army Life in the Civil War 1861–1865,* Second Edition (Franklin Hudson Publishing Co., 1920), 258.

[304] Ibid.

[305] *OR,* Ser.1, Vol. 48, pt. 1, 560.

[306] Captain W.L. Stuart, Murfreesboro, Tennessee [to father of George L. Barton], January 18, 1865, Chicago Historical Society, Chicago, Illinois.

---

[307] Leander Stillwell, *The Story of a Common Soldier of Army Life in the Civil War 1861-1865,* Second Edition (Franklin Hudson Publishing Co., 1920), 260.

[308] *OR,* Ser. 1, Vol. 44, pt. 1, 794.

[309] Leander Stillwell, *The Story of a Common Soldier of Army Life in the Civil War 1861-1865,* Second Edition (Franklin Hudson Publishing Co., 1920), 260.
[310] *History of Greene County, Illinois,* (Chicago: Donnelly, Gassette, Loyd Publishers, 1879), 490.

[311] Ibid.

[312] Leander Stillwell, *The Story of a Common Soldier of Army Life in the Civil War 1861-1865,* Second Edition (Franklin Hudson Publishing Co., 1920), 262.

[313] Ibid., 263.

[314] Ibid., 274.

[315] Ibid., 275.

[316] Ibid.

SIXTY-FIRST INFANTRY REGIMENT.

THREE YEARS' SERVICE.

FIELD AND STAFF.

Name and Rank.	Residence.	Date of rank or enlistment.	Date of muster.	Remarks.
Colonels.				
Jacob Fry	Greene co	Nov. 1, 1861	Mar. 7, 1862	Resigned May 14, 1863, as Lieutenant Colonel
Simon P. Ohr	Springfield	May 14, 1864	Not must'r'd	Died Sept. 14, '64, as Lt. Col.
Daniel Grass	Lawrenceville	Sept. 15, 1864	"	Disch. May 15, '65, as Lt.Col.
Jerome B. Nulton	Greensbury	July 11, 1865	July 18, 1865	Mustered out Sept. 8, 1865.
Lieutenant Colonels.				
Jacob Fry	Carrollton	Feb. 5, 1862	Feb. 5, 1862	Resigned May 14, 1863
Simon P. Ohr	Springfield	May 14, 1863	July 2, 1863	Promoted
Daniel Grass	Lawrenceville	Sept. 14, 1864	Oct. 4, 1864	"
Majors.				
Simon P. Ohr	Springfield	Mar. 7, 1862	Mar. 7, 1862	Promoted
Daniel Grass	Lawrenceville	May 14, 1863	July 17, 1863	"
Jerome B. Nulton	Greensbury	Sept. 15, 1864	Oct. 17, 1864	"
Daniel S. Keeley	Carrollton	July 26, 1865	Aug. 1, 1865	Mustered out Sept. 8, 1865.
Adjutants.				
Francis M. Posey	Indian'p'lis, Ind	Feb. 5, 1862	Feb. 5, 1862	Pro. Capt. Co. A. Mar. 6, '62
Albert Cramer	B'nt'n B'rr's, Mo	Mar. 7, 1862	Mar. 7, 1862	Resigned Oct. 8, 1862
Henry S. Goodspeed	Avon	Oct. 9, 1862	Jan. 6, 1863	Promoted Captain Co. I.
Allen C. Haskins	Chicago	Aug. 26, 1863	Aug. 26, 1863	Pro. Capt. Co. I, July 11, '65.
Francis M. Mytinger		July 31, 1865	Aug. 6, 1865	Mustered out Sept. 8, 1865.
Quartermasters.				
Francis P. Vedder	Carrollton	Feb. 5, 1862	Feb. 5, 1862	Dismissed with loss of pay May 21, 1862, for absence without leave.
William M. Potts	White Hall	Apr. 15, 1862	Apr. 15, 1862	Mustered out Apr. 14, 1865.
Surgeons.				
Leonidas Clemmons	Chicago	Feb. 5, 1862	Feb. 5, 1862	Resigned Aug. 31, 1862
Julius P. Anthony	Sterling	Sept. 30, 1863	Nov. 8, 1863	Mustered out Sept. 8, 1865.
First Ass't Surgeon.				
George H. Knapp	Jerseyville	Nov. 20, 1861	Feb. 5, 1862	Resigned Feb. 13, 1864
Chaplains.				
Edward Rutledge	Jacksonville	May 16, 1862		Resigned Sept. 3, 1862
Benjamin B. Hamilton	White Hall	Oct. 30, 1862	Nov. 1, 1862	Resigned Mar. 3, 1865

NON-COMMISSIONED STAFF.

Name and Rank.	Residence.	Date of rank or enlistment.	Date of muster.	Remarks.
Sergeant Majors.				
Charles H. Ayres	White Hall.....	Jan. 5, 1864	Jan. 29, 1864	Prom. 1st Lieut. Co. A .....
William Caldwell	Kane............	Feb. 29, 1864	Apr. 30, 1864	Mustered out Sept. 8, 1865.
Q. M. Sergeants.				
Jonathan Burns	Winchester	Feb. 20, 1864	Apr. 30, 1864	Prom. 2d Lieut. Co. F ....
Samuel B. Jellison....	Decatur	....	....	Reduced to ranks Co. F, Oct. 18, 1863.........
Nathan Zimmerman..	Persifer	Feb. 10, 1865	Feb. 10, 1865	Mustered out Sept. 8, 1865.
Commis. Sergeants.				
William H. Bonfoy ...	Kane............	Jan. 5, 1864	Jan. 20, 1864	Prom. 2d Lieut. Co. E ....
Thomas F. Pierce.....	White Hall.....	Mar. 1, 1864	Apr. 25, 1864	Mustered out Sept. 8, 1865.
Hospital Stewards.				
William J. Winner....	Vermont	Mar 21, 1862	Mar. 26, 1862	Dishonor'bly disch'ged by sente'ce G.C.M.Mar.25,'63
Henry M. Morrison...	Wilmington	Dec. 21, 1861	Feb. 5, 1862	Mustered out Feb. 7, 1865..
Frederick H. Rix.....	Dillon	Sept. 27, 1864	Sept. 27, 1864	Mustered out Sept. 8, 1865.
Principal Musician.				
Joseph J. Ball........	Vermont	Mar. 20, 1864	Apr. 30, 1864	Mustered out Sept. 8, 1865.

COMPANY A.

Name and Rank.	Residence.	Date of rank or enlistment.	Date of muster.	Remarks.
Captains.				
Simon P. Ohr	Springfield.....	Feb. 5, 1862	Feb. 5, 1862	Promoted Major, Mar.7,'62
Francis M. Posey.....	Indianap'ls,Ind	Mar. 7, 1862		Mustered out Mar. 7, 1865.
William H. Armstrong	Carrollton......	July 11, 1865	Not must'r'd	Resigned July 15, 1865, as 1st Lieut . ...
Green P. Hanks	Wilmington....	Aug. 2, 1865	Aug. 10, 1865	Mustered out Sept. 8, 1865.
First Lieutenants.				
David G. Culver.......	White Hall.....	Feb. 5, 1862	Feb. 5, 1862	Wounded in battle of Shiloh, and died Apr. 14, '62.
William M. Potts......	"	Apr. 15, 1862	Apr. 15, 1862	Promoted Q. M., May 1, '63
William H. Armstrong	Carrollton	May 1, 1863	Aug. 26, 1863	Promoted ....
Charles H. Ayers	White Hall.....	Aug. 2, 1865	Aug. 10, 1865	Mustered out Sept. 8, 1865.
Second Lieutenants.				
William H. Armstrong	Carrollton	Feb. 5, 1862	Feb. 5, 1862	Promoted ....
William J. Allen	White Hall.....	Aug. 2, 1865	Aug. 10, 1865	Mustered out Sept. 8, 1865.
First Sergeant.				
Marshall Potts........	White Hall.....	Dec. 7, 1861	Feb. 5, 1862	Promoted 1st Lieutenant.
Sergeants.				
Samuel F. Winters....	White Hall.....	Oct. 28, 1861	Feb. 5, 1862	Disch. Feb. 11, '63; disabil.
Thomas J. Warren	Carrollton......		"	Promoted 1st Lt. Co. D ...
Henry M. Morrison...	Wilmington....	Dec. 21, 1861	"	Prom. Hospital Steward.
John B. Dodson.......	Greene co	Nov. 5, 1861	"	Disch. June 15, '62; disabil.
Corporals.				
Creighton Tucker.....	....	Dec. 14, 1861	Feb. 5, 1862	Deserted Aug. 10, 1863 ...
John Dinwiddie.......	White Hall.....	Oct. 25, 1861	"	Private. Died at Memphis, Oct. 18, 1863.........
Benjamin F. Higbee.	"	"	"	Died at Helena, Ark., Aug. 18, 1863
William H. Garrison.	Greene co......	Nov. 18, 1861	"	Re-enlisted as Veteran ...
Thornton T. Crabtree	"	Oct. 25, 1861	"	Private. Absent, sick, at M. O. of Regiment.
Edward Worthington.	White Hall.....	Nov. 4 1861	"	M. O. Feb. 7, '65, as Serg't.
Allen W. Jackson.....	"	Oct. 28, 1861	"	Re-enlisted as Veteran ...
Tyler B. Cochran.....	Wilmington....	Nov. 29, 1861	"	Died, St. Louis, May 23,'62
Musicians.				
Morton Campbell.....	White Hall.....	Dec. 9, 1861	Feb. 5, 1862	Died, St. Louis, Oct. 16, '63.
Nelson J. Polaski	"	Jan. 3, 1862	"	Re-enlisted as Veteran ...

Name and Rank.	Residence.	Date of rank or enlistment.	Date of muster.	Remarks.
Privates.				
Ayres, Charles H	White Hall	Oct. 25, 1861	Feb. 5, 1862	Re-enlisted as Veteran
Allen, Runy	Carrollton	Dec. 27, 1861	"	
Ashlock, John N		Jan. 27, 1862	"	Re-enlisted as Vet.; w'nd'd
Ballard, L. Nelson	White Hall	Dec. 9, 1861	"	Re-enlisted as Veteran
Blankfield, James		Dec. 18, 1861	"	
Copeland, Alfred	Jerseyville	Feb. 4, 1862	"	Disch. Nov. 28, 1862; disabil
Crow, Stephen	Greenfield	Jan. 30, 1862	"	Disch. Oct. 19, '63; disabil.
Cade, Bardiel	St. Louis, Mo.	Dec. 4, 1861	"	Deserted Mar. 17, 1863
Clariday, William	Greene co	Jan. 29, 1862	"	Died, Quincy, June 22,'62.
Cookson, John		Oct. 25, 1861	"	Wounded at Shiloh. Discharged Feb. 6,'63;disab'l
Dobson, Thomas	Manchester	Jan. 3, 1862	"	Mustered out Feb. 7, 1865.
Engle, William	Wilmington	Dec. 6, 1861	"	Re-enlisted as Veteran
Engle, George M. D		Dec. 21, 1861	"	Mustered out Feb. 7, 1865.
Emery, George W	Waverly	Dec. 23, 1861	"	Killed at Shiloh, Apr. 6,'62.
Edwards, Thomas	Athensville	Feb. 3, 1862	"	Died at Pittsburg Landing, Tennessee.
Francis, William	White Hall	Feb. 7, 1862	"	Died, Memphis, Sept. 13, '63
Griswold, George	"	Dec. 12, 1861	"	Disch. Oct. 8, '62; disabil.
Garrison, Gregory	"	Jan. 2, 1862	"	Killed at Shiloh, Apr. 6, '62
Holland, John	"	Feb. 5, 1862	"	Died, St. Louis, Mar. 25, '62.
Harrison, John S	"	Nov. 5, 1861	"	Re-enlisted as Veteran
Hager, Edward L	"	Nov. 13, 1861	"	Died May 30, '62; wounds.
Humphrey, James M.	"	Nov. 18, 1861	"	Re-enlisted as Veteran.
Huffman, William	"	Dec. 16, 1861	"	
Hanks, Green P	Wilmington	Dec. 28, 1861	"	" "
Holland, William D	Carrollton	Feb. 1, 1862	"	" "
Jewell, Charles		Oct. 25, 1861	"	
Johnson, John D	Jacksonville	Nov. 29, 1861	"	Disch. June 10,'62; disabil.
Jones, William	Manchester	Dec. 10, 1861	"	Killed at Shiloh, Apr. 6, '62.
Jones, Robert	Wilmington	Dec. 21, 1861	"	
Kissinger, James H	Winchester	Dec. 10, 1861	"	Died at Jackson, Tenn., Sept. 26, 1862.
Kelly, Silas	Manchester	Jan. 3, 1862	"	Re-enlisted as Veteran
Lockhart, Samuel	White Hall	Dec. 17, 1861	"	Disch. Aug. 7, '62; disabil.
Long, Israel	Carrollton	Dec. 27, 1861	"	Disch. June 21, '62; disabil.
Lister, Isaiah F	"	Jan. 8, 1862	"	Disch. July 23, '62; disabil.
Long, Franklin	"	Jan. 16, 1862	"	Mustered out Feb. 7, 1865
Mullins, John	"	Nov. 5, 1861	"	Died at Snyder's Bluff, Miss., June 28, 1863
Marshall, John	"	Oct. 28, 1861	"	Re-enlisted as Veteran
Malone, Kindred H	White Hall	Dec. 17, 1861	"	Discharged
Moore, William		Dec. 10, 1861	"	Re-enlisted as Veteran
McCoy, William H	Jerseyville	Feb. 1, 1862	"	Died at Pittsburg Landing, Tenn., Apr. 6, '62.
Mason, George W	Carrollton	Nov. 2, 1861	"	Re-enlisted as Veteran
Noyes, James S	State of Mass.	Dec. 12, 1861	"	Disch. Sept. 4,'62; wounds.
Nichols, John	Carrollton	Dec. 9, 1861	"	Mustered out Feb. 7, 1865.
Overberry, Zadoo	White Hall	Nov. 2, 1861	"	Deserted Feb. 20, 1863.
Pyndreon, Joseph	LaSalle co	Dec. 9, 1861	"	Deserted Aug. 7, 1863
Pruitt, Richard	Wilmington	Dec. 30, 1861	"	Re-enlisted as Veteran
Pierce, Thomas F	White Hall	"	"	Wo'nded. Re-enl. as Vet.
Pulaski, William A		Feb. 4, 1862	"	Mustered out Feb. 7, 1865
Roberts, John	Jerseyville	Jan. 29, 1862	"	Disch. Jan. 29, '63; disabil.
Romines, John	Wilmington	Oct. 25, 1861	"	Re-enlisted as Veteran
Reamer, Squire	White Hall	"	"	
Rose, Fountain E	Glasgow	"	"	" "
Rose, Jeremiah J		"	"	" "
Robbins, James A	Carrollton	Oct. 31, 1861	"	Tr. to V. R. C., May 15, '64. M. O. Feb. 4, 1865
Rogers, John K	White Hall	Jan. 2, 1862	"	Disch. Sept. 4, '62; disabil.
Reeday, John H		Jan. 15, 1862	"	Mustered out Feb. 7, 1865.
Rigg, Samuel J	Athensville	Feb. 3, 1862	"	Re-enlisted as Veteran
Starky, Leonard M	Wilmington	Jan. 29, 1862	"	Wounded. Re-enl. as Vet.
Swaggerty, James M.	Carrollton	Nov. 29, 1861	"	
Spalding, Luctus O	White Hall	Dec. 9, 1861	"	Disch. Jan. 8, '63; wounds.
Swallow, Jacob		Dec. 27, 1861	"	Died at Pittsburg Landing, Tennessee
Shaw, James M	Jerseyville	Dec. 30, 1861	"	Died, Little Rock, May 26, '64
Wells, David W	White Hall	Oct. 25, 1861	"	Died at Pittsburg Landing, Tenn., Apr. 1, 1862
Walker, Dennis R	Carrollton	Oct. 28, 1861	"	Disch. May 27, '62; disabil.
Woods, John	White Hall	Oct. 30, 1861	"	Died, St. Louis, Apr. 10, '62.
Williams, Isaac		Nov. 29, 1861	"	Re-enlisted as Veteran
Warner, Samuel A	"	Dec. 2, 1861	"	Disch. Nov. 8, '62; disabil.
Welch, Dennis	"	Dec. 13, 1861	"	Died, Corinth, Nov. 1, '62.
Williams, James N	Carrollton	Jan. 3, 1862	"	Dishon. disch. Feb. 17, 1864.

Name and Rank.	Residence.	Date of rank or enlistment.	Date of muster.	Remarks.
Veterans.				
Ayers, Charles H	White Hall	Jan. 5, 1864	Jan. 20, 1864	Promoted Serg't Major...
Allen, Reuney				Mustered out Sept. 8, 1865..
Ashlock, John A	Carrollton	Mar. 1, 1864	Apr. 25, 1864	M. O. Aug. 15,'65; was pris.
Allen, William J	Taylorville	Jan. 5, 1864		Prom. Serg't, then 2d Lieut
Allen, Reuben	White Hall	"	"	M. O. Sept. 8, '65, as Corp'l.
Blanchfield, James	Carrollton	"	Jan. 25, 1864	Disch. Mar. 18, 1865: accidental wounds..
Ballard, Lewis N	White Hall	"	Jan. 25, 1824	M. O. Sept. 8,'65, as Corp'l.
Campbell, Amburgh		"		Mustered out Sept. 8, 1865.
Engle, William	Breese	"	Jan. 20, 1864	
Fears, Sylvester J	Carrollton	"	Apr. 25, 1864	M. O. Sept. 8,'65, as Corp'l.
Garrison. William	White Hall	"	"	Mustered out Sept. 8, 1865.
Hanks, Green P	Breese	"	Jan. 20, 1864	Prom. 1st Sgt, then Capt.
Huffman, William	White Hall	"	"	M. O. Sept. 8,'65, as Serg't.
Harrison, John S	"	"	Apr. 25, 1864	M. O. Sept. 8,'65, as 1st Sgt.
Holland, William D	Carrollton	"	"	Mustered out Sept. 8, 1865
Humphrey, James M	White Hall	"	"	M. O. May 30, '65, as Corp'l.
Jewell, Charles	Carrollton	"	"	M. O. Sept. 8,'65, as Serg't.
Kelly, Silas	Manchester	"	"	Mustered out May 30, 1865.
Moore, William	White Hall	"	"	Mustered out Sept. 8, 1865.
Mason, George W	Carrollton	"	"	M. O. May 30,'65; pris. war.
Marshall, John	"	"	"	
Pierce, Thomas F	White Hall	Mar. 1, 1864	"	Prom. Com. Sergeant......
Pruitt, Richard	Breese	Feb. 1, 1864	"	Mustered out Sept. 8, 1865.
Polaski, Nelson J	White Hall	"	"	
Rose, Jeremiah J	Glasgow	Jan. 5, 1864	Jan. 24, 1864	M. O. May 30,'65: pris. war.
Reamer, Squire P	White Hall	Feb. 1, 1864	Apr. 25, 1864	M. O. Sept. 8, '65, as Corp l.
Riggs, Samuel J	"	Mar. 1, 1864	"	M. O. Sept. 8,'65, as Serg't.
Romines, John	"	Feb. 1, 1864	"	M. O. May 30,'65; pris. war.
Rose, Fountain E	Glasgow	"	"	Disch. Aug. 2, '64; disabil.
Siples, Josiah	White Hall	Mar. 1, 1864	"	M. O. Sept. 8,'65, as Serg't.
Starkey, Leonard M	Breese	Feb. 1, 1864	"	M. O. May 30,'65: pris. war.
Swaggerty, James M	Scottsville	"	"	Mustered out Sept. 8, 1865.
Williams, Isaac	White Hall	Mar. 1, 1864	"	"
Recruits.				
Allen, John	White Hall	Feb. 10, 1862		Died, St. Louis, May 22, '62.
Allen, Reuben				Re-enlisted as Veteran..
Ashlock, George W	Richmond	Apr. 6, 1865	Apr. 6, 1865	Mustered out Sept. 8, 1865.
Burton, Thomas B	Loami	Dec. 28, 1863	Dec. 28, 1863	Never joined Co. Died at Memphis, Jan. 31, 1864
Brown, Henry	White Hall	Jan. 30, 1865	Feb. 1, 1865	Mustered out Sept. 8, 1865.
Bonas, William L	Carrollton	Dec. 11, 1863	Jan. 31, 1864	Deserted March 4, 1865
Campbell, Amburgh	White Hall	Feb. 22, 1862		Re-enlisted as Veteran.
Clark, William	Woodville			Mustered out Sept. 8 1865
Cox, Peter A	N. Western	Sept. 14, 1864	Sept. 14, 1864	Mustered out July 20, 1865.
Dempsey, John	Jacksonville	Dec. 31, 1863	Dec. 31, 1863	Mustered out Sept. 8, 1865.
Engle or England, Jeff	"	Dec. 25, 1862		Absent, in confinement, sentence G. C. M
Fears, Sylvanus J	Carrollton	Feb. 24, 1862		Re-enlisted as Veteran.
Fettigg, Alvin	"	Mar. 25, 1864	Apr. 28, 1864	Mustered out Sept. 8, 1865.
Freeman. George H	Woodville	Dec. 20, 1863		M. O. Sept. 8,'65, as Corp'l.
Gates, Samuel	"	Jan. 2, 1864	Feb. 2, 1864	Died, Little Rock, Sep. 16,'64
Green, Leonard A	"			Mustered out Sept. 8, 1865.
Grover, John	Hardin	Nov. 13, 1863	Dec. 31, 1863	Deserted July 20, 1865......
Howard, Elisha L	Greenfield	Mar. 21, 1864	Apr. 21, 1864	Died at Duvall's Bluff, Ark., Dec. 20, 1864
Hornaday, Nathan	Vedder	Feb. 7, 1864	Feb. 22, 1864	Mustered out Sept. 8, 1865.
Hutchinson, William	Woodville	Jan. 2, 1864	Feb. 2, 1864	" "
Hastings, James W	"			" "
Harp, Lewis B	Mackinaw	Sept. 28, 1864	Sept. 28, 1864	Mustered out July 20, 1865.
Jones, Francis M	Carrollton	Dec. 21, 1863		Mustered out Sept. 8, 1865.
Kesinger, Reuben	Greene co	Jan. 30, 1865	Feb. 1, 1865	
Kesinger, John M	Ball	Sept. 28, 1864	Sept. 28, 1864	Died, Murfreesboro, Tenn.
Kelly, James	N. Western	Sept. 14, 1864	Sept. 14, 1864	Mustered out July 20, 1865
Laken, George W	Vedder	Feb. 6, 1864	Feb. 22, 1864	Died, Memphis, Mar. 25, '64
Lakin, Elijah				Died at Duvall's Bluff, Ark., Oct. 16, 1864 ....
Lee, Elisha W	Carrollton	Feb. 7, 1862		Died, Quincy, May 24, 1862.
McPherson, Francis M	Manchester	Feb. 24, 1862		Disch. Aug. 6,'62: disabil.
Marshall, John S	Greene co	Nov. 11, 1863	Dec. 31, 1863	Mustered out Sept. 8, 1865.
Manning, James M	Jerseyville	Dec. 21, 1863	Jan. 12, 1864	" "
McKinnett, Orris	Locust	Apr. 12, 1865	Apr. 12, 1865	" "
Pinkerton, Willis H	Carrollton	Nov. 26, 1863	Dec. 31, 1863	Died, Little R'ck, Feb. 24,'64
Prosser, William	Oratin	Jan. 18, 1864	Feb. 22, 1864	Mustered out Sept. 8, 1865.
Price, Robert M	Danville	Nov. 26, 1863	Dec. 31, 1863	" "
Pinkerton, Revell	Eastern	Dec. 29, 1863	Dec. 29, 1863	" "
Rutherford, Wm. H	Belleview	Mar. 21, 1864	Mar. 21, 1864	Died, C'p Butler, May 8,'64
Ryno, George W	Bluffdale	Jan. 18, 1864	Feb. 22, 1864	Mustered out Sept. 8, 1865.

Name and Rank.	Residence.	Date of rank or enlistment.	Date of muster.	Remarks.
Siples, Josiah	White Hall	Feb. 20, 1862	....	Re-enlisted as Veteran...
Simons, Arthur	Eastern	Dec. 29, 1863	Dec. 29, 1863	Died at Duvall's Bluff, Ark., May 8, 1864
Smith, Jacob		Jan. 2, 1864	Feb. 2, 1864	Mustered out Sept. 8, 1865.
Sanders, William	Richmond	" "	" "	M. O. Sept. 8, '65, as Corp'l.
Swainey, William	Woodville	" "	" "	Mustered out Sept. 8, 1865.
Stackman, Henry		" "	" "	" "
Snyder, William	Worth	Feb. 10, 1865	Feb. 10, 1865	" "
Tongate, William W.	Loami	Dec. 28, 1863	Dec. 28, 1863	" "
Taylor, Hugh R.	Woodville	Jan. 2, 1864	Feb. 2, 1864	" "
Thurston, David J.	Vedder	Jan. 18, 1864	Feb. 22, 1864	" "
Thompson, Alexander	Eastern	Dec. 29, 1863	Dec. 29, 1863	Died at Franklin, Tenn., Apr. 16, 1865.
Thorp, Albert G.	Chatham	Dec. 28, 1863	Dec. 28, 1863	Disch. June 28,'65; disabil.
Vinson, Thomas W.	Woodville	Jan. 2, 1864	Jan. 2, 1864	Mustered out Sept. 8, 1865.
Walpole, John S	Jerseyville	Nov. 10, 1863	Dec. 31, 1863	" "
Warrimack, Riley	Woodville	Dec. 11, 1864	Jan. 31, 1864	" "
Warren, Robert	" "	Jan. 2, 1864	Feb. 2, 1864	" "
Wood, William J	Vedder	Feb. 1, 1864	Feb. 22, 1864	" "
Wheisman, George W	Cratin	Jan. 18, 1864		
Wood, Luke	Vedder	" "	" "	M. O. Sept. 8,'65, as Corp'l.
Williams, James K	Illinois Point.	Dec. 29, 1863	Dec. 29, 1863	Deserted Jan. 13, 1864......
York, Thomas.	Ball	Sept. 28, 1864	Sept. 28, 1864	Mustered out July 20, 1865.
Recruits trans. from 83d Ill. Inf.				
Brown, John F		Apr. 1, 1863	Apr. 1, 1863	Mustered out Sept. 8, 1865.
Burnett, John E	Henderson	Dec. 28, 1863	Dec. 29, 1863	" "
Benson, Hanson K	Persifer	Feb. 10, 1865	Feb. 10, 1865	" "
Benson, Harvey	Persifer	Jan. 4, 1864	Jan. 4, 1864	" "
Castle, Rufus A	Cedar	Dec. 28, 1863	Dec. 29, 1863	" "
Henry, William	Oneida	Dec. 29, 1863		" "
Hough, William	Peoria	Jan. 19, 1865	Jan. 19, 1865	" "
Mitchell, Alexander	Knoxville	Mar. 12, 1864	Mar. 12, 1864	" "
Massie, Eli P		Nov. 23, 1863	Nov. 23, 1863	" "
Mattron, Ovi P	Abingdon	Jan. 5, 1864	Jan. 5, 1864	" "
Packard, Carlos	Rivoia	Feb. 24, 1865	Feb. 25, 1865	" "
Ramp, David	Haw Creek	Feb. 24, 1864	Feb. 24, 1864	" "
Wilcox, Nathaniel R.	Knoxville	Nov. 30, 1863	Nov. 30, 1863	M. O. Sept. 8, '65, as Corp'l.
Zimmerman, Nathan	Persifer	Feb. 16, 1865	Feb. 16, 1865	Promoted Q. M. Sergeant.
Recruits transf'd from 123d Ill. Inf.				
Alwell, Thomas	Charleston	Mar. 16, 1864	Mar. 16, 1864	Mustered out Sept. 8, 1865.
Anderson, Thomas W.	Dement	Mar. 6, 1865	Mar. 7, 1865	" "
Epperson, Rhodes	Charleston	Jan. 4, 1864	Feb. 8, 1864	" "
Fleetwood, John	Hickory	Mar. 16, 1865	Mar. 16, 1865	" "
Ferguson, Andrew F	Sullivan	Feb. 22, 1865	Feb. 22, 1865	" "
Fleming, Charles	Charleston	Mar. 21, 1864	Mar. 21, 1864	" "
Kendall, George	" "	Mar. 16, 1864	Mar. 16, 1864	" "
Timmons, Cornelius	" "	Jan. 1, 1864	Jan. 2, 1864	" "
Watkins, William	Westfield			" "
White, Henry	Dement	Mar. 6, 1865	Mar. 7, 1865	" "

COMPANY B.

Name and Rank.	Residence.	Date of rank or enlistment.	Date of muster.	Remarks.
Captains.				
Martin J. Mann	New Provid'nce	Feb. 5, 1862	Feb. 5, 1862	Resigned Apr. 3, 1863 ......
Samuel T. Carrico	Carrollton	May 1, 1863	July 18, 1863	Resigned May 29, 1865......
Alfred D. Nash		July 13, 1865	July 20, 1865	Mustered out Sept. 8, 1865.
First Lieutenants.				
George Chism	New Provid'nce	Feb. 5, 1862	Feb. 5, 1862	Resigned Oct. 16, 1862......
Sammel T. Carrico	Carrollton	Oct. 16, 1862	Nov. 1, 1862	Promoted ......
Lorenzo J. Miner		May 1, 1863	July 18, 1863	Killed in action, Dec 15, '64.
John Thorn		Aug. 21, 1865	Not must'r'd	M. O. Sept. 8,'65; as priv..
Second Lieutenants.				
Samuel T. Carrico	Carrollton	Feb. 5, 1862	Feb. 5, 1862	Promoted ......
Charles W. Mann.	New Provid'nce	Oct. 16, 1862	Nov. 1, 1862	Dismissed May 26, 1863 ....
Privates.				
Adams, James D	Carrollton	Nov. 13, 1861	Feb. 5, 1862	Re-enlisted as Veteran...

Name and Rank.	Residence.	Date of rank or enlistment.	Date of muster.	Remarks.
Allen, Henry B	Pearl	Feb. 3, 1862	Feb. 5, 1862	Disch. Aug. 21, '62; disabil.
Byrand, George C	Carrollton	Nov. 15, 1861	"	Re-enlisted as Veteran.
Bradley, John A	"	Nov. 3, 1861	"	M. O. Feb. 7, '65, as Corp'l.
Bartlett, Lewis	"		"	Died, St. Louis, Mar. 25, '62.
Bowers, Jacob	"	Dec. 3, 1861	"	Re-enlisted as Veteran
Benner, John S	"	Dec. 5, 1861	"	Disch. July 7, '62; disabil.
Bush, Conrad	"		"	Died at Carrollton, Ill., Feb. 23, 1862
Bilbrook, William T	"	Jan. 7, 1862	"	Disch. Nov. 19, '62; disabil.
Breini, Joseph	"	Feb. 3, 1862	"	Died at Duvall's Bluff, Ark., Oct. 5, 1863
Crane, Robert Henry	New Provid'nce	Nov. 3, 1861	"	Deserted Dec. 26, 1862
Clark, Richard L	"		"	Died at White Hall, Ill., May 2!, 1862
Copley, John	Carrollton	Dec. 28, 1861	"	Disch. June 19, '62; wounds.
Clark, James H	"	Jan. 7, 1862	"	Disch. July 9, '62; disabil.
Clark, Elijah J	"		"	Died at Savannah, Tenn., Apr. 20, 1862
Campbell, William R	Whitehall	Jan. 18, 1862	"	Re-enlisted as Veteran.
Covier, Paul	Carrollton	Jan. 23, 1862	"	
Donnelly, James	"	Oct. 24, 1861	"	Killed himself accident'ly, Oct. 21, '62, at Bolivar, Ten
Devault, Isaac C	"	Nov. 3, 1861	"	Re-enlisted as Veteran
Donnally, John	"	Dec. 14, 1861	"	Killed at Gregory's Landing, Ark., Sept. 5, 1864
English, Warren	"	Nov. 7, 1861	"	Disch. Nov. 8, '62, as Serg't; disability
Elmore, William	"	Nov. 3, 1861	"	Disch. Dec. 16, '62; wounds.
Elmore, Ralph	"		"	Re-enlisted as Veteran
England, James	"	Dec. 9, 1861	"	Disch. July 21, '62; disabil.
Gamble, Martin V	"	Feb. 7, 1862	"	Died, St. Louis, Sept. 1862.
Guthery, George	"	Feb. 3, 1862	"	Mustered out Feb. 7, 1865.
Gunn, George S	"	Nov. 2, 1861	"	Re-enlisted as Veteran
Gamble, Aaron C	"	Nov. 3, 1861	"	Disch. Oct. 2, '62, as Serg't; disability
Green, Jacob	"	Dec. 27, 1861	"	Re-enlisted as Veteran
Hill, Jacob M	"	Feb. 1, 1862	"	Deserted Oct. 10, 1862
Hilderbrandt, Joseph	"	Nov. 18, 1861	"	Tr. to V. R. C., Sept. 3, '63
Hill, Phillip R	"	Dec. 19, 1861	"	Deserted May 10, '64, 2d des.
Hess, Luther D	Pearl	Dec. 21, 1861	"	Died at Pittsburg Landing, May 10, 1862
Irvin, Charles	Carrollton	Nov. 20, 1861	"	Mustered out Feb. 7, 1865.
Johnson, Alexander T	"	Nov. 3, 1861	"	Disch. Dec. 10, '62; disabil.
Johnson, John S	"	Dec. 3, 1861	"	Tr. to V. R. C., Sept. 3, '63, M. O. Feb. 4, 1865
Jones or Ivens, John	"	Dec. 14, 1861	"	Mustered out Feb. 7, 1865.
Jowidan, William T	"	Jan. 1, 1862	"	Disch. May 7, '62; disabil.
Jackson, John B	Pearl	Dec. 20, 1861	"	Mustered out Feb. 7, 1865.
Johnson, Alexander	Carrollton	Feb. 1, 1862	"	Died at Henderson, Ky., June 7, 1862
King, William B	"	Nov. '18 1861	"	Re-enlisted as Veteran
Keayton, John	"	Nov. 20, 1861	"	
Kennedy, T. W	"	Oct. 4, 1861	"	Disch. Apr. 25, '62; disabil.
Kuhn, Henry	"	Nov. 30, 1861	"	Re-enlisted as Veteran
Kasinger, S. J	Pearl	Jan. 20, 1862	"	Died at Pittsburg Landing, Apr. 19, 1862
Kirkwood, George T	Carrollton	Feb. 4, 1862	"	Dropped as deserter, Jan. 10, 1864
Lowhouse, John V		Oct. 21, 1861	"	Died at Duvall's Bluff, Ark., Aug. 31, 1863
Laubscher, Jacob	Carrollton	Nov. 30, 1861	"	Re-enlisted as Veteran
Lorance, Jesse W	White Hall	Dec. 2, 1861	"	"
Matheny, John R	Carrollton	Oct. 18, 1861	"	"
Martin, Thomas E	"	Oct. 17, 1861	"	Disch. Aug. 2, '62; disabil.
Mann, Charles W	"	Nov. 3, 1861	"	Prom. 1st Serg., then 2d Lt.
March, John	"	Dec. 2, 1861	"	Re-enlisted as Veteran
Musselman, Jonathan	"	Dec. 28, 1861	"	Mustered out Feb. 7, 1865.
Morgan, Hiram	Pearl	Jan. 1, 1862	"	Died at Pittsburg Landing, Tenn., May 13, 1862
March, George W	Carrollton	Jan. 4, 1862	"	Re-enlisted as Veteran
Maier, John	"	Jan. 20, 1862	"	Mustered out Feb. 7, 1865.
McClimans, J. D	"	Dec. 16, 1861	"	Died at White Hall, Ill., May 15, 1862
Nelson, John F	"	Dec. 11, 1861	"	Disch. Aug. 8, '62; disabil.
Ott, John	"	Nov. 16, 1861	"	Mortally wounded at Shiloh Apr. 6, 1862
Pope, William M	Kane	Oct. 28, 1861	"	Died St. Louis, Aug. 8, '62.
Perry, Commodore R	Carrollton	Nov. 9, 1861	"	Disch. Oct. 25, '63; disabil.
Pennington, Ephraim	"	Dec. 31, 1861	"	Died in Missouri, Sept. 6, '62
Rains, Thomas B	"	Nov. 3, 1861	"	Disch. Sept. 16, '62; disabil.

Name and Rank.	Residence.	Date of rank or enlistment.	Date of muster.	Remarks.
Rogers, William	Carrollton	Nov. 3, 1861	Feb. 5, 1862	Re-enlisted as Veteran ...
Reno, James	"	Nov. 16, 1861	"	Died at Bolivar, Tenn.. May 13, 1862.
Raines, William	Hardin.	Jan. 9, 1862	"	Disch. July 25, '62; disabil.
Reyno, George W	Carrollton	Jan. 20, 1862	"	Disch. Sept. 18, '62; disabil.
Siller, Louis.	"	Nov. 30, 1861	"	Re-enlisted as Veteran ...
Smith, Henry	"	Dec. 14, 1861	"	Died. St. Louis, Feb. 27, '62.
Stuber, Joseph	"	Dec. 17, 1861	"	Died May 10, 1862
Stailey, John W.	"	Jan. 4, 1862	"	Re-enlisted as Veteran ...
Smith, Frank	Hardin	Jan. 10, 1862	"	Disch. June 25, '64; di-abil.
Stine, Tilford T.	Carrollton	Feb. 4, 1862	"	Disch. Oct. 2, '62; disabil ...
Taylor, Hezekiah W.	"	Dec. 9, 1861	"	Disch. July 22, '62; disabil.
Thompson, Samuel D.	"	Jan. 4, 1862	"	Died at St. Louis May 12, 1862; wounds
Whiteside, William J.	"	Dec. 24, 1861	"	Disch. Nov. 8, '63; disabil..
Wear, Pleasant M.	"		"	Re-enlisted as Veteran. ..
Whiteside, Rich F.	Wilmington	Jan. 9, 1862	"	1st Sgt. Tr. to V.R.C. Sept. 3, 1863
Ward, Jasper N.	Carrollton	Jan. 11, 1862	"	Re-enlisted as Veteran. ..
Veterans.				
Adams, James D.	Carrollton	Feb. 1, 1864	Mar. 11, 1864	Mustered out Sept. 8, 1865.
Bowers, Jacob	"	"	"	Deserted Apr. 26, 1864
Bryan, George C	"	"	"	M. O. May 30, '65; pris. war.
Campbell, William R.	White Hall	"	"	Mustered out July 13, 1865.
Covier, Paul	Carrollton	"	"	Deserted Sept. 26, 1864 ....
Devault, Isaac C.	Malta, Ohio	"	"	M. O. May 29, '65, as 1st Sgt.; was prisoner
Elkington, Joseph H.	Carrollton	Feb. 29, 1864	"	M. O. June 14, '65; was pris.
Ellmore, Ralph.	Athensville	Feb. 1, 1864	"	Mustered out Sept. 8, 1865.
Goodpasture, Daniel J	Carrollton	Feb. 29, 1864	"	M. O. Sept. 8, '65, as Corp'l.
Green, Jacob	"	Jan. 4, 1864	Jan. 20, 1864	Mustered out Sept. 8, 1865.
Gunn, George S	"	Feb. 1, 1864	Mar. 11, 1864	Disch. June 26, '65, as Sgt.; disability
King, William B	N. Providence	Jan. 4, 1864	Jan. 20, 1864	M. O. Sept. 8, '65, as Serg't..
Keayton, John	Carrollton			Deserted Oct. 18, 1864
Kuhn, Henry	"	Feb. 1, 1864	Mar. 11, 1864	Deserted Sept. 26, 1864 ....
Lawbscher, Jacob	"			Died at Franklin, Tenn.. May 29, 1865.
Lorance, Jesse W	"	"	"	Mustered out Sept. 8, 1865
March, George W	"	Jan. 4, 1864	Jan. 20, 1864	"
March, John L	"	Feb. 1, 1864	Mar. 11, 1864	" "
Matheny, John R.	"			"
Nash, Alfred D	White Hall	Feb. 29, 1864	"	Prom. Captain July 27, '15.
Rogers, William	N. Providence	Jan. 4, 1864	Jan. 20, 1864	M. O. Sept. 8, '65, as Corp'l.
Siller, Louis	Carrollton	Feb. 1, 1864	Mar. 11, 1864	Mustered out Sept. 8, 1865.
Stailey, John W	Cincinnati, O.	Jan. 4, 1864	Jan. 20, 1864	
Wear, Pleasant M	Mt. Vernon, Mo.	Feb. 1, 1864	Mar. 11, 1864	M. O. Sept. 8, '65, as Corp'l.
Ward, Jasper N.	Carrollton	"	"	M. O. Sept. 8, '65, as Serg't.
Ward, William T	Auburn	Feb. 29, 1864	"	M. O. Sept. 8, '65, as Corp'l
Recruits.				
Benner, John	Rhoades' Point	Feb. 20, 1865	Feb. 21, 1865	Mustered out Sept. 8, 1865.
Clark, James	Greene co	Feb. 15, 1862	Mar. 7, 1862	Disch. Aug. 21, '62; disabil.
Damron, Milton T	Hittle	Sept. 30, 1864	Sept. 30, 1864	Mustered out July 20, 1865.
Elkington, Joseph H.	Greene co	Feb. 21, 1862	Mar. 7, 1862	Re-enlisted as Veteran. ..
Goodpasture, Daniel J	"	Feb. 18, 1862		
Kemper, Levi	Jerseyville	Nov. 23, 1863	Dec. 31, 1863	Mustered out Sept. 8, 1865..
McMillan, Isaac	Greene co	Feb. 17, 1862	Mar. 7, 1862	Died, St. Louis May 10, '62.
Nash, Alfred D.	"	Feb. 26, 1862		Re-enlisted as Veteran ...
Oswald, Louis	Eastern	Feb. 4, 1865	Feb. 11, 1865	Mustered out Sept. 8, 1865.
Rodgers, James	White Hall	Feb. 10, 1865	Feb. 16, 1865	"
Richards, James P.	Pioneer	Jan. 23, 1864	Feb. 22, 1864	"
Smith, James	Carrollton	Nov. 23, 1863	Dec. 31, 1863	"
Stubblefield, Fielding	Bluffdale.	Nov. 11, 1864	Nov. 12, 1864	"
Thaxton, Parm.	Carrollton	Nov. 17, 1863	Dec. 31, 1863	Vet. recruit. M. O. Sept. 8, 1865, as Corporal.
Trimble, Bembridge.	White Hall.	Feb. 11, 1865	Feb. 20, 1865	Mustered out Sept. 8, 1865
Thorn, John	Bridgeport	Feb. 29, 1864	Mar. 3, 1864	"
Vix, Yancy	Waver y	Jan. 31, 1865	Feb. 2, 1865	Deserted Apr. 15, 1865 . ....
Ward, William T	Carrollton	Feb. 6, 1862	Mar. 7, 1862	Re-enlisted as Veteran. ..
Ward, Francis M.	Bluffdale.	Nov. 11, 1864	Nov. 12, 1864	Mustered out Sept. 8, 1865 .
Whitesides, James H.	"			
Whiteside, Lorenzo D	"	Feb. 5, 1862	Mar. 7, 1862	Disch. Sept. 1, '63; disabil.
Wood, William	Barr's Store.	Feb. 10, 1865	Feb. 16, 1865	Mustered out Sept. 8, 1865..
Waltrip, James.	Sand Ridge	Jan. 31, 1865		"

Name and Rank.	Residence.	Date of rank or enlistment.	Date of muster.	Remarks.
Recruits transferred from 98th Ill. Inf.				
Anderson, John H...	Meridian	Mar. 11, 1865	Mar. 11, 1865	Mustered out Sept. 8, 1865.
Abbott, William H....	York	Feb. 23, 1865	Feb. 23, 1865	
Bond, William N...	Olney......	Feb. 28, 1864	Feb. 28, 1964	Abs., sick, at M O.of Reg.
Badgley, Atlas...	Hurricane......	Mar. 7, 1865	Mar. 7, 1865	Mustered out Sept. 8, 1865.
Berry, Jacob L...	Olney......	Feb. 9, 1864	Feb. 9, 1864	" "
Brothers, Robert A..	Denver	Dec. 7, 1863	Dec. 7, 1863	" "
Butler, Odom	Olney......	Feb. 16, 1864	Feb. 16, 1864	Vet. recruit. M. O. Sept. 8, 1865, as Sergeant. ......
Bowers, Isaac	Seminary	Mar. 7, 1865	Mar. 7, 1865	Mustered out Sept. 8, 1865.
Bolin, Delana.........	Harlem	Feb. 23, 1865	Feb. 23, 1865	" "
Conley, Thompson. ..	Laclede	Dec. 7, 1863	Dec. 7, 1863	" "
Cash, Henry	Flora	Dec. 1, 1863	Dec. 1, 1863	" "
Cox, Stephen O...	Parkersburg..	Oct. 24, 1863	Nov. 23, 1863	" "
Churchward, Alonzo.	Olney......	Dec. 2, 1863	Dec. 27, 1863	M. O. Sept. 8, '65, as Corp'l.
Craig, Jesse W...	"	Feb. 24, 1864	Feb. 24, 1864	Mustered out Sept. 8, 1865.
Campbell, James	"	Feb. 16, 1864	Feb. 16, 1864	" "
Erskine, Thomas.	Stanford.	Dec. 8, 1863	Dec. 8, 1863	" "
Ensor, James H	Olney......	Feb. 26, 1863	Feb. 26, 1863	" "
Harris, Woten	Ramsey	Mar. 7, 1865	Mar. 7, 1865	" "
Jaggers, Nathan......	Fairview......	Feb. 16, 1864	Feb. 16, 1864	" "
Kent, Thomas J......	Madison ..	Jan. 25, 1864	Jan. 25, 1864	" "
Kent, James	Marion co	Mar. 6, 1864	Mar. 7, 1864	" "
Luedacre, Christain..	Olney......	Feb. 27, 1864	Feb. 27, 1864	" "
Mattoon, Wilbur.....	Monee......	Mar. 8, 1865	Mar. 8, 1865	" "
Murray, William	Kaskaskia.....	Mar. 7, 1865	Mar. 7, 1865	" "
McDonald, Caleb W..	Seminary			" "
McClure, Thomas	Martinsville....	Oct. 11, 1864	Oct. 11, 1864	
Nash, Thomas J	Flora......	Nov. 23, 1864	Nov. 23, 1864	M. O. Sept. 8, '65, as Corp'l.
Newland, Eugene C ..	Palestine.	Nov. 20, 1863	Nov. 20, 1863	Mustered out Sept. 8, 1865...
Newland, Amasa A...	"	Dec. 8, 1863	Dec. 8, 1863	M. O. Sept. 8, '65, as Corp'l.
Odell. Adair G.	Pixley......	Feb. 22, 1864	Feb. 22, 1864	Mustered out Sept. 8, 1865.
Pittman, George	Olney......	Feb. 27, 1864	Feb. 27, 1864	" "
Pierce, Sylvester D...	Parkersburg ..	Nov. 23, 1863	Nov. 23, 1863	" "
Pennington, Josiah ..	Kaskaskia.	Mar. 6, 1865	Mar. 6, 1865	" "
Ray, Thomas..........	....	Sept. 20, 1863		Deserted July 28, 1865, before transfer ....
Rusk, John W.........	Stanford	Nov. 23, 1863	Nov. 23, 1863	Mustered out Sept. 8, 1865.
Ratcliffe, Albert......	Olney	Feb. 26, 1864	Feb. 26, 1864	" "
Sartin, Thomas W....	Hosier	Dec. 9, 1863	Dec. 9, 1863	" "
Sartin, John.........	Flora	Dec. 1, 1863	Dec. 1, 1863	" "
Sartin, Joseph H......	Hosier.	Dec. 9, 1863	Dec. 9, 1863	" "
Scott, James R........	Olney......	Mar. 30, 1864	Mar. 30, 1864	" "
Starnater, Alexander	Madison.	Mar. 8, 1864	Mar. 8, 1864	Discharged May 15, 1865 ..
Smith, Louis	Oblong	Mar. 9, 1865	Mar. 9, 1865	Mustered out Sept. 8, 1865.
Tanner, John R.......	Flora	Nov. 23, 1863	Nov. 23, 1863	" "
Travis, Noah K.......	Clay City.	Dec. 20, 1863	Dec. 20, 1863	Discharged July 31, 1865 ..
Truce, Luben........	Bonpas	Feb. 15, 1864	Feb. 15, 1864	Mustered out Sept. 8, 1865.
Umfleet, Benjamin F.	Monee	Mar. 9, 1865	Mar. 10, 1865	" "
Wood, Gideon	Hoosier......	Feb. 18, 1864	Feb. 18, 1864	" "
Weagel, Henry W	Olney......	Feb. 27, 1864	Feb. 27, 1864	" "
Youngling, David.....	"	Dec. 5, 1863	Dec. 5, 1863	" "

COMPANY C.

Name and Rank.	Residence.	Date of rank or enlistment.	Date of muster.	Remarks.
Captains.				
Warren, Ihrie.........	Jerseyville.....	Feb. 5, 1862	Feb. 5, 1862	Died Sept. 9, 1862...
John T. Hesser.	"	Sept. 9, 1862	Sept. 9, 1862	Discharged May 15, 1865 ..
First Lieutenants.				
John T. Hesser.......	Jerseyville.....	Mar. 7, 1862	....	Promoted ....
Marshall S. Parker...	"	Sept. 9, 1862	....	Resigned Apr. 3, 1863...
John W. Judd.........	Jersey co	Apr. 3, 1863	....	Discharged May 15, 1865...
Second Lieutenants.				
John T. Hesser.	Jerseyville.....	Feb. 5, 1862	Feb. 5, 1862	Promoted ....
Marshall S. Parker. ..	"	Mar. 7, 1862		"
John W. Judd......	Jersey co	Sept. 9, 1862	Sept. 9, 1862	"
Henry Nevis.........	"	Apr. 3, 1863	Apr. 23, 1863	Resigned June 10, 1865 ...
John Cooley..........	"	Aug. 2, 1865	Aug. 10, 1865	Mustered out Sept. 8, 1865.

Name and Rank.	Residence.	Date of rank or enlistment.	Date of muster.	Remarks.
Privates. Allen, Robert M.	Jersey co	Nov. 7, 1861	Feb. 5, 1862	Wounded at Shiloh. Not heard from since
Briggs, George L.	"	Dec. 21, 1861	"	Disch. July 9, '63; disabil.
Bell, Henry	"	Dec. 18, 1861	"	Mustered out Feb. 7, 1865.
Beale, John B.	"	Jan. 4, 1862	"	Received furlough. Never returned
Bates, William P.	"	Jan. 13, 1862	"	Re-enlisted as Veteran
Bates, John W	"		"	Died at St. Louis, May 15, '62
Cook, William H.	"	Nov. 7, 1861	"	Mustered out Feb. 7, 1865.
Cyter, John H	"		"	Died at Duvall's Bluff, Sept. 2, 1863
Campbell, John A	"		"	Re-enlisted as Veteran
Cooley, John	"	Nov. 11, 1861	"	
Chadwell, Thomas H.	"	Nov. 9, 1861	"	Disch. June 7, '63; disabil.
Case, James	"	Nov. 30, 1861	"	Disch. May 2, '62; disabil.
Chism, R. P	"	Dec. 6, 1861	"	Re-enlisted as Veteran
Crain, James B	"	Dec. 9, 1861	"	Disch. Apr. 26, '62; disabil.
Carson, John	"	Jan. 13, 1862	"	Mustered out Feb. 5, 1865.
Collip, Frederick.	"	Jan. 18, 1862	"	Disch. Jan. 7, '64; disabil.
Conner, Bark.	"	Feb. 4, 1862	"	Disch. Apr. 30, '62; disabil.
Davis, Amos.	"	Nov. 7, 1861	"	Re-enlisted as Veteran
Dodson, Francis M.	"	Nov. 11, 1861	"	
Dehner, Jacob	"	Nov. 29, 1861	"	Mustered out Feb. 7, 1865.
Dalils, Thomas N.	"	Dec. 5, 1861	"	Re-enlisted as Veteran
Edington, William.	"	Nov. 7, 1861	"	Disch. Apr. 30, '62; disabil.
Ennel, John.	"	Nov. 29, 1861	"	Re-enlisted as Veteran.
Elmore, William	"	Dec. 6, 1861	"	
Embley, Edgar	"	Feb. 4, 1862	"	Discharged Dec. 16, 1862, as Corporal; disability
Faulkner, John R.	"	Nov. 7, 1861	"	Re-enlisted as Veteran
Finleye, William B.	"		"	" "
Ferguson, Green B.	"	Dec. 12, 1861	"	
Francis, John.	"	Dec. 19, 1861	"	Died at St. Louis, Mar. 14, '62
Forbes, James B	"	Dec. 23, 1861	"	Tr. to Mulligan's Brigade.
Gaul, William	"	Nov. 7, 1861	"	Re-enlisted as Veteran
Goff, Julius S.	"	Dec. 11, 1861	"	Died at St. Louis, Mar. 14, '62
Gallagher, Edward C.	"	Jan. 1, 1862	"	Killed at Shiloh, Apr. 6, '62.
Griffin, William R	"	Jan. 14, 1862	"	Disch. Oct. 8, '62; disabil.
Grather, William M	"	Jan. 13, 1862	"	Disch. July 9, '62; disabil.
Hall, Edward E.	"	Nov. 7, 1861	"	Re-enlisted as Veteran
Handling, Orange	"	Dec. 6, 1861	"	Deserted June 3, 1864; 2d desertion
Hegans, Nelson.	"	Dec. 17, 1861	"	Died at Savannah, Tenn., Apr. 12, 1862; wounds
Judd, John W.	"	Nov. 7, 1861	"	Promoted 2d Lieutenant.
Jackson, Charles.	"	Nov. 23, 1861	"	Disch. July 3, '64; disabil.
Linnel, William.	"	Jan. 28, 1862	"	Re-enlisted as Veteran
Lee, John W	"	Nov. 7, 1861	"	
Loney, John P	"	Feb. 5, 1862	"	
Martin, John	"	Jan. 23, 1862	"	Died at Snyder's Bluff, Miss., July 25, 1863
Mott, Morgan H.	"	Nov. 7, 1861	"	Disch. Feb. 11, '63; disabil.
Margerum, George W	Greene co	"	"	Corp'l. Wounded at Shiloh. Not heard of since.
Minor, Benjamin F.	Jersey co	Nov. 11, 1861	"	Serg't. Died at Memphis, Feb. 1, 1864
Martin, Leonard	"		"	Corp'l. Killed at Shiloh, Apr. 6, 1862
Miner, Lorenzo J.	"	Nov. 7, 1861	"	Serg't. Discharged for promotion Aug. 13, 1863.
Myrick, Oliver T	"	Dec. 16, 1861	"	Mustered out Feb. 7, 1865.
Milford, B. C.	"	Dec. 19, 1861	"	Disch. Oct. 8, '62; disabil.
Mack, Patrick	"	Jan. 9, 1862	"	Re-enlisted as Veteran
McDow, William	"	Jan. 28, 1862	"	" "
McQuiddy, James D.	"	Jan. 25, 1862	"	" "
Nugent, Edward	"	Nov. 7, 1861	"	
Nevins, Henry	"		"	Prom. 2d Lt., from Serg't.
Nichols, Jasper N	"	Feb. 4, 1862	"	Re-enlisted as Veteran
Ohler, Coleman.	"	Dec. 12, 1861	"	
O'Reilly, Matthew	"	Dec. 31, 1861	"	
Post, Wickliffe F.	"	Jan. 25, 1862	"	Disch. July 9, '62; disabil.
Parker, Marshall S.	"	Nov. 7, 1861	"	Promoted 2d Lieutenant.
Perry, Comodore.	"	Dec. 19, 1861	"	Deserted Aug. 8, 1862.
Powers, William	"	Jan. 3, 1862	"	Re-enlisted as Veteran
Piggott, Joseph T	"	Dec. 26, 1861	"	Disch. Nov. 29, '62; disabil.
Robbins, Richard.	"	Nov. 7, 1861	"	Re-enlisted as Veteran
Reed, James H.	"	Jan. 28, 1862	"	Disch. Aug. 15, '63; disabil.
Shepherd, John D	Greene co	Nov. 7, 1861	"	Died May 3, 1862
Savage, John O	Jersey co	"	"	Tr. to Inv. Corps, Jan. 15, '64

Name and Rank.	Residence.	Date of rank or enlistment.	Date of muster.	Remarks.
Slover, Samuel	Jersey co	Nov. 11, 1861	Feb. 5, 1862	Mustered out Feb. 7, 1865
Sweeney, William H	"	Dec. 11, 1861	"	Re-enlisted as Veteran
Smith, Joseph	"	Jan. 6, 1862	"	In hospital Apr. 6, 1862; supposed died
Sanson, George W	"	"	"	Discharged Oct. 19, 1862
Stone, Joseph B	"	Jan. 13, 1862	"	Re-enlisted as Veteran
Schuller, Joseph F	"	Jan. 17, 1862	"	Mustered out Feb. 7, 1865
Todrany, William	"	Dec. 31, 1861	"	"
Thurston, John L	"	Jan. 6, 1862	"	"
Vinson, Isaac N	"	Nov. 7, 1861	"	Re-enlisted as Veteran
Wentworth, John F	"	"	"	"
Welch, John P	"	Dec. 11, 1861	"	Mustered out Feb. 7, 1865
Wentworth, George E	"	Dec. 4, 1861	"	Re-enlisted as Veteran
Yuard, Hugh	"	Nov. 11, 1861	"	M. O. Feb. 7, '65, as Serg't.
Veterans.				
Bates, William P	Jerseyville	Feb. 1, 1864	Mar. 11, 1864	M. O. May 30, '65; pris. war.
Chism, Thomas H	"	Feb. 29, 1864	"	M.O. Sept. 8, '65, as Corp'l.
Cope, Alexander	"		"	Mustered out Sept. 8, 1865.
Campbell, John A	"	Feb. 1, 1864	"	M. O. Dec. 28, 1865, to date Sept. 8, 1865
Chism, Ransom P	"	"	"	Mustered out Sept. 8, 1865.
Cooley, John	"	"	"	Prom. 1st Sgt., then 2d Lt.
Dodson, Francis M	"	"	"	Mustered out Sept. 8, 1865.
Dallas, Thomas N	"	"	"	"
Davis, Amos	"	"	"	M. O. May 30, '65; pris. war.
Ennel, John	"	"	"	"
Elmore, William	"	"	"	M.O. Sept. 8, '65, as Corp'l.
Finley, William	"	"	"	Mustered out Sept. 8, 1865.
Faulkner, John R	"	"	"	M.O. June 12, '65; was pris.
Ferguson, Green B	"	"	"	Mustered out Sept. 8, 1865.
Gaul, William	"	"	"	Deserted Aug. 13, 1865
Hall, Edward E	"	Jan. 4, 1864	Jan. 20, 1864	Pro. Sgt., then 1st Lt. Co. I
Lee, John W	"			Mustered out Sept. 8, 1865.
Looney, John P	"	Feb. 29, 1864	Mar. 11, 1864	"
Linnell, William	"	Feb. 1, 1864	"	M. O. June 7, '65, as Serg't; was prisoner.
Machel, John	"	Feb. 29, 1864	"	M. O. June 12, '65; was pris.
Milford, Henry F	"	"	"	M. O. May 30, '65; was pris.
Mack, Patrick	"	Feb. 1, 1864	"	M.O. Sept. 8, '65, as Serg't.
McQuiddy, James D	"	"	"	M. O. May 30, '65; was pris.
McDow, William	"		"	Ab't, sick, at M.O. of Regt.
Nichols, Jasper N	"	Feb. 29, 1864	"	M. O. Sept. 8, '65, as Corp'l.
Nugent, Edward	"	Feb. 1, 1864	"	Drowned July 4, 1862
Ohler, Coleman	"		"	Mustered out Sept. 8, 1865.
Piper, Oliver	"	Feb. 29, 1864	"	M. O. Sept. 8, '65, as Serg't.
Powers, William	"	Jan. 4, 1864	Jan. 20, 1864	M. O. Sept. 8, '65, as 1st Sgt.
O'Reilly, Matthew	"	Feb. 1, 1864	Mar. 11, 1864	Mustered out Sept. 8, 1865.
Robbins, Richard	"			M. O. Sept. 8, '65; pris. war
Staton, Henry L	"	Feb. 29, 1864	Feb. 29, 1864	Mustered out Sept. 8, 1865.
Stone, Joseph B	"	Feb. 1, 1864	Mar. 11, 1864	"
Sweeney, William H	"			M. O. May 30, '65; pris. war
Vinson, Isaac N	"	Feb. 26, 1864	Feb. 27, 1864	Mustered out Sept. 8, 1865.
Wentworth, John F	"	Feb. 1, 1864	Mar. 11, 1864	M. O. May 30, '65; was pris.
Wentworth, George E	"	Jan. 4, 1864	Jan. 20, 1864	Mustered out Sept. 8, 1865.
Recruits.				
Adams, Asa	Groveland	Oct. 10, 1864	Oct. 10, 1864	Disch. June 27, '65; disabil.
Chism, Thomas H	Jersey co	Feb. 22, 1862		Re-enlisted as Veteran
Cope, Alexander	"			
Conoway, John	Otter Creek	Sept. 5, 1864	Sept. 6, 1864	Deserted July 23, 1865
Dodson, Theodore	Jerseyville	Jan. 26, 1864	Feb. 24, 1864	Mustered out Sept. 8, 1865.
Erwin, Samuel P	Jersey co	Nov. 7, 1861		Died, St. Louis, May 12, '62.
Hesser, Joseph	Jerseyville	Sept. 27, 1864	Sept. 27, 1864	Mustered out July 29, 1865.
Hinson, Sydney	Hittle	Oct. 1, 1864	Oct. 1, 1864	
Jenkins, Peter	Alton	Apr. 5, 1865	Apr. 5, 1865	Mustered out Sept. 8, 1865.
Kuykendall, Rodolph	"			"
Kuykendall, Simon	"		"	"
Kuykendall, Lafayette	"			Deserted July 23, 1865
Lawless, Michael	Little Rock, Ark	Dec. 30, 1863	Jan. 4, 1864	Died at Murfreesboro, Tenn., Apr. 7, 1865
Machel, John	Jersey co	Feb. 21, 1862	Feb. 21, 1862	Re-enlisted as Veteran
Milford, Henry F	"	Feb. 17, 1862	Feb. 17, 1862	"
Mytinger, Francis M	Kane	Jan. 4, 1864	Jan. 4, 1864	Prom. Adjutant, Aug. 6, '65
Piper, Oliver	Jersey co	Feb. 28, 1862	Feb. 28, 1862	Re-enlisted as Veteran
Pritchall, Benjamin H	"	Feb. 24, 1862	Feb. 24, 1862	Died at Pittsburg Landing, May 8, 1862.
Reynolds, John	Shelby co	Apr. 6, 1865	Apr. 7, 1865	Mustered out Sept. 8, 1865.

Name and Rand.	Residence.	Date of rank or enlistment.	Date of muster.	Remarks.
Scoggins, John F	Elsah	Oct. 5, 1864	Oct. 6, 1864	Died at Franklin, Tenn., Aug. 6, 1865 ....
Staton, Henry L	Jersey co........	Feb. 27, 1862	....	Re-enlisted as Veteran ...
Recruits transferred from 98th Ill. Inf.				
Butts, Michael	Laclede	Feb. 28, 1865	Feb. 28, 1865	Mustered out Sept. 8, 1865.
Butts, Peter............	"	Apr. 12, 1865		" "
Evans, Joshua H	"	Feb. 21, 1864	Feb. 21, 1864	" "
Morris, William H ...	"	Feb. 28, 1865	Feb. 28, 1865	" "
McCaffrey, James	"			" "
Neeld, Elias G	Monee..........	Mar. 8, 1865		" "
Premas, Frank........	Laclede	Dec. 7, 1863	Dec. 7, 1863	" "
Quanlin, Thomas	"	Feb. 28, 1865	Feb. 28, 1865	" "
Scott, Robert G......	Chicago	Feb. 29, 1864	Feb. 29, 1864	" "
Scott, Amos..........	Laclede	Feb. 28, 1865	Feb. 28, 1865	" "
Truax, Stillwell	"	Dec. 7, 1863	Dec. 7, 1863	M. O. Sept. 8, '65, as Corp'l.
Wood, Thomas J	Edgewood	Feb. 8, 1864	Feb. 8, 1864	Mustered out Sept. 8, 1865.
Recruits transferred from 123d Ill. Inf.				
Atkins, Edward S.....	Charleston ...	Jan. 11, 1864	Feb. 8, 1864	M. O. Sept. 8, '65, as Serg't.
Barr, Albert...........	Lafayette	Mar. 14, 1865	Mar. 14, 1865	Mustered out Sept. 8, 1865
Brooks, John	Casey..........	Feb. 11, 1864	Feb. 11, 1864	M. O. Sept. 8, '65, as Corp l.
Beeson, Richard G ...	Johnson........	Mar. 7, 1865	Mar. 7, 1865	Mustered out Sept. 8, 1865.
Beurk, Charles M	Orange	Mar. 22, 1865	Mar. 22, 1965	" "
Bensley, Berkley	Worth	Jan. 17, 1865	Jan. 17, 1865	" "
Cook, Darwin B.......	Vermilion	Jan. 18, 1865	Jan. 18, 1865	" "
Cooper, Winfie d S ...	Charleston ...	Feb. 6, 1864	Mar. 26, 1864	" "
Durham, Alexander ..	Casey..........	Feb. 11, 1864	Feb. 11, 1864	" "
Davidson, George	Charleston ...	Mar. 21, 1864	May 3, 1864	" "
Dewitt, Solomon	York	Mar. 7, 1865	Mar. 7, 1865	" "
Furbee, Nathan L	Casey..........	Feb. 11, 1864	Feb. 11, 1864	M. O. Sept. 8, '65, as Corp'l.
French, John E	Saulsbury......	Nov. 17, 1863	Nov. 17, 1863	" "
Gray, John C.........	Jordan	Mar. 7, 1865	Mar. 14, 1865	Died at Franklin, Tenn ...
Gevans, Hiram	Georgetown ...	Mar. 22, 1865	Mar. 22, 1865	Mustered out Sept. 8, 1865.
Goodman, John M ...	Charleston ...	Feb. 1, 1864	Mar. 26, 1864	" "
Hayes, John	Lafayette	Mar. 17, 1865	Mar. 17, 1865	" "
Harlin, Jefferson R...	....	Dec. 1, 1862	Dec. 1, 1862	" "
Hayes, Isaac A. O	York	Feb. 11, 1865	Mar. 7, 1865	" "
James, Milton	Lafayette	Mar. 14, 1865	Mar. 14, 1865	" "
Lewis, Daniel	Johnson........	Mar. 9, 1865	Mar. 9, 1865	" "
Landurs, Etheal......	Garner	Apr. 12, 1865	Apr. 12, 1865	" "
Leitch, Robert N	Charleston ...	Feb. 21, 1864	Mar. 21, 1864	" "
Maffet, John H	....	Apr. 1, 1863	Apr. 10, 1863	" "
McNary, Thomas.....	Charleston ...	Feb. 11, 1864	Feb. 11, 1864	" "
Macy, Samuel........	"			" "
McCrotty, Robert M..	Chicago	Mar. 18, 1865	Mar. 18, 1865	" "
Ramsay, William R ..	Lafayette	Mar. 22, 1865	Mar. 22, 1865	" "
Stover, James H......		Mar. 17, 1865	Mar. 17, 1865	" "
Sours, David S		Mar. 13, 1865	Mar. 13, 1865	" "
Stowart, Alexander ..	Casey..........	Feb. 11, 1864	Feb. 11, 1864	" "
Shoemaker, William .		Apr. 1, 1864	May 2, 1864	" "
Stogdill, Huston W...	"	Feb. 11, 1864	Feb. 11, 1864	" "
Snyder, Joseph	Westfield	Feb. 11, 1865	Feb. 11, 1865	" "
Wintermote, Leon'd D	Dwight	Jan. 24, 1865	Jan. 24, 1865	" "
Williams, Elijah	Lafayette	Mar. 14, 1865	Mar. 14, 1865	" "
Williams, Henry W...	Greene co......	Feb. 7, 1865	Feb. 9, 1865	" "
Williams, David B....	Charleston ...	Feb. 24, 1864	Feb. 24, 1864	M. O. Sept. 8, '65, as Corp'l.
Yates or Tate, Wm. A.	Lafayette	Mar. 14, 1865	Mar. 14, 1865	Mustered out Sept. 8, 1865.

COMPANY D.

Name and Rank.	Residence.	Date of rank or enlistment.	Date of muster.	Remarks.
Captains.				
John H. Reddish	Jerseyville	Mar. 7, 1862	....	Resigned Apr. 3, 1863.......
Daniel S. Keeley	Carrollton......	Apr. 3, 1863	May 1, 1863	Prom. Major Aug. 1, 1865...
Thomas J. Warren....	....	Aug. 21, 1865	Aug. 21, 1865	Mustered out Sept. 8, 1865 .
First Lieutenants.				
John H. Reddish	Jerseyville	Feb. 5, 1862	Feb. 5, 1862	Promoted ....
Daniel S. Keeley	Carrollton......	Mar. 7, 1862	Mar. 7, 1862	" ....
Thomas J. Warren....	....	Apr. 3, 1863	Apr. 26, 1863	"
Leander Stillwell	Jersey co.......	Aug. 21, 1865	Aug. 21, 1865	Mustered out Sept. 8, 1865.

Name and Rank.	Residence.	Date of rank or enlistment.	Date of muster.	Remarks.
Second Lieutenants.				
James R. McWylder..	Clay City......	Mar. 7, 1862	Mar. 7, 1862	Resigned Sept. 3, 1862.....
W. M. Reddish	Fieldon	Sept. 3, 1862	Not must'r'd	Commission canceled ...
Enoch W. Wallace	Grafton		Feb. 4, 1863	Resigned Feb. 10, 1865 ....
Leander Stillwell ..	Jersey co	July 11, 1865	July 18, 1865	Promoted ....
Charles H. Oberdeik .	Grafton..........	Aug. 24, 1865	Not must'r'd	M. O. Sept. 8, '65, as Serg't.
Privates.				
Austin, Benjamin F .	Grafton.........	Dec. 6, 1861	Feb. 5, 1862	Died at Pittsburg Landing Apr. 30, 1862
Albert, Frank J	Jerseyville	Jan. 11, 1862	"	Missing in act'n Pittsburg Land'g, T. Report'd dead
Allenden, Ambrose P.	Grafton .:.....	Jan. 27, 1862	"	Re-enlisted as Veteran ...
Bethell, Lenton W....	Jersey co	Dec. 5, 1861	"	Sgt Sent hospital; never ret'ned. Rep't'd desert'r.
Bethell, Tilmon	"	"	"	Disch. June 28, '65; disabil.
Barton, John A	Otter Creek ..	Dec. 6, 1861	"	Re-enlisted as Veteran...
Brewer, Lemuel	Elsah	Dec. 9, 1861	"	
Bingham, Ransom C .	Otter Creek ..	Dec. 10, 1861	"	
Bartlett, Ira W	Grafton	Dec. 12, 1861	"	Disch. Aug. 1, '62, as Sergeant; disability ....
Burris, Ammon	"	Jan. 3, 1862	"	Re-enlisted as Veteran ...
Burcham or Burnham	F.S] "	Jan 11, 1862	"	Disch. Feb. 20, '63, as Corporal; disability ....
Corbin, Moses B......	Elsah	Nov. 6, 1861	"	Killed at Shiloh, Apr. 6, '62.
Carroll, James M	"	Dec. 27, 1861	"	
Dabbs, Emanuel......	Otter Creek ..	Feb. 3, 1862	"	Disch. July 22, '62; disabil..
Ellifrity, James	Fieldon	Dec. 13, 1861	"	Mustered out Feb. 7, 1865..
Ellifrity, Isaac	"	Jan. 22, 1862	"	Mustered out Sept. 8, 1865.
Eldridge, John	"	Dec. 16, 1861	"	Disch. July 13, '62; disabil.
Fillay, Lester B	Kane......	Jan. 3, 1862	"	Disch. May 2, '64; disabil.
Gates, Timothy M	Otter Creek ..	Dec. 5, 1861	"	Disch. Mar. 22, '63; disabil.
Gates, Francis M	Grafton......	Jan. 21, 1862	"	Re-enlisted as Veteran...
Green, Elisha H	Fieldon	Nov. 24, 1861	"	Disch. Apr. 3, '62; disabil.
Gorrell, William......	"	Dec. 14, 1861	"	Mustered out Sept. 8, 1865.
Gunther, William M..	Jersey co	Nov. 1, 1861	"	See Company O ....
Holliday, Hiram	Jerseyville ...	Nov. 11, 1861	"	Corp'l Died at Macon, Ga., Aug. 14, '62; pris. of war.
Harris, Andrew J.....	"	"	"	Reported dead ....
Harvill, John W	"	Dec. 14, 1861	"	Re-enlisted as Veteran ...
Harvill, Benjamin F..	"	Dec. 24, 1861	"	Disch. July 24, '63; disabil.
Hall, Edward.........	Fieldon	Feb. 3, 1862	"	Disch. Oct. 23, '62; disabil.
Hughes, Solomon	Alton.........	Dec. 21, 1861	"	Died at Savannah, Tenn.
Hagen, Thomas	Kane..........	Nov. 6, 1861	"	Died Jan. 27, 1864 ....
Hutchinson, James G.	Grafton........	Nov. 7, 1861	"	Deserted July 22, 1862...
Hill, Francis M......	Otter Creek ..		"	Disch. June 4, '62; disabil.
Jobson, John	"	Jan. 13, 1862	"	Died July 25, 1863.......
Reilley, Daniel S	Carrollton		"	Promoted 1st Lieutenant.
Klarr, Charles J	Fieldon	Jan. 14, 1862	"	Re-enlisted as Veteran ...
Karr, Hugh..........	Jerseyville ...	Jan. 23, 1862	"	Mustered out Feb. 7, 1865..
King, William	Elsah	Dec. 14, 1861	"	Re-enlisted as Veteran ...
Leavitt, Samuel......	Fieldon	Jan. 13, 1862	"	Died, M'nd City, May 10, '62.
Lippert, Henry	Grafton	Jan. 14, 1862	"	Disch. Aug. 10, '64; disabil.
Lee, William	Otter Creek ..	Dec. 10, 1861	"	Mustered out Feb. 7, 1865..
Miller, Joel P	Elsah	Dec. 13, 1861	"	Died at St. Louis, Mo......
Miller, William J	"	Dec. 21, 1861	"	M. O. May 18, '65; pris. war
Minor, Henry	Otter Creek ...	Jan. 3, 1862	"	Re-enlisted as Veteran ...
Medford, Jackson......	"	Dec. 21, 1861	"	Mustered out Feb. 7, 1865..
Murphy, Brackston...			"	Missing in act'n Pittsburg Land'g, T. Rep'rted dead
Montgomery, Ezekiel	Grafton........	Jan. 25, 1862	"	Died in Jersey county, Ill., Feb. 3, 1862..........
Oberdake, Charles H.	"	Jan. 3, 1862	"	Re-enlisted as Veteran ...
Pitchford, Ephraim ..	Greenfield.....	Jan. 7, 1862	"	Des'rted Dec. 19, '62, in act'n. Returned, awaiting trial.
Payne, Jonathan	Clay City.....	Dec. 21, 1861	"	Disch. Oct. 14, '62; disabil.
Potter, Phillip	Greenfield.....	Jan. 20, 1862	"	Re-enlisted as Veteran ...
Reddish, William M..	Venice	Dec. 14, 1861	"	M. O. Feb. 7, '65, as Serg't.
Richey, John..........	Otter Creek ..	Jan. 3, 1862	"	Re-enlisted as Veteran ...
Sapp, James...........	Fieldon	Nov. 6, 1861	"	Dishon. disch. Jan. 10, '61.
Scott, James	"	Nov. 11, 1861	"	Disch. Oct. 14, '62; disabil.
Smith, Samuel	"	Dec. 10, 1861	"	Died, St. Louis, Apr. 26, '62.
Schooley, James	Jerseyville ...	Dec. 14, 1861	"	Died Apr. 30, 1862; wounds.
Schultz, Albert........	Otter Creek ..	Jan. 3, 1862	"	Capt'd. Pittsburg Land'ng; exch'nged. Never rep't'd. Dropped as deserter....
Stillwell, Leander	"	Jan. 7, 1862	"	Re-enlisted as Veteran ...
Timmons, Jasper	Elsah	Jan. 17, 1862	"	
Smith, William C.	Newburn......	"	"	Dropped as deserter Aug. 18, 1862 ....

Name and Rank.	Residence.	Date of rank or enlistment.	Date of muster.	Remarks.
Timmons, Ephraim ..	Elsah.	Jan. 11, 1862	Feb. 5, 1862	Mustered out Feb. 7, 1865..
Wallace, Enoch W	Grafton	Dec. 6, 1861	''	Prom. 1st Sgt. then 2d Lt.
Worthey, William ...		Jan. 3, 1862	''	Discharged Apr. 30, 1862..
Wilder, James R. M ..	Clay City......	Nov. 1, 1861	''	Promoted 2d Lieutenant..
Veterans.				
Allender, Ambrose P.	Grafton	Feb. 1, 1864	Apr. 30, 1864	Mustered out Sept. 8, 1865.
Burns, Jonathan......	Winchester	Feb. 20, 1864	''	Promoted Q. M. Sergeant.
Banfield, William	Grafton.......	Feb. 24, 1864	''	M. O. Sept. 8, '65, as Serg't.
Barton, John A.......	Otter Creek ..	Feb. 1, 1864	''	Dishon. disch. June 22, '65.
Brewer, Lemuel	Grafton........	''	''	Mustered out Sept. 8, 1865.
Bingham, Ransom O .	Otter Creek ..	''	''	M. O. July 18, '65; was pris.
Burris, Ammon	Grafton........	''	''	M. O. Sept. 8, '65, as Corp'l.
Gates, Francis M	Otter Creek ..	''	''	M. O. Sept. 8, '65, as Serg't.
Hill, Jacob J	Jerseyville	''	''	M. O. Sept. 8, '65, as Corp'l.
Harvill, John W......	Fieldon........	''	''	M. O. Sept. 8, '65, as Serg't.
Jones, James W	Carrollton	Feb. 24, 1864	''	M. O. Sept. 8, '65, as Corp'l.
Klar, Charles	Fieldon........	Feb. 1, 1864	''	In milit'ry pris'... Nashville,
King, William H	Godfrey........	''	''	T., sentence G. C. M.....
Miner, Henry..........	Elsah........	''	''	Drowned in Cumberland River, Nov. 25, 1864 ......
Noe, Benjamin.......	Kane..........	Feb. 24, 1864	''	Mustered out Sept. 8, 1865.
Oberdick, Charles H .	Grafton........	Jan. 4, 1864	''	M. O. Sept. 8, '65, as 1st Sgt.
Potter, Phillip	Carrollton	Feb. 1, 1864	''	Died Dec. 8, '64; wounds..
Richey, John.........	Fieldon........	''	''	Mustered out Sept. 8, 1865 .
Ralston, Samuel L. ..	Jerseyville	Feb. 24, 1864	''	''
Stillwell, Leander	Otter Creek ..	Feb. 1, 1864	''	Prom. 1st Sg't, then 2d Lt.
Timmons, Jasper	Grafton........	''	''	Dishon. disch. Nov. 16, '65.
Recruits.				
Burns, Jonathan......				Re-enlisted as Veteran.
Burgess, W. B........	Jersey co	Feb. 19, 1862	Mar. 7, 1862	Disch. June 17, '62; disabil.
Burgess, W. B., Jr ...	Jerseyville....	Feb. 22, 1862	''	Tr. to V. R. C. Sept. 3, 1863.
Banfield, John	Otter Creek ...	Feb. 20, 1862		M. O. Mar. 6, 1865 ....
Banfield, William	''	Feb. 9, 1862	June 21, 1863	Disch. Apr. 26. '62; disabil.
Barrows, Akron	Elsah..........	Oct. 6, 1864	Oct. 8, 1864	Re-enlisted as Veteran ...
Curry, William	Greenfield	Feb. 24, 1862	Mar. 7, 1862	Mustered out Sept. 8, 1865 ..
Cochran, Samuel		Feb. 25, 1862		Disch. Dec. 16, '62; disabil.
Chapman, Lemuel N..	Newburg......	Mar. 30, 1864	Mar. 31, 1864	Disch. Oct. 18, '62; wounds.
Court, John...........	Litchfield	Mar. 15, 1865	Mar. 15, 1865	Mustered out Sept. 8, 1865.
Duggan, John	Fieldon........	Nov. 11, 1861	Mar. 7, 1862	Mustered out Mar. 22. 1865.
Dougherty, James	Otter Creek ..	Jan. 5, 1864	Apr. 11, 1864	Died at Duvall's Bluff, Ark. Sept. 22, 1864.
Dabbs, Emanuel		Nov. 5, 1864	Nov. 30, 1864	Mustered out Sept. 8, 1865 .
Durney, John........	Okaw..........	Mar. 31, 1865	Apr. 1, 1865	Deserted July 6, 1865.
Fowler, William S	Jerseyville	Feb. 19, 1862	Mar. 7, 1862	Mustered out Mar. 22, 1865.
Fickle, William	Virginia......	Feb. 13, 1865	Feb. 13, 1865	Mustered out Sept. 8, 1865.
Gilbert, David........	Elsah	Feb. 10, 1862	Mar. 7, 1862	Dropped as deserter Aug. 18, 1862.
Gorrell, John........	Virginia......	Feb. 13, 1865	Feb. 13, 1865	Mustered out Sept. 8, 1865.
Gorrell, Peter P		Nov. 10, 1863	Dec. 31, 1863	
Gass, Andrew J	Otter Creek ..	Oct. 1, 1864	Mar. 3, 1864	Mustered out July 20, 1865.
Golden, Michael	''	Jan. 11, 1862	June 21, 1863	Re-enlisted as Veteran.
Hill, Jacob J.........	''	Mar. 4, 1864	Apr. 28, 1864	Mustered out Sept. 8, 1865.
Hull, Quincy M......	Virginia......	Feb. 13, 1865	Feb. 13, 1865	Died at Murfreesboro, T., Mar. 21, 1865........
Hicks, George........				
Hall, Thomas J.......		Feb. 24, 1862	Mar. 7, 1862	Mustered out Mar. 22, 1865.
Inards, Silas.........	Fieldon........	Feb. 6, 1862	''	Disch. July 21, '62; disabil.
Jones, James W	Greenfield	Feb. 10, 1862	''	Re-enlisted as Veteran. ...
King, George W	Aiton.........	Jan. 5, 1864	Jan. 5, 1864	Mustered out Sept. 8, 1865.
McGrath, Owen	Carrollton	Feb. 10, 1862	Mar. 7, 1862	Mustered out Mar. 22, 1865.
Mills, Pendleton D ...		Feb. 6, 1862	''	Disch. May 29, '62; disabil.
Mayhall, James H	Kane..........	Nov. 23, 1863	Dec. 31, 1863	Mustered out Sept. 8, 1865.
Noe, Benjamin.......	Carrollton	Feb. 10, 1862	Mar. 7, 1862	Re-enlisted as Veteran. ...
Powell, William		Feb. 20, 1862	''	Disch. June 10, '63; disabil.
Powell, Joel	Otter Creek ..	Jan. 3, 1862	''	Disch. June 6. '62; disabil.
Paine, Jonathan	Clay City	Dec. 22, 1863	Jan. 12, 1864	Waiting trial for absence without leave M.O.Reg't.
Rowden, G. W........	Carrollton	Feb. 6, 1862	Mar. 7, 1862	Dropped as deserter Aug. 18, 1862...
Rowden, Daniel......	Jerseyville.....	Feb. 22, 1862	''	Died...............
Ralston, Samuel D....		Feb. 10, 1862	''	Re-enlisted as Veteran ...
Robinson, Joseph S...	Otter Creek ..			Disch. June 14, '62; disabil.
Richey, Vincent......	Litchfield	Mar. 15, 1865	Mar. 15, 1865	Mustered out Sept. 8, 1865.
Rudolph, William	Virginia......	Feb. 13, 1865	Feb. 13, 1865	
Seago, J. W.	Kane..........	Jan. 17, 1862	....	Died, St. Louis, May 24, '62.

Name and Rank.	Residence.	Date of rank or enlistment.	Date of muster.	Remarks.
Samples, Charles.....	Virginia	Feb. 13, 1865	Feb. 13, 1865	Mustered out Sept. 8, 1865.
Weaver, Adam........	....			" "
Recruits transferred from 83d Ill. Inf.				
Ashenhurst, Jos'ph W	Ohio Grove	Nov. 13, 1863	Nov. 23, 1863	M. O. Sept. 8 '65, as Corp'l.
Beachler, William P..	Ellison.........	Feb. 24, 1865	Feb. 25, 1865	Mustered out Sept. 8, 1865.
Blair, William G......	New Salem.....	Apr. 12, 1865	Apr. 12, 1865	" "
Blair, Daniel R.......	Oxford..........	Feb. 15, 1864	Mar. 26, 1864	" "
Boyer, Joseph	Rivola ..., ...	Feb. 24, 1865	Feb. 25, 1865	" "
Brady, Henry.........	Millersburg ...	Dec. 17, 1863	Dec. 18, 1863	" "
Briggs, Ransom S....	Oxford.........	Feb. 15, 1864	Mar. 26, 1864	M. O. Sept. 8, '65, as Corp'l.
Davis, George W......	Clarksville, T.	May 4, 1864	June 27, 1864	Mustered out Sept. 8 1865.
Green, Perry C.......	Oxford.........	Feb. 15, 1864	Mar. 26, 1864	" "
Hustan, David A......		Apr. 2, 1864	Apr. 2, 1864	" "
Hathaway, Humphrey	Rivola ..., ...	Feb. 24, 1865	Feb. 25, 1865	" "
Heasley, Johnson S..				" "
Bunting, Mitchell Y..	Sunbeam.......	Mar. 31, 1864	Apr. 25, 1864	" "
Johnson, Peter.......	Chicago	Oct. 17, 1864	Oct. 17, 1864	" "
Kennedy, Leander....	Green..........	Mar. 7, 1866	Mar. 8, 1865	" "
Lincoln, Randall	Coal Valley....	Oct. 11, 1864	Oct. 13, 1864	" "
Moore, Risner W	Ohio Grove....	Nov. 13, 1863	Nov. 23, 1863	" "
Moore, Daniel S	Sunbeam.......	Mar. 1, 1865	Mar. 2, 1865	" "
Marston, Fletcher ...		Feb. 26, 1864	Feb. 26, 1864	Abs't, sick, at M. O. of Regt.
McWilliams, John F..	Tompkins	Feb. 3, 1865	Feb. 21, 1865	Mustered out Sept. 8, 1865.
Piper, John H........	Pre-emption. ..	Mar. 31, 1864	June 24, 1864	
Piper, Henry J........		" "	Apr. 25, 1864	M. O. Sept. 8, '65, as Corp'l.
Potter, Orange A.....	Oxford	Feb. 15, 1864	Mar. 26, 1864	Mustered out Sept. 8, 1865.
Ross, Randall J.......	Monmouth.	Jan. 5, 1864	Jan. 7, 1864	" "
Richardson, Richard J	....	Jan. 25, 1864	Feb. 18, 1864	" "
Sanders, James.......	....	July 30, 1864	Aug. 26, 1864	" "
Sexton, Theodore.....	Green	Mar. 7, 1865	Mar. 8, 1865	" "
Smith, Thomas.......	....	July 29, 1864	Aug. 22, 1864	" "
Smith, Robert........	....	Jan. 25, 1864	Feb. 14, 1864	" "
Smith, Benjamin F...	Rivola	Feb. 24, 1865	Feb. 25, 1865	" "
Smith, Ezra F........	Rio	Jan. 31, 1865	Feb. 1, 1865	" "
Stroud, George W....	Oxford	Feb. 15, 1864	Mar. 26, 1864	" "
Stewart, William	Cameron.	Feb. 2, 1864	Feb. 27, 1864	M.O. Sept. 8, '65, as Corp'l.
Shelton, Thomas L...	Lafayette.......	Jan. 6, 1864	Feb. 14, 1864	Mustered out Sept. 8, 1864.
Stanley, Frank.......	Rio	Jan. 31, 1865	Feb. 1, 1865	" "
Taylor, Robert B.	Rock Island co.	Oct. 11, 1864	Oct. 13, 1864	" "
Thompson, Samuel F.	Piggsville.....	Feb. 26, 1864	Feb. 26, 1864	" "
Underwood, D'n P'dro	....	Mar. 16, 1865	Mar. 17, 1865	" "
Whipp, Henry........	Oxford	Feb. 15, 1864	Mar. 26, 1864	" "
Whitcomb, Silas O....	Lawrence	Apr. 12, 1865	Apr. 12, 1865	" "
Wallace, Hugh F	Monmouth	Feb. 23, 1864	Feb. 26, 1865	" "
Wallace, Samuel F...	....	Feb. 26, 1864		" "
Wheeler, Charles W..	" "	Oct. 30, 1863	Nov. 23, 1864	M. O. Sept. 8, '65, as Corp'l.
Williams, James M...	Mt. Pleasant. ..	Aug. 16, 1864	Aug. 16, 1864	Mustered out Sept. 8, 1865.
Wells, Henry T.......	Greenbush	Mar. 10, 1865	Mar. 11, 1865	" "
Wells, Girard W......	Roseville.	Mar. 16, 1865	Mar. 17, 1865	" "

COMPANY E.

Name and Rank.	Residence.	Date of rank or enlistment.	Date of muster.	Remarks.
Captains.				
Henry W. Manning...	Kane	Mar. 7, 1862	....	M.O. Mar. 26, '64; drunken'ss
Charles E. McDougall	Petersburg.....	Mar. 26, 1864	July 9, 1864	Mustered out Sept. 8, 1865.
First Lieutenants.				
Henry W. Manning...	Kane	Feb. 5, 1862	Feb. 5, 1862	Promoted ....
Jedediah Beals.	Beardstown....	Mar. 7, 1862	....	Died at Evansville, Ind., May 11, 1862.
Charles E. McDougall	Petersburg.....	July 1, 1862	Aug. 16, 1862	Promoted ....
Luther Grundy.	Kane...........	Mar. 26, 1864	....	Mustered out Sept. 8, 1865.
Second Lieutenants.				
James B. Ballow......	White Hall.....	Mar. 7, 1862	....	Died, St. Louis, Apr. 21, '62.
Charles E. McDougall	Petersburg.....	May 1, 1862	May 1, 1862	Promoted ....
John C. Judy	Sumner........	July 1, 1862	....	Prom., Co. G, Mar. 1, 1863..
Luther Grundy.......	Kane..........	Mar. 1, 1863	May 1, 1963	Promoted ....
William H. Bonfoy...	....	July 31, 1865	Aug. 6, 1865	Mustered out Sept. 8, 1865.

Name and Rank.	Residence.	Date of rank or enlistment.	Date of muster.	Remarks.
Privates.				
Atkins, Leven.	Kane	Nov. 2, 1861	Feb. 5, 1862	Mustered out Feb. 7, 1865..
Adams, John Q	"	Dec. 7, 1861	"	M. O. Feb. 7,'65, as Serg't..
Bonfry, William H	"	Nov. 2, 1861	"	Prom. Commis. Sergeant.
Ballow, James B	White Hall	Dec. 7, 1861	"	Promoted 2d Lieutenant.
Boyle, George	Kane		"	Re-enlisted as Veteran...
Bronson, Abram C	"	Dec. 9, 1861	"	Disch. May 22. '62; disabil.
Baird, Samuel W	Otter Creek	Dec. 14, 1861	"	Died at Helena, Ark., Aug. 12, 1863.
Baird, William S	White Hall	Dec. 28, 1861	"	Mustered out Feb. 7, 1865...
Brown, Stephen A	"	Jan. 18, 1862	"	Died, Little R'ck. Feb.24,'64
Caldwell, William	Kane	Nov. 2, 1861	"	Re-enlisted as Veteran...
Clark, William B.	White Hall	Dec. 7, 1861	"	
Cooke, Phillip R	Kane	Dec. 27, 1861	"	Disch. Jan. 28, '63; disabil.
Cooke, Mordecai C	"	Jan. 17, 1862	"	M. O. Feb. 7,'65, as Serg't.
Corey, Marshall S	"	Dec. 27, 1861	"	Killed, Shiloh, Apr. 6, '62..
Dugan, John W	"	Nov. 2, 1861	"	Re-enlisted as Veteran...
Estes, Harrison	"	Jan. 2, 1862	"	Dishon. disch, Nov. 25, '65.
Elkin, Edward W	Beardstown	Jan. 18, 1862	"	Died, Keokuk, Ia., May 4, '62
Foulbeaut, Filman J	Kane	Nov. 2, 1861	"	Re-enlisted as Veteran...
Forbush, Thomas M	"	Dec. 8, 1861	"	Disch. June 27.'62; disabil.
Grandy, Luther	"	Nov. 2, 1861	"	Promoted 2d Lieutenant.
Gentry, James A	"	Jan. 17, 1862	"	Re-enlisted as Veteran...
Glover, John W	Beardstown	Jan. 29, 1862	"	Died, St. Louis, May 27, '62.
Hayes, James	Kane	Dec. 26, 1861	"	Wounded at Shiloh. Discharged Apr. 6,'63; disabil
Hart, William H	White Hall	Dec. 28, 1861	"	Re-enlisted as Veteran...
Hudgspeth, Samuel.	Kane	Jan. 2, 1862	"	Disch. June 25, '62; disabil.
Howard, William L	Carrollton		"	Re-enlisted as Veteran...
Hill, Anthony	Beardstown	Jan. 18, 1862	"	Mustered out Feb. 7, 1865..
Irvin, Clifford	Kane	Dec. 26, 1861	"	Died Aug 24, 1863 ....
Keller, Frank	"	Nov. 18, 1861	"	Died at Jefferson Barracks Aug. 11, 1863
Lownds, John	"	Nov. 9, 1861	"	Re-enlisted as Veteran ...
Miller, James	"	Nov. 6, 1861	"	
McDougall, Charles E	Petersburg	Dec. 6, 1861	"	Promoted 2d Lieutenant...
Moore, Peter	Kane	Jan. 27, 1862	"	Mustered out Feb. 7, 1865..
McCann, George W	Otter Creek	Feb. 4, 1862	"	Re-enlisted as Veteran ...
Newman, Wesley	Kane	Dec. 24, 1861	"	
Potts, William	"	Jan. 21, 1862	"	Disch. Nov.23, '62, as Serg't; disability ....
Rawley, Daniel	Beardstown	Jan. 18, 1862	"	Mustered out Feb. 7, 1865..
Stone, Simon	Kane	Nov. 2, 1861	"	
Seward, Robert	"	Nov. 9, 1861	"	Re-enlisted as Veteran...
Scoggins, George	"	Nov. 20, 1861	"	Mustered out Feb. 7, 1865..
Snow, Thomas M	"	Dec. 24, 1861	"	Re-enlisted as Veteran...
Seward, George W	"	Jan. 6, 1862	"	Mustered out Feb. 7, 1865..
Snow, Ludwell	"	Jan. 8, 1862	"	Died, Bolivar, T., May 16.'62
Smith, Ira H	"	Jan. 7, 1862	"	M. O. Feb. 7,'65, as Corp'l..
Squires, William A	Beardstown	Jan. 18, 1862	"	Died, St. Louis, Mar. 30, '63.
Sansom, James L	Grafton	Jan. 29, 1862	"	M. O. Feb. 7, '65, as Serg't.
Sanders, George J	Beardstown		"	Mustered out Feb. 7, 1865..
Shoopman, Nick	"	Nov. 2, 1861	"	
Talbott, Amos	Kane	Dec. 7, 1861	"	Died, St. Louis, June 25, '62.
Thompson, Thomas J	White Hall	Jan. 20, 1862	"	Missing since battle of Shiloh ....
Vernon, William	Kane	Dec. 8, 1861	"	Disch. Nov.23, '62; disabil.
Walker, William R	White Hall	Jan. 18, 1862	"	Re-enlisted as Veteran...
Wells, Jacob D	Beardstown		"	Disch. Aug. 14,'62; disabil.
Woods, Madison	"		"	Mustered out Feb. 7, 1865..
Wells, Alpheus P	"	Jan. 24, 1862	"	Died, St. Louis, Apr. 11, '62.
Winfree, Asa F	"	Jan. 29, 1862	"	Mustered out Feb. 7, 1865..
Winckler, John W	Kane	Feb. 4, 1862	"	Discharged for wounds received at Shiloh ......
Whitesides, Joel	"		"	
Veterans.				
Boyle, George	White Hall	Feb. 29, 1861	Apr. 30, 1864	Deserted Sept. 26, 1864.....
Colwell, William	Kane	"	"	Prom. Sergeant Major....
Clark, William R	White Hall	"	"	Paroled prisoner. Died at Annapolis,Md.,June 11,'65
Dugan, John W	Kane	"	"	M. O. Sept. 8, '65, as 1st b'gt.
Foulboeuf,Philemon J	"	"	"	Disch. July 13,'65; pris war.
Gentry, James H	"	"	"	Corp'l. Died. Little Rock, May 21, 1864
Hart, William H	Bloomington	"	"	1st Serg't. Paroled pris. Died, Jacksonville, Ga..
Howard, William L	Carrollton	"	"	M. O. Sept. 8,'65, as Serg't.
Lownds, John	Kane	"	"	Mustered out Sept. 8, 1865
Miller, James	"	"	"	M. O. June 28,'65; pris. war.
McCann, George W	Jerseyville	"	"	Mustered out Sept. 8, 1865.

Name and Rank.	Residence.	Date of rank or enlistment.	Date of muster.	Remarks.
Menckel, John C......	Beardstown....	Feb. 29, 1864	Apr. 30, 1864	M. O. June 2d, '65; pris. war.
McCormick, John	"	"	"	M. O. Sept. 8, '65, as Corp'l.
Newman, Wesley	Kane	"	"	Mustered out Sept. 8, 1865.
Seward, Robert	....	"	"	Died, Andersonville prison, Apr. 15,'65. Gr. 12,827.
Snow, Thomas C. M ..	"	"	"	Mustered out Sept. 8, 1865.
Stone, George L	"	"	"	Mustered out July 13, 1865.
Walker, William R....	White Hall	Jan. 5, 1864	Jan. 20, 1864	M. O. Sept. 8, '65, as Berg't.
Recruits.				
Atkins, Charles B.....	Barr's Store....	Feb. 16, 1865	Feb. 17, 1865	Mustered out Sept. 8, 1865.
Atkins, Bartlett.	Union	"	"	"
Albion, William D	Macoupin co ..	Feb. 21, 1865	Feb. 25, 1865	"
Buxton, Peter........	Beardstown....	Feb. 21, 1862	Mar. 7, 1862	Mustered out Mar. 22, 1865.
Beals, Walter	"	Feb. 10, 1862		Disch. July 22, '62; disabil.
Barlow, Peter C......	Petty	Feb. 16, 1865	Feb. 17, 1865	Mustered out Sept. 8, 1865.
Burrows, John R	Bear Creek	"	"	"
Carey, Lawrence	Carrollton	Feb. 24, 1862	Mar. 7, 1862	Disch. July 3, '62; disabil.
Caruth, Joseph P.....	Gillespie	Feb. 16, 1865	Feb. 17, 1865	Mustered out Sept. 8, 1865.
Cobb, Jesse	Lancaster	Mar. 4, 1865	Mar. 6, 1865	"
Craven, James........	Sandy	Feb. 24, 1865	Feb. 25, 1865	"
Davis, Zachary G......	Carrollton	Mar. 5, 1862	Mar. 7, 1862	Informally disch.from 14th Ill. Trans. to that Reg't Apr. 24, 1862
Grant, Daniel B......	Beardstown....	Dec. 20, 1861	Feb. 5, 1862	Mustered out Mar. 22, 1865.
Giles, Samuel A......	Milton	Feb. 21, 1862		Tr. to V. R. C., May 8, '64.
Gregory, James H....	Bloomfield	Feb. 15, 1865	Feb. 16, 1865	Mustered out Sept. 8, 1865.
Green, John W........	Otter Creek	Sept. 5, 1864	Sept. 6, 1864	Mustered out May 23, 1865.
Hunt, William J	Kane	Feb. 26, 1862	Mar. 7, 1862	Deserted Mar. 10, 1863 .....
Hutchinson, David L.	Beardstown....	Feb. 21, 1862		Deserted Feb. 5, 1863.
Hartman, Zebulon	Bear Creek	Feb. 16, 1865	Feb. 17, 1865	Mustered out Sept. 8, 1865.
Judy, John C	Sumner	Dec. 10, 1861		Promoted 2d Lieutenant.
Jobe, Jacob	Bloomfield	Feb. 15, 1865	Feb. 16, 1865	Mustered out Sept. 8, 1865.
Jones, John	....	"	"	"
Kelly, John	Athens	Feb. 15, 1862	Mar. 7, 1862	Mustered out Mar. 22, 1865.
Menckel, John C......	Beardstown....	Feb. 14, 1862		Re-enlisted as Veteran.
McCormick, John......	"	Feb. 24, 1862	Feb. 24, 1862	"
Milner, John	Carrollton	Mar. 5, 1862	Mar. 7, 1862	Deserted Oct. 10, 1862 .....
Milton, William T....	Beardstown....	Feb. 21, 1862		Disch. Mar. 26, '62; disabil.
Meyer, Charles	"	Feb. 10, 1862		Mustered out Mar. 22, 1865.
Melford, Samuel J	Athens	Feb. 15, 1862		Died, St. Louis, May 5, '62.
McPherson, James H.	....	"		Died at Pittsburg Landing Apr. 1, 1862.
McGee, Z. T	Kane	Feb. 24, 1862		Deserted Mar. 21, 1862 ....
McBride, John S......	Milton	"	June 30, 1862	Deserted Oct. 10, 1862 ....
Noyes, Benjamin M ..	Bloomfield.	Feb. 9, 1865	Feb. 16, 1865	Mustered out Sept. 8, 1865.
Ruby, George T......	Beardstown....	Feb. 10, 1862	Mar. 7, 1862	Disch. June 14, '62; disabil.
Stone, George L	"	Feb. 26, 1862		Re-enlisted as Veteran ....
Shoopman, George W	Beardstown....	Feb. 10, 1862		Mustered out Mar. 22, 1865.
Shoopman, John H....	"	Feb. 29, 1862		"
Schmitker, Fred	"	Feb. 10, 1862		"
Smith, Bird	Glasgow	Feb. 21, 1862		Died, St. Louis, May 25, '62.
Smith, William B......	Kane	Feb. 19, 1862		Mustered out Mar. 22, 1865.
Trommen, Jacob	Beardstown....	Feb. 21, 1862		Died at Pittsburg Landing Apr. 29, 1862.
Varner, John	Rhoad's Pt	Feb. 21, 1865	Feb. 22, 1865	Mustered out July 17, 1865.
Welsner, Lorenzo D...	Greenfield......	Feb. 26, 1862	Mar. 7, 1862	Mustered out Mar. 22, 1865.
Wood, William	"	Feb. 15, 1865		Never joined Co. Deserted
Young, Francis M	Union	Feb. 16, 1865	Feb. 17, 1865	Mustered out Sept. 8, 1865.
Recruits transferred from 83d Ill. Inf.				
Alexander, Charles L.	Hale	Mar. 20, 1865	Mar. 22, 1865	Mustered out Sept. 8, 1865.
Burns, Jesse	Mt. Pleasant ..	Mar. 3, 1865	Mar. 4, 1865	"
Baird, James S	"	Nov. 20, 1863	Nov. 30, 1863	"
Black, Andrew	Monmouth	Feb. 25, 1864	Feb. 26, 1864	"
Brown, Daniel	Woodford co ..	"	"	"
Bailey, Daniel B	Sumner	Feb. 17, 1865	Feb. 17, 1865	"
Barrett, William H ...	Mt. Pleasant ..	Mar. 3, 1865	Mar. 4, 1865	"
Bromby, Jason	"	Jan. 25, 1864	Feb. 14, 1864	Deserted July 24, 1865 ......
Grosier, George R....	Roseville	Oct. 30, 1864	Nov. 25, 1863	M. O. Sept. 8, '65, as Serg't.
Corcoran, Richard....	"	Apr. 11, 1865	Apr. 13, 1865	Mustered out Sept. 8, 1865.
Coppersmith, Andrew	Greenbush	"	"	"
Dougherty, Oliver J..	Hale	Mar. 20, 1865	Mar. 22, 1865	"
Dorensey, Daniel	"	Mar. 10, 1865	Mar. 11, 1865	"
Foster, Minard	Swan	Apr. 4, 1865	Apr. 5, 1865	"
Graham, Benjamin F.	Ellison	Feb. 29, 1864	Mar. 2, 1864	M. O. Sept. 8, '65, as Corp'l.
Gardner, Archibald ..	Greenbush	Mar. 14, 1865	Mar. 15, 1865	Mustered out Sept. 8, 1865.
Guillinger, James F..	Spring Grove..	"	"	"
Gibson, Thomas	....	Dec. 14, 1863	Dec. 16, 1863	

Name and Rank.	Residence.	Date of rank or enlistment.	Date of muster.	Remarks.
Harper, James A	Spring Grove	Feb. 25, 1864	Feb. 26, 1864	M. O. Sept. 8, '65, as Serg't.
Haverfield, Samuel	Ohio Grove	Mar. 11, 1865	Mar. 15, 1865	Mustered out Sept. 8, 1865.
Hammond, James C	Monmouth	Feb. 25, 1864	Feb. 26, 1864	" "
Johnson, Fred. B		Jan. 6, 1864	Feb. 14, 1864	M. O. Sept. 8, '65, as Corp'l.
Kline, Hiram R	Roseville	Mar. 10, 1865	Mar. 11, 1865	Mustered out Sept. 8, 1865.
Knox, Sumner B	Ohio Grove	Mar. 14, 1865	Mar. 15, 1865	" "
Keller, Jacob	Farmington	Mar. 12, 1864	Apr. 25, 1864	" "
Lochard, John	Perryton	Mar. 10, 1865	Mar. 11, 1865	" "
Looby, Patrick	Sumner	Feb. 17, 1865	Feb. 18, 1865	" "
Moore, Josiah H		Dec. 24, 1863	Dec. 24, 1863	M. O. Sept. 8, '65, as Corp'l.
Moore, Joseph M				
Monroe, George N	Mt. Pleasant	Mar. 28, 1865	Mar. 29, 1865	Mustered out Sept. 8, 1865.
McFarin, James		Mar. 14, 1865	Mar. 15, 1865	" "
McDougall, James	Ohio Grove			
Morrison, Marion M	Sumner	Feb. 26, 1864	Feb. 26, 1864	" "
Michaels, Wesley N		Jan. 18, 1864	Jan. 19, 1864	" "
McCoy, Perry	Sumner	Jan. 20, 1864	Jan. 20, 1864	" "
McGeary, Joseph		Feb. 17, 1865	Feb. 17, 1865	" "
McCoy, Thomas M	"			
McLosky, Robert	Ohio Grove	Mar. 14, 1865	Mar. 15, 1865	" "
McCrary, Matt. R	Tompkins			" "
McCrary, Spencer M	Monroe			" "
Nichols, George		Mar. 3, 1865	Mar. 3, 1865	" "
Nichols, Alvin M	Sumner	Feb. 17, 1865	Feb. 17, 1865	" "
Peters, August	Chicago	Aug. 14, 1864	Aug. 15, 1864	" "
Russell, William	Mt. Pleasant	Mar. 3, 1865	Mar. 3, 1865	" "
Ritchie, Adam C	Haw Creek	Mar. 18, 1865	Mar. 19, 1865	" "
Snapp, Ezekiel	Swan	Apr. 4, 1865	Apr. 5, 1865	" "
Southern, Charles W	Ohio Grove	Mar. 14, 1865	Mar. 15, 1865	" "
Thompson, William N	Nov.	Nov. 13, 1863	Nov. 23, 1863	M. O. Sept. 8, '65, as Corp'l.
Thompson, William M	Sumner	Feb. 17, 1865	Feb. 17, 1865	Mustered out Sept. 8, 1865.
Tally, William T		Mar. 6, 1865	Mar. 7, 1865	" "
Turpin, Francis	Buena Vista	Apr. 14, 1865	Apr. 15, 1865	" "
Wells, Alfred B		Mar. 7, 1865	Mar. 8, 1865	" "
Waterhouse, Sam'l O.	LaHarpe	Mar. 30, 1865	Mar. 30, 1865	" "
Worden, Linder	Swan			" "
Wynn, Morgan	Ohio Grove	Mar. 14, 1865	Mar. 15, 1865	" "
Williams, James A		Mar. 17, 1864	Mar. 18, 1865	" "
Wilson, Christopher	Berwick	Mar. 16, 1863	Mar. 17, 1865	" "
Wiley, Samuel N		Feb. 29, 1864	Mar. 2, 1864	" "
Walter, Gibson M	Sumner	Feb. 17, 1865	Feb. 18, 1865	" "

COMPANY F.

Name and Rank.	Residence.	Date of rank or enlistment.	Date of muster.	Remarks.
Captains.				
Robert E. Haggard	Winchester	Mar. 24, 1863		Resigned Apr. 2, 1863
William L. Stuart	"	Apr. 2, 1863	July 9, 1864	Mustered out Sept. 8, 1865.
First Lieutenants.				
Robert E. Haggard	Winchester	Feb. 5, 1862	Feb. 5, 1862	Promoted
William L. Stuart	"	Mar. 24, 1862	Mar. 24, 1862	
Charles B. Smith	Bloomington	Apr. 2, 1863	May 8, 1863	Resigned Oct. 29, 1864
Nelson A. Corrington.	Greenfield	Oct. 29, 1864	Feb. 4, 1865	Resigned Aug. 5, 1865
Jonathan Burns	Winchester	Aug. 21, 1865	Not must'r'd	M. O. Sept. 8, '65, as 2d Lt.
Second Lieutenants.				
Charles B. Smith	Bloomington	Mar. 24, 1862	Mar. 24, 1862	Promoted
Elijah B. Corrington	Greenfield	Apr. 2, 1863	May 1, 1863	Killed in action Dec. 4, '64.
Jonathan Burns	Winchester	July 31, 1865	Aug. 6, 1865	Promoted
William M. Gray	"	Aug. 21, 1865	Not must'r'd	M. O. Sept. 8, '65, as Sergt.
Privates.				
Branum, Napoleon J.	Exeter	Jan. 25, 1862	Feb. 5, 1862	Discharged Feb. 12, 1863
Buchanan, James M	"	Dec. 20, 1861	"	
Bailey, William B	Winchester		"	Corp'l. Died at Paducah, Ky., July 7, 1862
Barton, George L	Milton	Jan. 9, 1862	"	Re-enlisted as Veteran
Balsley, John W	Winchester		"	
Clark, Oscar	Exeter	Jan. 22, 1862	"	
Cox, Micajah			"	Died, St. Louis, Apr. 1, '62.
Carlton, Isaiah	Winchester	Dec. 17, 1861	"	Re-enlisted as Veteran
Cumby, Isaac	"		"	Unofficially reported died Jan., '63 in Scott co., Ill.

Name and Rank.	Residence.	Date of rank or enlistment.	Date of muster.	Remarks.
Cohagen, Samuel D ..	Winchester	Dec. 20, 1861	Feb. 5, 1862	Re-enlisted as Veteran ...
Crump, Charles G ..	"	Dec. 21, 1861	"	
Cox, Thomas A.	"	Dec. 27, 1861	"	Disch. Aug. 3, '62; disabil.
Chance, William W..	Exeter	Jan. 4, 1862	"	Re-enlisted as Veteran ...
Crabtree, Joel...	Winchester	Jan. 17, 1862	"	Mustered out Feb 7, 1865..
Copper, Robert J.	"	Jan. 18, 1862	"	Died at Carrollton, Ill., Mar. 3, 1862......
Cox, John J.	"	Jan. 23, 1862	"	Serg't. Died at Mound City, Aug. 2, 1863 ....
Corrington, Nelson A.	Greenfield......	Feb. 5, 1862	"	Re-enlisted as Veteran ...
Corrington, Elijah B..	"	"	"	Pro. 1st Serg., then 2d Lt.
Corrington, Isaac N ..	"	"	"	Disch. Aug. 13, '62; disabil.
Dolahite, Andrew J...	Exeter	Jan. 17, 1862	"	Re-enlisted as Veteran ...
Flynn, Ezekiel	Winchester	Jan. 4, 1862	"	
Gray, William M	Manchester ...	Dec. 17, 1861	"	" .....
Hogatt, Crowder H ...	Winchester	Dec. 20, 1861	"	Deserted Aug. 18, 1862...
Hanback, George W ..	"	"	"	Re-enlisted as Veteran ...
Hale, Solon B	"	Dec. 21, 1861	"	Disch. Oct. 8, '62; disabil.
Hodges, James	"	Jan. 22, 1862	"	Disch. July 16, '62; wounds
Jackson, William.....	"	Dec. 17, 1861	"	Re-enlisted as Veteran ...
Lyman, Charles.	"	"	"	
Lewis, William G	"	"	"	Mustered out Feb. 7, 1865..
Lewis, John E	"	Dec. 21, 1861	"	M. O. Feb. 7, '65, as Serg't.
Lewis, Samuel Z	"	Dec. 27, 1861	"	Re-enlisted as Veteran ...
Morrow, William	"	Dec. 21, 1861	"	
McGinnis, Lemuel....	"	"	"	Died at Owl Creek, Tenn., May 19, 1862...
Minor, Francis M	"	Dec. 30, 1861	"	Re-enlisted as Veteran...
Overstreet, Reuben J.	Exeter.	Jan. 4, 1862	"	Died at Benton Barracks, Mo.. Sept. 12, 1862 ....
Osborn, Abram L....	"	Jan. 22, 1862	"	Re-enlisted as Veteran....
Prather, Andrew J ..	Winchester	Dec. 27, 1861	"	
Ross, Jonathan W....	"	Dec. 17, 1861	"	
Riley, John W	Exeter	Dec. 27, 1861	"	
Ryan, William	Winchester	Jan. 4, 1862	"	Disch. Nov. 10, '62; disabil.
Rayburn, Thomas	"	Jan. 7, 1862	"	Re-enlisted as Veteran ...
Reeser, Cyrus.......	"	Jan. 28, 1862	"	Disch. Dec. 2, '62; disabil..
Slavens, Thomas F ..	Exeter	Jan. 4, 1862	"	Died at Pittsburg Landing, Apr. 5, 1862 ...
Six, Abram D..........	Winchester	"	"	Disch. Jan. 7, '63, as Serg.; disability ...
Stuart, William L.....	"	Dec. 17, 1861	"	Promoted 1st Lieutenant .
Thompson, Wash'ton.	Exeter	"	"	Disch. Oct. 30, '62, as Corp.; disability ...
Torrey, Charles L	"	Jan. 17, 1862	"	Died at Pittsburg Landing, April 24, 1862...
Wilders, Sylvester B .	Winchester	Dec. 30, 1861	"	Disch. May 19, '62; disabil.
Woods, Patrick.	"	Jan. 2, 1862	"	Mustered out Feb. 7, 1865..
Veterans.				
Balsley, John W	Winchester	Feb. 9, 1864	Mar. 18, 1864	M. O. May 30, '65; pris. war.
Birdsell, William.	Jacksonville...	Mar. 25, 1864	Apr. 30, 1864	Died at Franklin, Tenn., May 5, 1865 ...
Barton, George L...	Winchester	Feb. 9, 1864	Mar. 18, 1864	M. O. Aug. 10, '65; pris. war.
Carlton, John.	Glasgow........	Feb. 29, 1864		Mustered out Sept. 8, 1865.
Cox, Franklin.........	Vermont.......	Mar. 25, 1864	Apr. 30, 1864	M. O. Sept. 8. '65, as Serg't.
Crump, Charles G	Winchester	Jan. 4, 1864	Jan. 20, 1864	M. O. Aug. 10, '65; pris. war.
Carlton, Isaiah.......	Glasgow........	"	"	Mustered out Sept. 8, 1865.
Cohagen, Samuel D ..	Winchester	"	"	M.O. May 30, '65, as Corp'l.; prisoner of war...
Chance, William W..	Exeter	"	"	M. O. Sept. 8, '65, as Serg't.
Corrington, Nelson A.	Greenfield......	Feb. 9, 1864	Mar. 18, 1864	Pro. 1st Serg., then 1st Lt.
Clark, Oscar	Exeter	"	"	M. O. Sept. 8, '65, as Corp'l.
Dollahite, Andrew J..	"	"	"	Deserted Sept. 26, 1864 ...
Daniels, John N	Winchester	"	"	M. O. May 30, '65; pris. war.
Flynn, Ezekiel	Bedford	Jan. 4, 1864	Jan. 20, 1864	Mustered out Sept. 8, 1865.
Gray, William M	Manchester ...	Feb. 9, 1864	Mar. 18, 1864	M.O. Sept. 8, '65, as 1st Sgt.
Hanback, George W ..	Winchester	Jan. 4, 1864	Jan. 20, 1864	M. O. Sept. 8, '65, as Serg.
Hazen, Reuben L.....	"	Feb. 9, 1864	Mar. 18, 1864	Mustered out Sept. 8, 1865.
Jackson, William.....	"	"	"	M. O. May 30, '65; pris. war.
Lewis, Samuel Z	"	"	"	Mustered out Sept. 8, 1865.
Lyman, Charles......	"	Jan. 4, 1864	Jan. 20, 1864	Deserted Nov. 6, 1864 ...
Lyman, Anson S.......	"	Feb. 9, 1864	Mar. 18, 1864	Mustered out Sept. 8, 1865.
Morrow, William	Roseville, O ...	Jan. 4, 1864	Jan. 20, 1864	" "
Minor, Francis M.....	Winchester	Feb. 9, 1864	Mar. 18, 1864	M. O. Sept. 8, '65; pris. war.
Malloy, Luke.........	Bedford			M.O. June 23, '65; pris. war.
McGinnis, William....	Winchester....	Mar. 25, 1864	Apr. 30, 1864	Mustered out Sept. 8, 1865.
McCarty, John.......	"	Feb. 29, 1864	Mar. 18, 1864	M. O. May 30, '65; pris. war.
Osborn, Abram L.....	Naples..........	Feb. 9, 1864	"	Mustered out Sept. 8, 1865.

Name and Rank.	Residence.	Date of rank or enlistment.	Date of muster.	Remarks.
Prather, Andrew J ...	Winchester	Jan. 4, 1864	Jan. 20, 1864	M. O. May 30, '65; pris. war.
Rayburn, Thomas ...	''	Feb. 9, 1864	Mar. 18, 1864	
Ross, Jonathan W ...	''	Jan. 4, 1864	Jan. 20, 1864	Mustered out Sept. 8, 1865.
Ruark, James H	Greenfield....	Feb. 29, 1864	Mar. 18, 1864	
Vaughn, John T......	Montezuma...	''	''	M. O. Sept. 8, '65, as Serg't.
Walters, Joseph	Vermont........	Mar. 25, 1864	Apr. 30, 1864	M. O. Sept. 8,'65, as Corp'l.
Recruits.				
Ashley, Aden J	Miner's Springs	Feb. 21, 1865	Feb. 22, 1865	Mustered out Sept. 8, 1865.
Birdsell, William ...	Iatan............	Mar. 24, 1862		Re-enlisted as Veteran...
Burns, Jonathan.....	Winchester	Jan. 4, 1862	Mar. 7, 1862	Promoted Q. M. Sergeant.
Bateson, Lewis J. ...	Vermont	Mar. 24, 1862	Mar. 24, 1862	Disch. Jan. 31,'63, as Corp.; disability.
Bartlett, Nimrod.....	Greenfield......	Feb. 10, 1862	Mar. 7, 1862	Disch. Nov. 9,'63; disabil.
Bruce, William H....	Milton..........	Feb. 6, 1862		Unofficially reported died at Savannah, Tenn.
Carlton, John.	Winchester	Feb. 18, 1862	''	Re-enlisted as Veteran ...
Cox. Franklin.......	Vermont'......	Mar. 24, 1862	June 21, 1863	
Corrington, Joel M..	....	Feb. 10, 1862	Mar. 7, 1862	Disch. May 7, '62; disabil.
Claten, James H	Glasgow......	Feb. 21, 1865	Feb. 22, 1865	M. O. Sept. 8,'65, as Corp'l.
Calahan, Isaac	Little Rock,Ark	Feb. 4, 1864	Mar. 18, 1864	Mustered out Sept. 8, 1865.
Carraher, Patrick....	Woodville	Jan. 28, 1864	Apr. 11, 1864	
Daniels, John N	Milton.........	Feb. 6, 1862	Mar. 7, 1862	Re-enlisted as Veteran ...
Dunsmore, Guilford.	Montezuma ...	Jan. 28, 1864		Mustered out Sept. 8, 1865.
Donley, Peter.........	Naples..........	''	May 3, 1864	M. O. May 11, '65. Never joined Company.........
Esters, James.........	Winchester	Mar. 24, 1862	....	Missing since battle of Shiloh, Tenn.
Evans, Benjamin F..	Barry	Mar. 8, 1864	Apr. 23, 1864	Mustered out Sept. 8, 1865.
Gilson, Daniel H	Greene co	Jan. 30, 1865	Feb. 1, 1865	
Hazen, Reuben L.....	Winchester	Feb. 6, 1862	Mar. 7, 1862	Re-enlisted as Veteran ...
Hughes, Oliver P....	Iatan	Mar. 24, 1862	June 19, 1863	M. O. Mar. 23,'65, as Corp'l.
Hester, Osmey M	Milton	Feb. 25, 1862	Mar. 7, 1862	Mustered out Mar. 23, 1865.
Hibbard, C. M.......	Vermont.......	Mar. 24, 1862		Disch. July 19,'62; wounds.
Haney, John	Glasgow......	Feb. 21, 1865	Feb. 22, 1865	M. O. Sept. 8,'65, as Corp'l.
Hatchett, Charles W.	New Franklin..	Feb. 17, 1864	Feb. 29, 1864	Mustered out Sept. 8, 1865.
Henry, William N....	Glasgow.......	Feb. 21, 1865	Feb. 22, 1865	
Jones, Richard D.....	Iatan...........	Mar. 24, 1862	June 30, 1863	M. O. Mar. 23,'65, as Corp'l.
Jellison, Samuel B...	Decatur	Dec. 10, 1861	Mar. 7, 1862	Red. from Q. M. Sgt. Pro. 1st Lieut. 1st Ark. Cav ..
Lyman, Anson S......	....	Feb. 6, 1862	''	Re-enlisted as Veteran ...
Langford, John C....	....	Mar. 23, 1863	June 21, 1863	M. O. May 30, '65, as Serg.; prisoner of war.
McCarty, John........	Winchester ...	Feb. 22, 1865	Mar. 7, 1862	Re-enlisted as Veteran ..
McGinnis, William...	....	Mar. 24, 1862	June 21, 1863	
Molloy, Luke........	Milton........	Feb. 6, 1862	Mar. 7, 1862	M. O. May 30,'65; pris. war.
McCarty, John M.	Winchester ...	Feb. 22, 1862	''	Disch. Oct. 12, '62; disabil.
Madigan, Martin	''	''	''	Deserted Aug. 7, 1862 ......
Miller, Benjamin	''	Feb. 6, 1862	''	Mustered out Mar. 23, 1865.
Miller, Christopher...	Hardin..........	Feb. 17, 1862	''	Disch. May 18,'62; blind ...
Miller, Lacy..........	Vermont........	Mar. 24, 1862		Died at Pittsburg Landing, Tenn., Apr. 23, 1862
McKinney, M. D......	Carrollton......	Nov. 1, 1861	Mar. 7, 1862	Deserted May 29, 1862 ...
McMahon, William..	Glasgow.......	Feb. 21, 1865	Feb. 22, 1865	M. O. Sept. 8, '65, as Corp'l.
Minor, James H.......	Naples..........	Jan. 28, 1864	Apr. 11, 1864	Mustered out Sept. 8, 1865.
McGlasson, Wm. L...	Glasgow.......	Jan. 21 1865	Feb. 22, 1865	''
McMahon, Levi.	''	Feb. 21, 1865	''	''
Ruark, James H	Greenfield......	Feb. 10, 1862	Mar. 7, 1862	Re-enlisted as Veteran ...
Rolston, Thomas D...	Manchester	Feb. 25, 1862		Deserted Aug. 7, 1862......
Ryan, Andrew	Jacksonville.'..	Nov. 26, 1863	Dec. 31, 1863	Mustered out Sept. 8, 1865.
Stewart, John.........	Winchester ...	Feb. 24, 1862	Mar. 7, 1862	Disch. Oct. 29, '64; disabil.
Seevers, George W ...	Iatan...........	Mar. 24, 1862	June 30, 1863	Mustered out Mar. 23, 1865.
Sims, James D........	....	''	''	
Stins, James W	Milton..........	Feb. 25, 1862	Mar. 7, 1862	Disch. June 2, '62; disabil.
Sturman, Charles H..	Greenfield......	Nov. 28, 1863	Dec. 31, 1863	Died, Duvall's Bluff, Ark., July 18, 1864
Shackleford, Chas. A.	....	Oct. 4, 1864		M. O. June 14,'65; pris. war
Sharp, Jethro N......	Glasgow.......	Feb. 21, 1865	Feb. 22, 1865	Mustered out Sept. 8, 1865.
Smith, William.......	''	''	''	Died at Franklin, Tenn., May 28, 1865
Taylor, Alexander....	Winchester	Dec. 16, 1861	Mar. 7, 1862	Disch. Nov. 10,'62; disabil.
Vaughn, John T......	Milton	Feb. 15, 1862		Re-enlisted as Veteran...
Vaughn, Jesse	Montezuma ...	Jan. 26, 1864	Apr. 11, 1864	Mustered out Sept. 8, 1865.
Vaughn, James	Eastern	Dec. 31, 1863	Jan. 31, 1864	Never joined Company...
Walters, Joseph	Vermont........	Mar. 24, 1862	June 21, 1863	Re-enlisted as Veteran ...
Wilson, John L	Iatan			Drowned in Hatchie River May 26, 1862
Whealdon, Nathan...	Vermont	''	....	Disch. Oct. 2, '62; disabil ...
Walters, James.......	''	''	....	Unoffic'lly report'd disch.
Winner, William J....	''	''	....	Prom. Hospital Steward.

Name and Rank.	Residence.	Date of rank or enlistment.	Date of muster.	Remarks.
Wilson, William H....	Glasgow.......	Feb. 21, 1865	Feb. 22, 1865	M. O. Sept. 8, '65, as Corp'l
Wilson, Robert N	Manchester....	Nov. 17, 1863	Dec. 31, 1863	Mustered out Sept. 8, 1865.
Wade, Joseph.........	Glasgow.......	Feb. 21, 1865	Feb. 22, 1865	" "
Recruits transferred from 123d Ill. Inf.				
Alenbaugh, S. S.......	Greenup.......	Feb. 11, 1864	Mar. 26 1864	Mustered out Sept. 8, 1865.
Brownell, Franklin...	"	Mar. 19, 1864	Mar. 19, 1864	" "
Buriner, George S....	Charleston ...	Jan. 10, 1864	Feb. 10, 1864	M. O. Sept. 8, '65, as Corp'l.
Bennett, Henry O.....	Westfield.......	Feb. 11, 1864	Feb. 11, 1864	Mustered out Sept. 8, 1865.
Barber, Clark C.......				" "
Baker, Thomas	Martinsville..	Feb. 1, 1864	Feb. 1, 1864	" "
Bales, James.........	Westfield.......	Feb. 11, 1865	Feb. 11, 1865	" "
Cook, Miles	Greenup.......	Mar. 19, 1864	Mar. 19, 1864	" "
Cunningham, William	Martinsville..	Feb. 1, 1864	Mar. 1, 1864	" "
Cornwell, James L....	Ashmore......	Jan. 1, 1864	Jan. 24, 1864	M.O.Sept. 8, '65; never rep'd
Clark, Henry H.......	Crookederunk.	Feb. 29, 1864	Mar. 29, 1864	Mustered out Sept. 8, 1865.
Coons, George H		Dec. 15, 1864	Dec. 15, 1864	" "
Dunn, Harvey L.......	Madison co., Ala	Dec. 25, 1863	Dec. 23, 1863	" "
Dow, Lorenzo.......	Greenup.......	Mar. 18, 1864	Apr. 19, 1864	Mustered out June 6. 1865..
Fry, Franklin........	Westfield.......	Jan. 20, 1864	Jan. 20, 1864	Mustered out Sept. 8, 1865.
Fisher, Charles H	Chicago......	Apr. 1, 1865	Apr. 1, 1865	" "
Hamilton, Albert		Feb. 11, 1864	Mar. 26, 1864	" "
Hammers, Albert.....	Jasper co......	Feb. 29, 1864	Mar. 29, 1864	" "
Kellum, John W	Greenup.......	Feb. 11, 1864	Mar. 26, 1864	" "
Knight, William M...	Charleston ...	Feb. 1, 1864	Feb. 1, 1864	" "
Mahaffrey, Joseph ...	Greenup.......	Feb. 11, 1864	Feb. 28, 1864	" "
McCabe, William C...		Mar. 16, 1865	Mar. 16, 1865	" "
Maleroy, David......	Jasper co......	Feb. 29, 1864	Feb. 29, 1864	" "
Maggart, Charles A...	Dolson	Feb. 1, 1864	Feb. 1, 1864	" "
Miller, Henry C......	Westfield.......	Feb. 4, 1864	Feb. 11, 1864	" "
Malroy, Rees	Casey.........			" "
Medcaff, William H...	Westfield.......	Feb. 11, 1864	"	" "
Medcaff, Nathan L...	"	"	"	" "
Newlin, Thomas	"	"	"	Abs't, sick, at M. O. of Reg
Parker, Nathaniel L..	"	"	"	Mustered out Sept. 8, 1865.
Rufner, Martin J.....	Greenup.......	"	Mar. 26, 1864	" "
Redman, Joseph	Westfield.......	"	Feb. 11, 1864	" "
Sturbuck, William H.	Greenup.......	"	Mar. 26, 1864	" "
Stump, Levi.........	"	Mar. 10, 1864	Mar. 10 1864	" "
Smith, Reuben R		Apr. 29, 1864	Apr. 29, 1864	" "
Tumbleson, William C		Feb. 4, 1864	Feb. 4, 1864	" "
Tomlinson, Sylvester	Westfield.......	Feb. 1, 1864	Feb. 1, 1864	" "
Troxsil, John S	Will co.......	Oct. 3, 1864	Oct. 8, 1864	" "
Wollard, William H...		Aug. 10, 1864	Aug. 10, 1864	" "
Wagner, Peter H.....		Jan. 11, 1864	Feb. 8, 1864	M. O. Sept. 8, '65, as Corp'l
Woodworth, Edwin B	Charleston ...	Mar. 21, 1864	May 3, 1864	Mustered out Sept. 8, 1865.
White, John T.......	Westfield.......	Feb. 11, 1865	Feb. 11, 1865	" "
Wilson, James		"	"	Abs't, sick, at M. O. of Reg.

COMPANY G.

Name and Rank.	Residence.	Date of rank or enlistment.	Date of muster.	Remarks.
Captains.				
Jerome B. Nulton	Greensbury....	Feb. 5, 1862	Mar. 7, 1862	Promoted Major...........
John C. Judy........	Sumner	Sept. 14, 1864	Oct. 19, 1864	Mustered out Sept. 8, 1865.
First Lieutenants.				
William B. Taylor	Greene co......	Mar. 7, 1862	Mar. 7, 1862	Resigned Sept. 3, 1862....
John C. Judy........	Sumner	Mar. 1, 1863	May 1, 1863	Promoted ....
Thomas H. Dayton ...	Greene co......	May 5, 1865	July 12, 1865	Prom.Cap. Co.H.Aug.10,'65
Presley T. Rice	"	Aug. 21, 1865	Not must'd.	M. O. Sept. 8, '65, as 2d Lt.
Second Lieutenants.				
Jacob L. Marshall ...	Greene co......	Mar. 7, 1862		Dismissed Apr. 13, 1863....
Thomas H. Dayton...	"	June 1, 1863	July 18, 1863	Promoted ....
Presley T. Rice......	"	July 11, 1865	July 18, 1865	"
John Powell	Jersey co	Aug. 21, 1865	Not must'd.	M. O. Sept. 8, '65, as Serg't
Privates.				
Abney, James........	Greene co......	Oct. 29, 1861	Feb. 5, 1862	Accident'ly kil'd.Dec.14,'62
Abney, Joseph.......	"	Nov. 9, 1861	"	Disch. Nov. 7, '62, as Corp'l; disability
Austin, Rollin S.......	"	Dec. 4, 1861	"	Disch. at Cincinnati, Ohio

Name and Rank.	Residence.	Date of rank or enlistment.	Date of muster.	Remarks.
Barber, William Alex.	Jersey co	Oct. 29, 1861	Feb. 5, 1862	Disch. Feb. 11, '63; disabil. Shot himself in big toe..
Brooks, William L....	Greene co	Dec. 3, 1861	''	Corporal. Died at Milliken's Bend, July 29, 1863.
Blake, George F.....	Jersey co	Dec. 7, 1861	''	Re-enlisted as Veteran ...
Carpenter, Reuben...	Greene co...	Oct. 29, 1861	''	
Cummings, Andrew...	''	Nov. 5, 1861	''	Died at Jackson, Tenn., July 1, 1862..........
Cummings, Noah J...	''	Dec. 5, 1861	''	Died at Keokuk, Iowa, of wou'ds rece'ed at Shiloh
Cummings, Jacob C..	''	Dec. 9, 1861	''	Killed at Shiloh, Apr. 6, '62.
Clark, Elias.	''	Dec. 11, 1861	''	Mustered out Feb. 7, 1865..
Cockrell, Nathan.....	''	Dec. 20, 1861	''	Re-enlisted as Veteran. .
Cope, John	''	Jan. 31, 1862	''	Unofficially reported died Sept. 20, '62, at Macon, Ga., while prisoner war.
Dayton, William S....	''	Oct. 29, 1861	''	Mustered out Feb. 7, 1865..
Davis, Huston	''	Nov. 5, 1861	''	Re-enlisted as Veteran ...
Dayton, Thomas H. ..	''	Oct. 29, 1861	''	Prom. Serg't, then 2d Lt..
Eppler, George........	''	Dec. 9, 1861	''	Re-enlisted as Veteran ...
Franby, Henry........	''	Nov. 9, 1861	''	Mustered out Mar. 24, 1865.
Fleak, John D..........	''	''	''	Died at Jefferson Barracks, Mo., Nov. 16, 1863.
Fickell, Francis M....	Jersey co.......	Dec. 2, 1861	''	Died at Alton, Ill., in military prison
Fields, Robert H......	Greene co....	Feb. 4, 1862	''	Repor'd desert'r Aug. 18, '62
Gounds, Joseph.....	'' ..	Oct. 29, 1861	''	Re-enlisted as Veteran ...
Gaffney, Thomas J. ..	'' ..		''	Disch. Sept. 24, '62; disabil.
Giberson, Hezekiah...	''	Dec. 13, 1861	''	Re-enlisted as Veteran ...
Henson, Samuel, Jr...	''	Jan. 20, 1862	''	Corporal. Died at Evansville, Ind., Jan. 14, 1862...
Hust, Keller	''	Oct. 29, 1861	''	Sergeant. Trans to Inv. Corps Sept. 1, 1863
Harmon, John W.	''	''	''	Musician. Died at St. Louis, May 14, 1862 ......
Hargett, Thomas......	''	Nov. 11, 1861	''	Re-enlisted as Veteran ...
Hondashelt, James N.	''	Jan. 6, 1862	''	Died while prisoner of war
Harmon, George A...	''	Oct. 29, 1861	''	Mustered out Feb. 7, 1865..
Johnnessee, James M.	''		''	
Jones, Robert H	''		''	Re-enlisted as Veteran ...
Kimball, Jesse	''	Oct. 22, 1861	''	Disch. Oct. 1, '62; disabil..
Kelch, Charles	Jersey co	Dec. 23, 1861	''	Died while prisoner of war
Lachmund, Christ....	Greene co....	Dec. 14, 1861	''	Re-enlisted as Veteran ...
Lenow or Lenoir, Geo.	''	Dec. 31, 1861	''	Report'd desert'r Aug. 18, '62
Marshall, J. L	''	Oct. 29, 1861	''	Promoted 2d Lieutenant .
McCalla, William M...	''		''	Disch. Aug. 6, '64; disabil..
Million, Adam S......	''	Dec. 2, 1861	''	Mustered out Feb. 7, 1865..
Miller, Thomas J.....	''	Dec. 3, 1861	''	Disch. from mil. pris., Alton, Ill., at exn'n of serv.
Mattison, James F....	''	Dec. 13, 1861	''	Died, St. Louis, May 5, 1862.
Owens, Robert........	''	Nov. 5, 1861	''	Miss'g after bat. of Shiloh.
O'Keefe, Patrick	Carrollton	Nov. 11, 1861	''	Disch. Feb. 11, '63; disabil.
Powell, John	Jersey co.....	Nov. 5, 1861	''	Re-enlisted as Veteran ...
Quigley, William L. ..	''	Jan. 3, 1862	''	Died at Hamburg, Tenn...
Reynolds, John L.....	Greene co.....	Oct. 29, 1861	''	Died at Jackson, Tenn., July 1, 1862
Revers, Frank	Calhoun co.....	''	''	Died at Snyder's Bluff, Miss., July 18, 1863........
Rice, Presley T.	Greene co......	Nov. 4, 1861	''	Re-enlisted as Veteran ...
Rayfield, Isaac	''	Nov. 9, 1861	''	Disch. Feb. 11, '63; disabil.
Rice, Joseph P.:......	''	Nov. 4, 1861	''	Serg't. Died at Pittsburg Landing, Apr. 1, 1862 ....
Rigsby, Nathaniel L..	''	Nov. 20, 1861	''	Re-enlisted as Veteran ...
Richardson, Henry...	''	Dec. 2, 1861	''	Corp. Deserted Aug. 14, '62.
Rowden, William A...	Jersey co.....	Dec. 10, 1861	''	Absent Aug. 18, 1862, and dropped from rolls ......
Robinett, James L....	Greene co......	Dec. 11, 1861	''	Killed at Shiloh, Apr. 6, '62.
Rayfield, William....	''	Dec. 13, 1861	''	Re-enlisted as Veteran ...
Stone, Daniel Ed.....	''	Oct. 29, 1861	''	Died, St. Louis, June 1, '62.
Stewart, John D	''		''	Re-enlisted as Veteran ...
Smith, David H.	''		''	Deserted Dec. 27, 1862......
Scoggins, William H..	''	Nov. 1, 1861	''	Re-enlisted as Veteran ...
Sturman, Thomas R..	Jersey co......	Nov. 5, 1861	''	Tr. to Inv. Corps May 31, '64
Stout, Elisha	Greene co......	Nov. 9, 1861	''	Kil'd near Jackson, Tenn., Dec. 19, 1862
Sanders, Simon M....	''	Nov. 19, 1861	''	Disch. Mar. 11, '63; disabil.
Stines, John F........	''	Dec. 2, 1861	''	Mustered out Sept. 8, 1865..
Stephenson, LeRoy...	''	Dec. 6, 1861	''	Re-enlisted as Veteran ...
Scoggins, George L..	Jersey co......	Jan. 7, 1862	''	''

Name and Rank.	Residence.	Date of rank or enlistment.	Date of muster.	Remarks.
Taylor, William B....	Greene co......	Oct. 19, 1861	Feb. 5, 1862	Promoted 1st Lieutenant.
Talley, William James	"	......	"	Re-enlisted as Veteran.
Townsend, Reuben...	"	Nov. 9, 1861	"	Died, St. Louis, July 18, '62.
Thomasson, Andrew J	"	Nov. 20, 1861	"	Mustered out Feb. 7, 1865.
Taylor, Tuoba.........	"	Oct. 29, 1861	"	"
Turpin, James W.	Jersey co	Dec. 7, 1861	"	Re-enlisted as Veteran ...
Varble, Phillip	Greene co......	Dec. 3, 1861	"	"
Whisman, George W.	Calhoun co.....	Oct. 29, 1861	"	Disch. June 17, '62; disabil.
Veterans.				
Briscoe, Aaron	Carrollton......	Feb. 26, 1864	Apr. 5, 1864	M. O. Sept. 8, '65, as Sergt.
Blake, George F	St. Paul, Minn.	Feb. 1, 1864	"	M. O. Sept. 8, '65. Det'ched
Clendenin, Oscar	Carrollton......	Feb. 26, 1864	"	M. O. Sept. 8, '65, as Serg't.
Crotchet, Perry	"	......	"	Drowned in Cumberland River, Nov. 25, 1864 .....
Carpenter, Reuben ...	"	Feb. 1, 1864	"	Died of wounds received Dec. 7, 1864 ......
Cockrell, Nathan......	"	"	"	Mustered out Sept. 8, 1865.
Davis, Hoston.........	"	"	"	"
Eppler, George	"	"	"	Discharged July 13, 1865...
Gound, Joseph........	"	"	"	Mustered out Sept. 8, 1865.
Giberson, Hezekiah..	Kane	"	"	"
Hargett, Thomas	Carrollton.....	"	"	"
Jones, Robert H	"	"	"	M. O. May 30, '65; pris. war.
Lofton, John	Jerseyville	Feb. 26, 1864	"	Mustered out Sept. 8, 1865.
Lachmund, Christ....	Carrollton......	Jan. 5, 1864	Jan. 20, 1864	M.O. Sept. 8, '65, as 1st Sg't.
Powell, John.........	Jerseyville	Feb. 1, 1864	Apr. 5, 1864	Died of wounds received Dec. 15, 1864
Rigsby, Nathaniel	Carrollton......	Jan. 5, 1864	Jan. 20, 1864	
Rayfield, William	"	Feb. 1, 1864	Apr. 5, 1864	Died of wounds received Dec. 15, 1864 ......
Rice, Presley T.......	"	"	"	Promoted 2d Lieutenant...
Scoggins, George L..	"	......	"	M. O. June 14, '65, as Corp'l; was prisoner.
Steward, John D......	"	"	"	Mustered out Sept. 8, 1865.
Stephenson, LeRoy...	Jerseyville	"	"	Died at Murfreesboro, T., Mar. 29, 1865
Scoggins, William H.	Carrollton......	"	"	Discharged Mar. 22, 1865...
Tally, William James.	"	......	"	Mustered out Sept. 8, 1865.
Turpin, James W.	Fieldon	"	"	M. O. July 3, '65; pris. war.
Varble, Phillip	Carrollton.....	"	"	Mustered out Sept. 8, 1865.
Recruits.				
Alexander, Samuel..	Greene co......	Feb. 7, 1863	......	Discharged Nov. 26, 1862...
Briscoe, Aaron	Jersey co......	Feb. 24, 1862	......	Re-enlisted as Veteran ...
Barlow, George	Greene co......			Deserted Jan. 24, 1863 ......
Bucknell, John		Feb. 20, 1862		Report'd desert'r Aug.18,'62
Baldwin, Jeremiah ..	Hittle	Sept. 27, 1864	Sept. 27, 1864	Mustered out July 20, 1865.
Clendenin, Oscar	Greene co......	Feb. 25, 1862		Re-enlisted as Veteran ...
Crotchett, Perry		Feb. 16, 1862		
Carter, John A.......	Otego	Apr. 12, 1865	Apr. 12, 1865	M. O. Sept. 8, '65, as Corp'l.
Crotchett, Amos	Hittle	Oct. 1, 1864	Oct. 1, 1864	Mustered out July 20, 1865.
Crane, James J.	L. Mackinaw..	Sept. 27, 1864	Sept. 27, 1864	"
Crotchett, William C.	"	"	"	"
Clark, George F.....	"	"	"	"
Crawford, John H....	State of Tenn..	June 3, 1863	June 21, 1863	Tr. to V. R. C., Feb. 21, '65.
Doyle, Perry	Stonington	Dec. 3, 1864	Dec. 8, 1864	Mustered out June 3, 1865.
Grimm, John	Fieldon	Nov. 14, 1863	Dec. 31, 1863	Mustered out Sept. 8, 1865.
Grasley, Simon	Jersey co......	Oct. 5, 1864	Oct. 6, 1864	
Jones, Noah W........	Jerseyville	Feb. 20, 1862	....	Died at Owl Creek, Tenn., June 1, 1863 ......
Jones, Price M........	Greene co......	"		Disch. Dec. 23, '62; disabil.
Lofton, John ...:....	Jersey co......	Feb. 18, 1862		Re-enlisted as Veteran ...
McGovern, James E.	Greene co......	Dec. 13, 1861	....	M. O. Mar. 22, '65, as Serg't.
Pearine, Jerome.....	Hittle	Sept. 28, 1864	Sept. 28, 1864	Mustered out July 20, 1865.
Roundtree, Solway R.	Jersey co......	Feb. 6, 1862		Disch. Sept. 12, '63, as Serg.
Rhodes, John	L. Mackinaw..	Sept. 27, 1864	Sept. 27, 1864	Died at Murfreesboro, T., Jan. 27, 1865...
Reeves, Samuel McR.	Petty	Feb. 21, 1865	Feb. 21, 1865	Mustered out Sept. 8, 1865.
Robinette, John R....	L. Mackinaw..	Sept. 27, 1864	Sept. 27, 1864	Mustered out July 20, 1865.
Skearnatz, Charles...	Lyons	Oct. 21, 1864	Oct. 21, 1864	Mustered out Sept. 8, 1865.
Thomasson, James A.	Greene co......	Feb. 17, 1862	....	Report'd desert'r Aug.18,'62
Trimble, Napoleon B.	"	Feb. 25, 1862		Discharged June 28, 1865...
Trimble, Bainbridge T	"	Feb. 22, 1862		Discharged Sept. 12, 1862 ..
Tully, John	Woodville	Oct. 17, 1864	Oct. 18, 1864	Mustered out Sept. 8, 1865.
Withrow, William	Jersey co......	Oct. 5, 1864	Oct. 6, 1864	"
Warren, George W...	Carrollton......	Feb. 11, 1865	Feb. 14, 1865	Mustered out July 20, 1865.
Warren, Winfield S...	L. Mackinaw...	Sept. 27, 1864	Sept. 27, 1864	"

Name and Rank.	Residence.	Date of rank or enlistment.	Date of muster.	Remarks.
Recruits transferred from 83d Ill. Inf.				
Adams, Fred J	Bushnell	Jan. 4, 1864	Jan. 8, 1864	M. O. Sept. 8, '65, as Corp'l.
Beachamp, Wm. M.	Maquon	Dec. 29, 1863	Dec. 29, 1863	Mustered out Sept. 8, 1865.
Bumbarger, Peter	Salem	Feb. 23, 1865	Feb. 23, 1865	'' ''
Bailey, John L		Dec. 10, 1862	Dec. 10, 1862	'' ''
Bennett, James		Dec. 1, 1863	Feb. 13, 1864	'' ''
Bailey, James D	Copley	July 12, 1864	Aug. 20, 1864	'' ''
Burges. Fred W		Jan. 25, 1865	Jan. 25, 1865	'' ''
Combs, John F	Maquon	Feb 17, 1865	Feb. 17, 1865	M O. Sept. 8, '65, as Corp'l.
Orabill, Jonathan	Salem	Feb. 3, 1865	Feb. 3, 1865	
Cowman, John				Mustered out Sept. 8, 1865.
Collins, Henry O		Nov. 30, 1863	Nov. 30, 1863	'' ''
Darr, John B	Galesburg	Feb. 10, 1844	Feb. 18, 1864	M. O. Sept. 8, '65, as Corp'l.
Darnell, George	Maquon	Dec. 28, 1863	Dec. 29, 1863	Mustered out Sept. 8, 1865.
Darnell, James	''	Feb. 17, 1865	Feb. 19, 1865	'' ''
Dalton, William		Jan. 18, 1865	Jan. 18, 1865	'' ''
Dalton, Lewis				'' ''
Dunnagun, B. O		Nov. 25, 1863	Feb. 15, 1864	'' ''
Durham, James A				'' ''
Dunnaway, Jesse		Dec. 24, 1862	Dec. 24, 1862	'' ''
Dunbar, George	Rio	Jan. 31, 1865	Feb. 1, 1865	'' ''
Dunbar, Francis M				'' ''
Everett, Ezra	Galesburg	Feb. 18, 1864	Feb. 18, 1864	M. O. Sept. 8, '65, as Serg't.
George, William A		Nov. 9, 1864	Nov. 29, 1863	'' ''
Gla-gow, Jesse		Nov. 25, 1862	Nov. 25, 1862	Mustered out Sept. 8, 1865.
Gibbs, William A		Aug. 20, 1864	Feb. 25, 1863	'' ''
Hilligoss, Geo. or Gar-	Salem	Jan. 19, 1865	Jan. 19, 1865	'' ''
Hilligoss, Wm.... [ey	''	Jan. 21, 1865	Jan. 21, 1865	'' ''
Holloway, Jonathan		Feb. 3, 1865	Feb. 3, 1865	'' ''
Haines, John	''	Feb. 6, 1865	Feb. 6, 1865	'' ''
House, William A.	Knox co	Nov. 30, 1863	Nov. 30, 1863	'' ''
Hooper, Joseph		Dec. 28, 1863	Feb. 28, 1864	'' ''
Kerns, Samuel		Apr. 7, 1865	Apr. 7, 1865	'' ''
Lusk, Thomas		May 29, 1863	June 11, 1863	'' ''
Logan, Jasper		Apr. 11, 1865	Apr. 12, 1865	'' ''
McCune, John A	Monmouth	Nov. 20, 1863	Nov. 20, 1863	'' ''
Moore, St. Clair	Maquon	Dec. 28, 1863	Dec. 29, 1863	'' ''
Morse, John O		Mar. 15, 1864	Mar. 15, 1864	'' ''
Moore, William	Fairview			'' ''
Morehead, William	Maquon	Feb. 2, 1864	Feb. 2, 1864	'' ''
Minard, William		Dec. 18, 1863	Feb. 15, 1864	'' ''
McClarry, James F.	Galesburg	Feb. 10, 1864	Feb. 18, 1864	'' ''
Ondendirk, William.	Knox co	Feb. 12, 1865	Feb. 14, 1865	'' ''
Palmer, Ludwell O.	Coal Valley	Apr. 11, 1865	Apr. 12, 1865	'' ''
Porter, George W.		Mar. 8, 1865	Mar. 8, 1865	'' ''
Porter, Julius P	Union			'' ''
Pickenspaugh, Wm	Maquon	Feb. 17, 1865	Feb. 17, 1865	'' ''
Powers, Willis		Dec. 28, 1863	Feb. 28, 1864	'' ''
Pease, Stillman, A	Victoria	Feb. 1, 1864	Mar. 25, 1864	'' ''
Pease, Alonzo J		Feb. 18, 1865	Feb. 19, 1865	'' ''
Redding, Michael		Oct. 6, 1862	Nov. 13, 1862	'' ''
Shaw, Lee W	Honey Creek	Apr. 11, 1865	Apr. 12, 1865	M. O. Sept. 8, '65, as Corp'l.
Sullivan, Jeremiah.		Oct. 6, 1862	Nov. 13, 1862	Mustered out Sept. 8, 1865.
Stevenson, Alonzo	Knox co	Feb. 13, 1865	Feb. 14, 1865	'' ''
Underwood, William M		Dec. 24, 1862	Dec. 24, 1862	'' ''
West, Samuel D	Truman	Nov 2, 1864	Nov. 2, 1864	M. O. Sept. 8, '65, as Corp'l.
Whiting, George J	St. Louis, Mo.	Feb. 16, 1864	Feb. 16, 1864	Mustered out Sept. 8, 1865.
Williams, Benj. F		Nov. 25, 1863	Feb. 15, 1864	'' ''
Recruits transf'd from 98th Ill. Inf.				
Anderson, James M	Oblong	Feb. 15, 1865	Feb. 15, 1865	Mustered out Sept. 8, 1865.
Laws, Lot	Petty's	Dec. 7, 1863	Dec. 7, 1863	'' ''
Lowback, Eli	Olney	Feb. 28, 1864	Feb. 28, 1864	'' ''

COMPANY D.

Name and Rank.	Residence.	Date of rank or enlistment.	Date of muster.	Remarks.
Captains.				
Daniel Grass	Lawrenceville	Dec. 2, 1862	Dec. 2, 1862	Promoted Major July 18, '63
Andrew J. Knight	Mattoon	June 1, 1864	July 16, 1863	Resigned Aug. 12, 1864
Elias C. Davis	Sumner	Aug. 12, 1864	Not must'r'd	Disch. May 15, '65, as 2d Lt.
Thomas H. Dayton		Aug. 2, 1865	Aug. 10, 1865	Mustered out Sept. 8, 1865.

Name and Rank.	Residence.	Date of rank or enlistment.	Date of muster.	Remarks.
First Lieutenants.				
Daniel Grass.............	Lawrenceville .	Mar. 7, 1862	Mar. 7, 1862	Promoted ....
Andrew J. Knight......	Mattoon..........	Dec. 2, 1862	Dec. 2, 1862	"
George W. Bryans.....	....	June 1, 1863	June 18, 1863	Resigned Jan. 9, 1865......
John T. Jones...........	Coles co........	Aug. 2, 1865	Aug. 1, 1865	Mustered out Sept. 8, 1865.
Second Lieutenants.				
George W. Bryans.....		Dec. 2, 1862	Feb. 1, 1863	Promoted...............
Elias C. Davis....	Sumner.... ...	June 1, 1863	July 18, 1863	"
Privates.				
Anderson, Joseph W.	Decatur	Dec. 10, 1861	Mar. 7, 1862	Disch Apr. 29, '63; disabil.
Burgess, Charles S...	Lawrence co ...		"	Re-enlisted as Veteran....
Boles, William	Coles co	Jan. 23, 1862	"	Died Oct. 2, 1862; wounds.
Corder, Louis T	Prairie City....	"	"	Re-enlisted as Veteran ...
Cox, Paris D	Cumberland co	"	"	
Choat, Samuel H		"	"	.....
Cummings, Isaac	Lawrence co .	Jan. 8, 1862	"	Died, Jeffers'n'Barracks, May 18, 1862...........
Campbell, Alexander.	Jersey co	Feb. 18, 1862	"	Died at Good Samaritan, M., Apr. 3, 1862........
Davis, Edwin............	Sumner.........	Dec. 10, 1861	"	Disch. June 18, '62; disabil.
Davis, Elias P...........	"	"	"	Died...................
Davis, Elias C...........	"	"	"	Pro. 1st Serg., then 2d Lt..
Dutton, John C.		"	"	Re-enlisted as Veteran..
Estes, Thomas	Coles co........	Feb. 5, 1862	"	Deserted Feb. 15, 1863....
Followell, Robert M..	Macon co.......	Dec. 10, 1861	"	Re-enlisted as Veteran...
Falkner, Joseph	Jersey co......	"	"	Disch. Aug 28. '62; disabil.
Farrar, William G	Lawrence co...	"	"	Re-enlisted as Veteran...
Fickes, George	Coles co	Jan. 23, 1862	"	Disch. Aug.2, '62; disabil.
Gallagher, Edward....	Macon co	Dec. 10, 1861	"	Deserted Aug. 18, 1862 ...
Goodwin, Burrell T...	Cumberland co	Jan. 23, 1862	"	Disch. Oct. 18, '62; disabil.
Goodwin, Bradford C.	"	"	"	Re-enlisted as Veteran.
Goodwin, Andrew J ..	"	"	"	Disch. Feb. 11, '63; disabil.
Grotts, George F	Jersey co	Feb. 25, 1862	"	Re-enlisted as Veteran..
Hart, William P	Coles co........	Jan. 23, 1862	"	"
Heath, Asahel..........	Lawrenceville .	Jan. 8, 1862	"	Died at Jefferson Barracks, May 12, 1862......
Jones, William	Decatur	Dec. 10, 1861	"	Deserted July 18, 1862....
Jellison, Samuel B....	"	"	"	Promoted Q. M. Sergeant.
Joslen, Amos N	"	"	"	Mustered out Mar. 22, 1865.
Judy, John C...........	Sumner.........	"	"	Transferred to Co. E......
Knight, Andrew J	Mattoon......	Jan. 23, 1862	"	Promoted 2d Lieutenant .
Lundrey, John	Etna............	"	"	Deserted Aug. 18, 1862....
Landrus, Joseph H...	Mattoon........	"	"	Re-enlisted as Veteran ...
Lyons, Robert.....	Jerseyville	Feb. 28, 1862	"	Died at Jackson, Tenn., Sept. 22, 1862.........
Mienre, Charles........	Lawrenceville .	Dec. 10, 1861	"	Disch. June 2, '62; disabil.
Miles, John T	Carrollton......	Mar. 1, 1862	"	Deserted Aug. 18, 1862....
Petty, John M..........	Lawrence co...	Jan. 8, 1862	"	Died ....
Pruitt, Aaron..........	Jersey co.......	Feb. 23, 1862	"	Miss'g afterbattleof Shiloh
Richey, Stephen M...	"	"	"	Mustered out Mar. 22, 1865.
Roberts, Fieldin B....	Greene co......	Nov. 2, 1861	"	Re-enlisted as Veteran ...
Schultz, Samuel	Lawrence co...	Dec. 10, 1861	"	Disch. Jan. 16, '64; disabil.
Salisbury, George W.	" "	"	"	Re-enlisted as Veteran...
Smith, Joel B..........	" "	"	"	Deserted Apr. 23, 1862 ...
Smith, Samuel C......	Cumberland co	Mar. 3, 1862	"	Transferred to 14th Ill. Inf., Apr. 15, 1862
Sullender, Henry	Coles co.......	Jan. 23, 1862	"	Mustered out Mar. 22, 1865.
Shoars, Nelson A.....	Lawrence co...	"	"	Disch. Feb. 12, '64; disabil.
Smith, John J..........	" ...	Jan. 8, 1862	"	Serg't. Died at Sumner, Ill., June 24, 1864......
Sutherland, Clark	" "	"	"	Disch. Jan. 13, '63; disabil.
Thorn, Clinton.........	" "	"	"	Re-enlisted as Veteran...
Turopaw, George W.	Jersey co	Dec. 10, 1861	"	Corporal. Died ....
Tolbert, William	Jerseyville	Feb. 18, 1862	"	Disch. Nov. 9, 62; disabil.
Walters, William W ..	Lawrence co...	Jan. 8, 1862	"	Mustered out Mar. 22, 1865.
Whitsel, Peter D......	Fayette co	Jan. 23, 1862	"	Re-enlisted as Veteran ...
Veterans.				
Barton, Benjamin F..	Bloomington ..	Feb. 26, 1864	Apr. 30, 1864	Mustered out Sept. 8, 1865..
Barton, John W.......	" "	"	"	M. O. Sept. 8, '65, as Serg't.
Burgess, Charles S..	Sumner	Jan. 24, 1864	"	
Corder, Lewis T	Johnston........	"	"	M. O. July 18, 1865, as 1st Sergeant; pris. of war ..
Choat, Samuel H......	Neoga	"	"	Died Dec. 7, 1864; wounds.
Cox, Paris D	Johnston	"	"	Mustered out Sept. 8, 1865.
Dutton, John C.......	Sumner.........	"	"	
Followell, Robert M .	Decatur	Jan. 4, 1864	Jan. 30, 1864	M. O. Sept. 8, 1865, as Corp'l

Name and Rank.	Residence.	Date of rank or enlistment.	Date of muster.	Remarks.
Farrar, William G	Sumner	Jan. 21, 1864	Apr. 30, 1864	M. O. May 39, 1865, as Corporal; prisoner of war ..
Grotts, George F	Jerseyville ...	Feb. 26, 1864	"	Mustered out Sept. 8, 1865.
Goodwin, Bradford C.	Johnston	Jan. 24, 1864	"	
Hart, William P.......	Neoga	"	"	M. O. Sept. 8, 1865, as Serg't
Jones, John T.........	Johnston	"	"	Prom. Serg't, then 1st Lt..
Landrus, Joseph H...	....	"	"	M. O. May 30, '65; pris. war.
Pugh, Isaac W	Neoga	"	"	" "
Roberts, Fielden B....	Carrollton	"	"	
Salsbury, George W..	Sumner	"	"	Abs't sick, at M.O. of Reg't.
Thorn, Clinton.......	....	"	"	M. O. May 30,'65; pris. war.
Whitsel, Peter D.....	Vandalia.	"	"	M. O. Sept. 8, '65, as Corp'l.
White, Alexander.....	Lexington	Feb. 20, 1864	"	M. O. Sept. 8, '65, as 1st Sgt.
Recruits.				
Anderson, Phillp J...	....	Dec. 1, 1862	....	Mustered out Sept. 8, 1865.
Barton, Benjamin F .	Bloomington...	Jan. 23, 1862	Mar. 24, 1862	Re-enlisted as Veteran ...
Barton, John W	" "	Feb. 5, 1862	" "	
Barton, George W	" "			Disch. June 18,'62: disabil.
Blakely, Charles	Jerseyville			Mustered out Aug. 18, 1865.
Baker, W. H. H	Sumner	Sept. 1, 1862		M. O. Sept. 8,'65, as Serg't.
Bryans, George W	Lawrenceville.	Oct. 1, 1862		Promoted 2d Lieutenant..
Dutton, Stewart	Sumner	Sept. 1, 1862		Trans. to V. R. C. May 15, 1864. Disch. Apr. 12, 1865.
Eldred, Samuel D.....	Greene co	"		Trans. to V. R. C., Jan. 5, 1865. M. O. Sept. 15, 1865.
Evans, John B	Lawrenceville.	Nov. 1, 1862		Mustered out Sept. 8, 1865.
Foster, George W	Bloomington...	Feb. 5, 1862	May 7, 1862	Disch. July 1, '62; disabil..
Fox, John F	....	Nov. 5, 1864		Mustered out Sept. 8, 1865.
Fenton, John A.	Plana	Sept. 1, 1864	Sept. 1, 1864	
Gray, Salathiel	Sumner	Sept. 1, 1862		M. O. Sept. 8, '65; pris. war.
Glass, Lewis J	Lincoln	Nov. 16, 1863	Dec. 31, 1863	Disch. Aug. 20, '65; disabil.
Gaines, Stephen G....	Russellville ...	Nov. 1, 1862		Deserted Mar. 2, 1863 ......
Graves, Henry	....	Oct. 10, 1862		Trans. to V. R. C. May 15, '64
Hampton, Robert	Bloomington...	Feb. 5, 1862		Disch. June 23,'62; disabil.
Hollen, Joseph	Jerseyville ...	May 24, 1862		Mustered out July 20, 1865.
Highsmith, John O..	Lawrenceville.	Nov. 1, 1862		Died ....
Hallet, John..........	Russellville ...			Died at Andersonville prison, Feb. 9, 1865.....
Hodges, John R.......	" "	" "		M. O. May 30, '65; pris. war
Jones, John T........	Coles co	Jan. 23, 1862		Re-enlisted as Veteran ..
Lemons, John	Sumner	Sept. 1, 1862		Disch. June 23, '62; disabil.
McClintock, John. ...	Bloomington	Feb. 5, 1862		Died ....
McDaniels, Charles ..	Springfield....	Feb. 20, 1862		Mustered out Sept. 8, 1865.
Olney, Henry E.......	Eastern	Dec. 1, 1863	Jan. 31, 1864	Vet. Rec. M. O. Sept. 8, '65.
Pugh, Isaac W	Cumberland co.	Jan. 23, 1862		Re-enlisted as Veteran ...
Perry, James H.......	Sumner	Sept. 1, 1862		Trans. to V. R. C. M. O. July 3, 1865............
Russell, Zachariah T.	Petty's	Sept. 26, 1864	Sept. 26, 1864	Mustered out July 20, 1865.
Rix, Frederick H	Dillon	Sept. 27, 1864	Sept. 27, 1864	Prom. Hospital Steward..
Thurston, Lewis C....	Russellville ...	Aug. 30, 1862	Dec. 18, 1862	Mustered out Sept. 8, 1865.
Truckey, Anthony	Russellville ...	Nov. 1, 1862	Dec. 5, 1862	
White, Alexander....	Bloomington...	Feb. 5, 1862		Re-enlisted as Veteran...
Woolford, John W ...	" "	" "		Died ....
Walker, Henry	" "	" "		Disch. Aug. 21, '62; disabil.
Waggoner, Phillip. ..	Lawrence co...	Dec. 10, 1861		Died at Jefferson Barracks, Mo., May 31, 1862..
Winkles, Levi.	Lawrenceville.	Dec. 1, 1862		Mustered out Sept. 8, 1865.
Whitsel, George M...	Lawrence co...	Nov. 1, 1863	Nov. 23, 1863	" "
Willett, Runyon	....	Sept. 2, 1862		M. O. May 30,'65; pris. war.
Wilber, Benjamin F..	Russell	Sept. 22, 1864	Sept. 26, 1864	Mustered out July 20, 1865.
Recruits transferred from 83d Ill. Inf.				
Bruce, Nath'l or M. H.	Sumner	Feb. 17, 1865	Feb. 17, 1865	Mustered out Sept. 8, 1865.
Hohn, William M	Cameron	Jan. 28, 1864	Jan. 28, 1864	" "
Palmer, Allen........	Monmouth	Mar. 3, 1864	Mar. 3, 1864	" "
Recruits transf'd from 98th Ill. Inf.				
Adamson, Andrew J..	Madison.......	Jan. 1, 1864	Jan. 1, 1864	M. O. Sept. 8, '65, as Corp'l.
Baker, Henry W	Georgetown ...	Feb. 9, 1864	Feb. 9, 1864	" "
Brown, Columbus ...	Monee	Mar. 11, 1865	Mar. 11, 1865	Mustered out Sept. 8, 1865..
Burk, John W	Georgetown ...	Feb. 9, 1864	Feb. 9, 1864	" "
Barnes, George W ...	....			" "
Bryan, Lafayette	Louisville	Mar. 15, 1865	Mar. 21, 1865	" "
Bryan, Lunkford.....	LaSalle co			" "
Bridges, William	Hyde Park	Jan. 18, 1865	Jan. 18, 1865	" "
Crawford, Henry	....	July 26, 1863	July 26, 1863	" "
Davis, Caleb R	Louisville	Mar. 21, 1864	Mar. 21, 1864	M. O. Sept. 1, '65, as Corp'l.

Name and Rank.	Residence.	Date of rank or enlistment.	Date of muster.	Remarks.
Davidson, George	Hurricane	Mar. 14, 1865	Mar. 14, 1865	Abs., sick, M. O. of Reg't.
Dean, James R	Elbridge	Mar. 21, 1865	Mar. 21, 1865	Mustered out Sept. 8, 1865.
Dawson, Nathaniel	Eagle	Mar. 8, 1865	Mar. 9, 1865	" "
Farmer, Aaron R	Fayette co	Mar. 7, 1865	Mar. 7, 1865	" "
Graham, Arthur T	Newton	Feb. 23, 1864	Mar. 26, 1864	M. O. Sept. 8, '65, as Corp'l.
Gallicn, Samuel L	Fayette co	Mar. 6, 1865	Mar. 6, 1865	Mustered out Sept. 8, 1865.
Gibson, Stephen A	Georgetown	Feb. 9, 1864	Feb. 9, 1864	" "
Gregory, John W	Newton	Oct. 25, 1863	Nov. 24, 1863	" "
Hull, David	Seminary	Mar. 7, 1865	Mar. 7, 1865	" "
Harris, Zacharias O	Hurricane			" "
Henry, Martin T	Eagle	Feb. 21, 1865	Feb. 22, 1865	" "
Hopkins, Martin	Kaskaskia	Mar. 6, 1865	Mar. 7, 1865	Died July 6, 1865
Jack, Samuel	Crooked Creek.	Mar. 1, 1865		Mustered out Sept. 8, 1865.
Jones, John	Louisville	Mar. 28, 1864	Mar. 28, 1864	M. O. Sept. 8, '65, as Corp'l.
Kilburn, Marion	Newton	Feb. 23, 1864	Mar. 26, 1864	Mustered out Sept. 8, 1865.
Kinkade, William T		Aug. 27, 1864	Feb. 16, 1865	" "
Lambert, Thomas W	Marion co	Mar. 3, 1865	Mar. 3, 1865	" "
Laine, Joseph	Richland co	Sept. 10, 1864	Dec. 29, 1864	Mustered out Sept. 22, 1865
Lewis, Filman L	Louisville	Dec. 28, 1863	Dec. 28, 1863	Disch. July 15, '65; disabil.
Mallet, Charles	Eagle	Mar. 8, 1865	Mar. 8, 1865	Mustered out Sept 8, 1865.
Maxwell, Thomas N	Wade	Mar. 26, 1864	Mar. 26, 1864	" "
Martin, James N	Lancaster,	Mar. 17, 1865	Mar. 18, 1865	" "
McDonald, Andrew J	Seminary	Mar. 7, 1865	Mar. 7, 1865	" "
McCorkle, Lafavette	Lucas	Oct. 31, 1864	Oct. 31, 1864	" "
Martin, Robert M	Palestine	Oct. 26, 1863	Nov. 23, 1863	" "
Mize, Thompson	Watts	Mar. 9, 1865	Mar. 9, 1865	" "
McIlwain, Edward	Crooked Creek.	Nov. 16, 1863	Nov. 16, 1863	" "
McCulloch, Leander	Newton	Feb. 23, 1864	Mar. 26, 1864	" "
Pridemore, Andrew J	Mackinaw	Mar. 7, 1865	Mar. 7, 1865	" "
Rayneer, Thomas C	Manhattan	Apr. 12, 1865	Apr. 12, 1865	" "
Ray, Morris or Moses	Hurricane	Mar. 7, 1865	Mar. 7, 1865	" "
Rollins, George		Dec. 25, 1864	Jan. 25, 1864	" "
Rose, Madison O	Green Garden	Mar. 10, 1865	Mar. 10, 1865	" "
Rentfrow, George W	Centralia	Feb. 29, 1864	Mar. 2, 1864	" "
Rentfrow, John M. O	"	Feb. 21, 1865	Feb. 22, 1865	" "
Sears, Sterling	Hurricane	Mar. 11, 1865	Mar. 11, 1865	" "
Smith, Thomas A	Franklin co			" "
Smith, Joseph H	Georgetown	Feb. 9, 1864	Feb. 9, 1864	" "
Smith, John	Watts	Mar. 9, 1865	Mar. 9, 1865	" "
Tucker, John		Nov. 13, 1862	Nov. 13, 1862	" "
Tindale, Napoleon B.	Palestine	Oct. 26, 1864	Nov. 23, 1864	" "
Wood, Pallas L		Feb. 8, 1864	Feb. 8, 1864	M. O. Sept. 8, '65, as Corp'l
Williams, George W	Monee	Mar. 7, 1865	Mar. 7, 1865	Mustered out Sept. 8, 1865.
Werner, Albert L		Oct. 26, 1863	Nov. 23, 1863	" "
Wallace, John L	Mound	Jan. 14, 1864	Jan. 25, 1864	" "
Wilson, Albert	Jasper co	Mar. 7, 1865	Mar. 7, 1865	" "
Young, James	Cameron co,T'n	Dec. 27, 1863	Dec. 27, 1863	" "

COMPANY I.

Name and Rank.	Residence.	Date of rank or enlistment.	Date of muster.	Remarks.
Captains.				
James Lawrence.	Chicago	Mar. 28, 1862	Apr. 1, 1862	Resigned Feb. 25, 1864
Henry S. Goodspeed .	Avon	Feb. 25, 1864	Aug. 8, 1864	Mustered out Mar. 24, 1865.
Allen O. Haskins	Chicago	May 5, 1865	July 12, 1865	Mustered out Sept. 8, 1865.
First Lieutenants.				
Frederick Mattern	Chicago	Mar. 28, 1862		Resigned July 8, 1852
Charles J. Dawes	"	July 8, 1862	July 8, 1862	Resigned Apr. 3, 1863
Allen O. Haskins	"	May 1, 1863	Aug. 26, 1863	Promoted Adjutant.
Edward E. Hall		Feb. 25, 1864		Mustered out Sept. 8, 1865.
Second Lieutenants.				
James Lawrence.	Chicago	Mar. 7, 1862		Promoted
Joseph H. Buffington.	Jerseyville	Mar. 28, 1862		Resigned June 5, 1862
Henry S. Goodspeed.	Avon	June 5, 1862		Promoted Adjutant
Theodore Phillips	Van Buren, Ia.	Aug. 2, 1865	Aug. 10, 1865	Mustered out Sept. 8, 1865.
Privates.				
Allen, Albert H	Chicago	Feb. 2, 1862	Mar. 7, 1862	Wounded and missing at Shiloh
Barker, James	Frederick	Dec. 30, 1861	"	Reported a deserter Aug. 18, 1862
Ballegoyen, Henry	Chicago	Jan. 22, 1862	"	Discharged July 2, 1862, as Corporal; wounds

Name and Rank.	Residence.	Date of rank or enlistment.	Date of muster.	Remarks.
Bullock, Ebenezer H.	White Pig'n, M.	Feb. 22, 1862	Mar. 7, 1862	Reported a deserter Aug. 18, 1862.
Colton, Charles P.....	Princeton	Dec. 8, 1861	"	Re-enlisted as Veteran...
Dalhauser, Anthony..	Eagleton.	Jan. 11, 1862	"	Died at Quincy, Ill., May 27, 1862; wounds.
Dawes, Henry.........	Chicago	Dec. 17, 1861	"	Musician. Re-enlisted as Veteran..
Elkner, Edward G	"	Jan. 17, 1862	"	Corporal. Killed at Shiloh, Apr. 6, 1862.
Fendler, Claude.......	"	Mar. 6, 1862	"	Disch. Nov. 11, '63; disabil.
Galpin, Arthur........	Freeport.	Dec. 3, 1861	"	Mustered out Mar. 7, 1865..
Goodspeed, Henry S .	Avon	Feb. 1, 1862	"	Prom. Serg't, then 2d Lt..
Haskins, Allen C.....	Chicago	Feb. 18, 1862	"	Promoted 1st Lieutenant.
Havenstiene, Phillip .	Eagleton	Jan. 17, 1862	"	Reported a deserter Aug. 18, 1862.
Heiner, Elias..........	"	Jan. 11, 1862	"	Mustered out Mar. 24, 1865.
Hester, Thomas W....	Carrollton	Feb. 22, 1862	"	Died in Pike co., Ill., Dec. 21, 1863.
Hunt, Herbert	Chicago	Dec. 21, 1861	"	Discharged Aug. 22, 1862, as Sergeant; disability ....
Jarvis, Edwin M	Athens. ...:....	Feb. 22, 1862	"	Deserted Apr. 10, 1862. See Jarvis, Morris, recruit ..
Kahle, Frederick C ...	Freeport	Jan. 21, 1862	"	Re-enlisted as Veteran ...
Knapp, Samuel H....	Chicago	Dec. 3, 1861	"	Disch. Oct. 24, '62; disabil.
Lawrence, John S ...	"	....	"	Reported a deserter Aug. 18, 1862.
Lincoln, Levitt........	"	Dec. 27, 1861	"	Serg't. Died at Duvall's Bluff, Dec. 7, 1864.
Lindberg, Paul James	Blue Island	Dec. 17, 1861	"	Disch. Aug. 12, '62; disabil.
Lytle, James F........	Carrollton......	Feb. 22, 1862	"	Died at Benton Barracks, Mo., Mar 23, 1862.
Mattern, Frederick ...	Chicago	Dec. 10, 1861	"	Promoted 1st Lieutenant.
McClure, Ezekiel W .	York, N. Y	Jan. 22, 1862	"	Serg't. Reported a deserter Aug. 18, 1862............
Murray, Thomas J....	White Hall.....	Mar. 1, 1862	"	Died at Jefferson Barracks, Mo., May 24, 1862..
Muth, Phillip..........	Eagleton.	Jan. 11, 1862	"	Re-enlisted as Veteran...
Oscar, John	Delhi	Jan. 3, 1862	"	" " .....
Perlewitz, August	Chicago	Dec. 3, 1861	"	" " .....
Ross, William P.,Jr ..	"	Feb. 1, 1862	"	Mustered out Mar. 24, 1865.
Schorse, Franz.	Milwaukee, W ..	Dec. 31, 1861	"	
Smith, Seth B.	Carrollton	Feb. 25, 1862	"	Died at Jefferson Barracks, Mo., July 13, 1862..
Strahan, Henry.	Chicago	Jan. 4, 1862	"	Disch. Aug. 12, '64; disabil..
Southoff, John	Jerseyville ...	Mar. 1, 1862	"	Disch. Oct. 24, '62; disabil.
Strausenbach, Edw'rd	Eagleton	Jan. 11, 1862	"	Re-enlisted as Veteran...
Thaxton, Parham	Carrollton	Feb. 7, 1862	"	Mus'n. Discharged Feb. 11, 1863; disability ....
Tucker, John W	"	Feb. 25, 1862	"	Re-enlisted as Veteran...
Van Wert, John.......	Chicago	Feb. 13, 1862	"	Disch. June 27, '62; disabil.
Vogel, John	Eagleton.	Jan. 11, 1862	"	Died at Monterey, Tenn., June 8, 1862
Wendemuth, John....	"	"	"	Re-enlisted as Veteran...
Wink, Isaac D	St. Clairville, O.	Feb. 22, 1862	"	Mustered out Mar. 24, 1865.
Witting, Charles E ...	Benton B'ks,Mo	Feb. 19, 1862	"	Serg't. Died at Jefferson Barracks, May 15, 1862 ...
Wells, Peter S..	Chicago	Mar. 1, 1862	"	Disch. June 17, '62; disabil.
Veterans.				
Aber, Franz...	Chicago	Mar. 30, 1864	Apr. 30, 1864	Mustered out Sept. 8, 1865.
Boon, John	Frederick	Mar. 1, 1864	"	M. O. May 30, '65; pris. war.
Bannon, Matthew....	Joliet	Mar. 30, 1864	"	M. O. Sept. 8, '65, as Corp'l.
Ball, Joseph J	Vermont		"	Prom. Principal Musician.
Colton, Charles P....	Princeton	Mar. 1, 1864	"	M. O. Sept. 8, '65, as Serg't.
Cunningham, Allison.	Vermont .....:.	Mar. 30, 1864	"	Mustered out Sept. 8, 1865..
Dawes, R. H. P.......	Chicago	Mar. 1, 1864	"	
France, John	Redsville, Mo ..	Mar. 30, 1864	"	" " .....
Jones, John B	Browning		"	Died Dec. 23, '64; wounds..
Kahle, Frederick......	LaSalle	Mar. 1, 1864	"	1st Serg't. Died Dec. 27, 1864; wounds .....
Kimball, Henry......	Vermont	Mar. 30, 1864	"	Mustered out Sept. 8, 1865..
Kline, John V	Chicago		"	Disch. June 27, '65; disabil.
Londry, William......	Browning	"	"	Mustered out Sept 8, 1865..
Londry, John W	"	"	"	Kil'd, Nashville, Dec. 15, '64.
Muth, Phillip.........	LaSalle	Mar. 1, 1864	"	M. O. Sept. 8, '65; wounded.
Oscar, John C	Delhi		"	M. O. July 18, '65; was pris.
Phillips, Theodore. ..	Winchester	Mar. 30, 1864	"	Promoted 2d Lieutenant...
Perlewitz, August	Chicago	"	"	M. O. June 12, '65; was pris.
Shay, John	Iowa City, Ia...	"	"	In arrest at M. O. of Reg't.
Strausenbach, Edw'd.	Eagle	Mar. 1, 1864	"	M. O. Sept. 8, '65, as Corp'l.

Name and Rank.	Residence.	Date of rank or enlistment.	Date of muster.	Remarks.
Tiffany, Hugh........	Crystal Lake...	Mar. 30, 1864	Apr. 30, 1864	M. O. May 30,'65; pris. war.
Tucker, Francis M...	Mt. Sterling ...	Mar. 1, 1864	"	Serg't. Paroled pris. Died at Vicksburg, Apr. 15,'65.
Tucker, John W.....	Carrollton	"	"	M. O. Sept. 8,'65, as Corp'l.
Wisdom, Granville L.	Browning	Mar. 30, 1864	"	M. O. Sept. 8,'65, as 1st Sgt.
Wendemuth, John....	Chicago	Mar. 1, 1864	"	Mustered out Sept. 8, 1865..
Recruits.				
Aber, Franz.........	Greene co ...	Mar. 14, 1862	Mar. 14, 1862	Re-enlisted as Veteran ...
Adams, Edwin O....	Hittle	Sept. 30, 1864	Sept. 30, 1864	Mustered out July 20, 1865.
Allen, Joseph H....	Frederick	Mar. 25, 1862	June 21, 1863	Mustered out Mar. 24, 1865.
Anderson, Samuel M	Frederick	Feb. 15, 1862		
Allen, James F......	Chicago	Mar. 23, 1862		Disch. Oct. 20, '62; disabil.
Boon, John.........	Frederick	Feb. 15, 1862	June 21, 1863	Re-enlisted as Veteran ...
Bannon, Matthew...	Kankakee co...	Mar. 18, 1862	June 30, 1863	" "
Ball, Joseph J......	Vermont	Mar. 11, 1862	June 21, 1863	" "
Buffington, O. O.....	Evanston.....	Mar. 18, 1862		Pro. Corp.,1st Sgt. W'nd'd at Shiloh. M.O.Mar.24,'65.
Bauman, Jacob.......	Kankakee	"	....	Wounded and missing at Shiloh............
Black, Samuel......	Frederick	Feb. 15, 1862	June 30, 1863	Mustered out Mar. 24, 1865.
Cunningham, Allison	Vermont	Mar. 11, 1862		Re-enlisted as Veteran ...
Caldwell, Patrick...	Carrollton	Feb. 15, 1862	June 21, 1863	Mustered out Mar. 24, 1865.
Campbell, Lewis O.	Browning	Sept. 27, 1864	Sept. 27, 1864	Mustered out July 20, 1865.
Dawes, Charles J...	Chicago	Dec. 24, 1861		Promoted 1st Lieutenant.
Duke, Abram......	Frederick	Feb. 15, 1862		Disch. May 2, '62; disabil.
Ellison, Alexander....	Chicago	Mar. 16, 1862		Reported a deserter Aug. 18, 1862.
Easley, Reese.......	Fulton co ...	Mar. 11, 1862	June 21, 1863	M.O. Mar. 24,'65; wounded.
France, John........			June 30, 1863	Re-enlisted as Veteran ...
Harris, Isaac.........	Vermont	Feb. 15, 1862	June 21, 1863	Pro.Sgt. Reduc'd to ranks. DiedDuv'll's Bl'ff,Oct.19'64
Jones, John B.......	Browning ...	Mar. 11, 1862	June 21, 1863	Re-enlisted as Veteran ...
Jarvis, Morris......	....	Feb. 22, 1862		Retained to make up time lost ....
Kimball, Henry	Vermont	Mar. 11, 1862	Mar. 11, 1862	Re-enlisted as Veteran ...
Kline, John V	Chicago	Mar. 7, 1862		
Kirby, George O	Evanston.....	Mar. 18, 1862		Wounded at Shiloh .....
Kirkham, Charles ...	Frederick	Feb. 15, 1862		Disch. Mar. 30,'63; disabil.
Londry, John Wl.....	Browning	Mar. 11, 1862	June 30, 1863	Re-enlisted as Veteran ...
Londry, William		"	"	" "
Low, William A	Frederick	Feb. 15, 1862	....	Missing since battle of Shiloh ....
Misenhelmer, Marion.	"	"	June 21, 1863	Mustered out Mar. 24, 1865.
Misenhelmer, Isaac...		"	"	
McGaughey, Christ...	Carrollton.....	"	"	Mustered out Mar. 14, 1865.
Miller, John	......	Mar. 28, 1862		Reported a deserter, Aug. 18, 1862.
Montgomery, T. B...	Athens.....	Mar. 18, 1862		Deserted Feb. 24, 1864 .....
Phillips, Theodore..	V'nBuren co..Ia	Mar. 28, 1862	June 30, 1863	Re-enlisted as Veteran ...
Pulver, George O ...	Chicago	Oct. 19, 1864	Oct. 19, 1864	Mustered out. Sept. 8, 1865.
Paine, George R	Elkhorn	Sept. 24, 1864	Sept. 24, 1864	" "
Rider, Nicholas	Carrollton	Mar. 2, 1862	June 21, 1863	Mustered out Mar. 24, 1865.
Ryan, Charles W	Frederick	Feb. 15, 1862		Died in prison at Montgomery, Ala.
Shay, John	Iowa City, Ia...	Mar. 5, 1862	June 21, 1863	Re-enlisted as Veteran ...
Spangler, Cyrus	Frederick	Feb. 15, 1862		Mustered out Mar. 24, 1865.
Spillers, Isaac........	"	"		Disch. Dec. 9,'62; disabil.
Tiffany, Hugh.....		Mar. 6, 1862	June 21, 1863	Re-enlisted as Veteran ...
Thompson, P. B.....	White Hall	Mar. 1, 1862		Dishon. disch. Sept. 6,'63, sentence G. C. M
Tucker, Francis	Frederick	Mar. 15, 1862		Prom. Corp'l. Re-enlisted as Veteran ......
Talbott, James......	Chicago	Mar. 31, 1862		Died, Keokuk, June 23, '62.
Tucker, Anderson B..	Elkhorn	Sept. 24, 1864	Sept. 24, 1864	Mustered out Sept. 8, 1865.
Vaughn, James.....		Oct. 21, 1863	Jan. 20, 1864	Died, Paducah, Mar. 18,'65.
Wisdom, Granville L.	Browning	Mar. 11, 1862	June 21, 1863	Re-enlisted as Veteran ...
Wilson, William S	"	"		Missing since battle of Shiloh ....
Recruits trans. from 83d Ill. Inf.				
Allen, Henry T......		Jan. 5, 1864	Jan. 7, 1864	M. O. Sept. 8,'65, as Serg't.
Bostwick, Theodore H	Berwick	Jan. 28, 1864	Jan. 28, 1864	M. O. Sept. 8, '65, as Corp'l.
Butler, Abraham	Greenbush	Mar. 10, 1865	Mar. 11, 1865	Mustered out Sept. 8, 1865.
Barber, Robert B....		"	"	" "
Brown, William H....	Chicago	Mar. 1, 1865	Mar. 1, 1865	M. O. Sept. 8,'65, as Corp'l.
Brown, James.....		Mar. 22, 1865	Mar. 22, 1865	M. O. Sept. 8, '65, as Serg't.
Bachus, James W....	Oxford	Feb. 28, 1865	Feb. 28, 1865	Mustered out Sept. 8, 1865.
Bell, James S		Feb. 24, 1865	Feb. 24, 1865	" "
Clark, James..........		Feb. 4, 1864	Feb. 5, 1865	M. O. Sept. 8,'65, as Corp'l.

Name and Rank.	Residence.	Date of rank or enlistment.	Date of muster.	Remarks.
Clark, John		Feb. 4, 1864	Feb. 5, 1865	M. O. Sept. 8, '65, as Serg't.
Crosier, Charles	Ohio Grove	Nov. 27, 1863	Nov. 27, 1863	Mustered out Sept. 8, 1865.
Cochran, Andrew W	Worth	Feb. 24, 1865	Feb. 24, 1865	" "
Conant, William W	Rivola		Feb. 25, 1865	" "
Courson, James	Greenbush	Apr. 11, 1865	Apr. 11, 1865	" "
Cunningham, Thomas	"	Mar. 10, 1865	Mar. 10, 1865	" "
Futhey, Leander	Roseville	Apr. 7, 1865	Apr. 7, 1865	" "
Foster, Silas R	Rivola	Feb. 24, 1865	Feb. 24, 1865	" "
Givens, James		Apr. 20, 1864	June 29, 1864	" "
George, Samuel A	Sumner	Feb. 24, 1865	Mar. 22, 1865	" "
Hogue, Joseph D	Mt. Pleasant		Feb. 24, 1865	" "
Hogue, William H	Tompkins	Nov. 20, 1863	Nov. 20, 1863	" "
Houts, John B	Greenbush	Mar. 10, 1865	Mar. 11, 1865	" "
Houts, Henry	"	Mar. 15, 1865	Mar. 16, 1865	" "
Huditurgh, Isaac H	Lenox	Mar. 10, 1865	Mar. 11, 1865	" "
Hitchcock, Miles	Greenbush	Mar. 12, 1865	Mar. 18, 1865	" "
Hitchcock, Charles	"	Mar. 17, 1865	"	M. O. Sept. 8, '65, as Corp'l.
Hathway, John	Green	Mar. 7, 1865	Mar. 7, 1865	Mustered out Sept. 8, 1865.
Heasley, Joseph L	Rivola	Mar. 24, 1865	Mar. 25, 1865	" "
Harris, William H		Apr. 11, 1865	Apr. 12, 1865	" "
Imnul, James	Greenbush	Mar. 10, 1865	Mar. 16, 1865	" "
Jones, Ambrose	Chicago	Mar. 1, 1865	Mar. 1, 1865	" "
Kelly, Weden	Greenbush	Mar. 10, 1865	Mar. 11, 1865	" "
Lepray, David	"	Mar. 15, 1865	Mar. 16, 1865	" "
Laundaker, Peter	"	Mar. 17, 1865	Mar. 18, 1865	" "
Likens, Samuel		Mar. 7, 1865	Mar. 8, 1865	" "
McClure, Henry B	Roseville	Mar. 6, 1865	Mar. 7, 1865	" "
Miller, Samuel				" "
Morris, Michael	Greenbush	Mar. 10, 1865	Mar. 11, 1865	" "
Moor, George W	Roseville	Mar. 6, 1865	Mar. 7, 1865	M. O. Sept. 8, '65, as Corp.
McGowan, Archie	Swan	Mar. 17, 1865	Mar. 18, 1865	Mustered out Sept. 8, 1865.
McNally, William	Chicago			" "
Ostrander, Charles A.	Roseville	Mar. 6, 1865	Mar. 7, 1865	" "
Owens, James		Mar. 3, 1865	Mar. 4, 1865	" "
Osborn, Aud'w or Jas	Mt. Pleasant			" "
Pinkerton, David	Bremen	Dec. 30, 1864	Dec. 30, 1864	" "
Peck, Andrew	Greenbush	Mar. 10, 1865	Mar. 11, 1865	" "
Parkins, William H	Perryton	Mar. 11, 1865	Mar. 12, 1865	" "
Pointer, Marshall	Chicago	Feb. 24, 1865	Feb. 25, 1765	" "
Ritchie, Lafayette		Mar. 1, 1865	Mar. 2, 1865	" "
Russell, John R	Abingdon	Dec. 14, 1863	Dec. 14, 1863	" "
Rothman, John	Chicago	Feb. 24, 1865	Feb. 25, 1865	" "
Sailer, Joseph H	Roseville	Jan. 23, 1864	Jan. 23, 1864	" "
Shofer, Robert	Union	Mar. 8, 1865	Mar. 8, 1865	" "
Singleton, Joseph R.	"	Mar. 4, 1865	Mar. 4, 1865	" "
Singleton, Allen P	"			" "
Sturgeon, John		Mar. 8, 1865	Mar. 8, 1865	" "
Stacker, Thomas	Greenbush	Mar. 10, 1865	Mar. 11, 1865	" "
Smith, Lucius E	Green	Mar. 7, 1865	Mar. 8, 1865	" "
Tuttle, Simeon H	Roseville	Mar. 6, 1865	Mar. 7, 1865	" "
Taylor, William B	"			" "
Vanvelzer, Francis	Greenbush	Mar. 16, 1865	Mar. 17, 1865	" "
Watson, Hiram		Mar. 2, 1864	Mar. 4, 1864	" "
Wolf, George W	Green	Mar. 10, 1865	Mar. 11, 1865	" "
Welsh, William	Greenbush	Mar. 7, 1865	Mar. 8, 1865	" "
Recruit transferred from 98th Ill. Inf.				
Bartholomew, John	Clay City	Dec. 22, 1863	Jan. 12, 1864	Never rep'rt'd since trans.

COMPANY K.

Name and Rank.	Residence.	Date of rank or enlistment.	Date of muster.	Remarks.
Captains.				
Alfred J. Judy	Sumner	Jan. 1, 1864	Jan. 14, 1864	Resigned Oct. 31, 1864
John G. McCoy	Mt. Erie	Oct. 31, 1864	Mar. 14, 1865	Mustered out Sept. 8, 1865.
First Lieutenants.				
John G. McCoy	Mt. Erie	Jan. 8, 1864	Jan. 14, 1864	Promoted
George Best	"	Oct. 31, 1864	Mar. 16, 1865	Mustered out Sept. 8, 1865.
Second Lieutenants.				
George Best	Mt. Erie	Jan. 8, 1864	Jan. 14, 1864	Promoted
Henry L. Davenport	Sumner	Oct. 31, 1863	Mar. 16, 1865	Mustered out Sept. 8, 1865.

Name and Rank.	Residence.	Date of rank or enlistment.	Date of muster.	Remarks.
First Sergeant.				
William H. Brown	Petty's..........	Dec. 29, 1863	Jan. 14, 1864	Mustered out Sept. 8, 1865.
Sergeants.				
John A. Hite	Christy.........	Dec. 29, 1863	Jan. 14, 1864	Vet. rec. M. O. Sept. 8, '65. Reduced to ranks at his own request
Shirley Trotter.	Bedford	"	"	Vet. rec. M. O. Sept. 8, '65.
Henry L. Davenport..	Christy.......	"	"	Promoted 2d Lieutenant.
John A. Crumbacher.	Bedford	"	"	Mustered out Sept. 8, 1865.
Corporals.				
James Leech..........	Petty's..........	Dec. 29, 1863	Jan. 14, 1864	Died, C'p Butler, Jan. 18, '64.
Mahlon Duke..........	Bedford	Dec. 24, 1863	"	Vet. rec. M. O. Sept. 8, '65, as Sergeant.
Thomas F. Greer.	Christy.......	Dec. 29, 1863	"	M. O. Sept. 8, '65, as Serg't.
Henry L. Adams......	Elm	Dec. 3, 1863	"	Died, C'p Butler, Jan. 19, '64
Wm. H. H. Waggoner	Petty's..........	Dec. 29, 1863	"	Mustered out Sept. 8, 1865.
Rufus G. Winchester.	Johnsonville ..	Jan. 1, 1864	"	Private. Died at Cairo, Jan. 20, 1864
James M. Harlan......	Christy.......	Dec. 29, 1863	"	M. O. Sept. 8, '65, as priv.
Benjamin O. Wilder..	Mt. Erie	Jan. 1, 1864	"	Disch. Jan. 1, '65, as priv.; disability..............
Privates.				
Adams, James A	Elm	Dec. 3, 1863	Jan. 14, 1864	M. O. Sept. 8, '65, as Corp'l.
Ake, William C.......	Mt. Erie	"	"	Mustered out Sept. 8, 1865.
Anderson, John	Elm	Jan. 1, 1864	"	Vet. rec. M. O. Sept. 8, '65.
Baker, Bezin M.......	Petty's..........	Dec. 29, 1863	"	M. O. Sept. 8, '65, as Corp'l.
Bauer, Joseph	"	Jan. 4, 1864	"	Died, C'p Butler, Jan 25, '64.
Berkshire, Ezra	"	"	"	Mustered out Sept. 8, 1865.
Berkshire, Israel.	"	"	"	"
Bradshaw, Ira W	Mt. Erie	Dec. 24, 1864	"	"
Calvin, Reason L.	"	"	"	"
Campbell, Henry L...	Bedford	"	"	"
Cassidy, Joseph K....	"	"	"	Died, C'p Butler, Jan. 24, '64.
Candle, Zachary T. ...	Christy.......	Jan 4, 1864	"	Mustered out Sept. 8, 1865.
Connerly, Kinyon	Bond	Dec. 29, 1863	"	Disch. June 12, '65; disabil.
Davis, John.	"	"	"	Disch. June 14, '64; disabil.
Day, George	Lucan	"	"	Mustered out Sept. 8, 1865.
Deselms, David.......	Bedford	Dec. 24, 1863	"	Died, Mound City, Oct. 17, 64
Evans, Jesse P	"	"	"	Mustered out Sept. 8, 1865.
Galbreath, Edwin.....	Mt. Erie	"	"	"
Griffith, Jonas B......	Johnsonville..	Dec. 3, 1863	"	Vet. rec. Missing since Dec. 25, 1864. Supposed drowned in White River
Gudgel, John S.	Christy	Dec. 29, 1863	"	Mustered out Sept. 8, 1865.
Gunion, James C	Bedford	Jan. 1, 1864	"	Died, Little R'k, June 24, '64
Halcom, Benjamin L.	Christy.......	Jan. 4, 1864	"	Mustered out Sept. 8, 1865.
Harman, James M	Johnsonville ..	Jan. 1, 1864	"	"
Heath, Tobias........	Christy.......	Jan. 4, 1864	"	"
Henderson, Wiley	Bedford	Jan. 1, 1864	"	"
Holmes, Calvin.	Mt. Erie	"	"	"
Jennings, Seth M.....	Petty's..........	Dec. 29, 1863	"	"
Judy, Joseph R.	"	"	"	"
Kimmel, John	Bond.	"	"	Died at Cairo, Feb. 1, 1864
King, William A......	Christy.......	"	"	Disch. May 16, '64; disabil.
Landis, William	"	Jan. 4, 1864	"	Mustered out Sept. 8, 1865.
Lathrop, Thomas K..	Petty's	Dec. 29, 1863	"	"
Laws, Lewis	Christy.......	"	"	Died, Paducah, Feb. 8, '65.
Laws, William M.....	"	Jan. 4, 1864	"	Mustered out Sept. 8, 1865
Loos, Thomas F	Petty's	"	"	"
Malone, John H	Christy.......	"	"	Disch. June 28, '65; disabil.
Mann, Henry B.......	Elm	Dec. 24, 1863	"	Mustered out Sept. 8, 1865.
Mann, Henry H.......	Petty's.........	Dec. 29, 1863	"	"
Maris, John F	Johnsonville	Dec. 24, 1863	"	"
Merrick, James C.....	Mt. Erie	Dec. 3, 1863	"	"
Miller, Oliver M.....	"	Dec. 24, 1863	"	M. O. Sept. 8, '65, as Corp'l.
Miller, William.	"	"	"	
Moore, Robert T	Jeffersonville .	"	"	Mustered out Sept. 8, 1865.
Morse, Henry C.	Ziff............	"	"	Died at Cairo, Apr. 2, 1864.
Musgrave, William H.	Petty's.........	Jan. 4, 1864	"	....
Mushrush, Robert	"	Dec. 24, 1863	"	Mustered out Sept. 8, 1865.
Owen, Hiram P.	Ziff............	Dec. 3, 1863	"	"
Patterson, Nicholas J.	"	Dec. 24, 1863	"	"
Pitman, Joseph P	Bedford	Jan. 1, 1864	"	"
Reeves, Lorenzo.	Christy.......	Dec. 29, 1863	"	Died, C'n Butler, Jan. 16, '64
Robinson, Albertus...	Bedford	Jan. 1, 1864	"	Died at his home ....
Robertson, Thomas J.	"	Dec. 3, 1863	"	Disch. Nov. 20, '64; disabil.
Roderick, John S. ...	Petty's.........	Dec. 29, 1863	"	Mustered out Sept 8, 1865.
Roderick, Thomas L.	....	"	"	

Name and Rank.	Residence.	Date of rank or enlistment.	Date of muster.	Remarks.
Rubencamp, Andrew J	Mt. Erie	Jan. 1, 1864	Jan. 14, 1864	Vet. rec. Dishon. disch. Nov. 8, 1864. ....
Rush, Benjamin F....	Christy	Jan. 4, 1864	"	Died at Duvall's Bluff, Aug. 13, 1864......
Rutherford, John C....	"	Dec. 29, 1863	"	Disch. June 28, '65; disabil.
Sample, William	"	"	"	M. O. Sept. 8, '65, as Corp'l.
Shaw, Eli	Petty's	Jan. 4, 1864	"	Disch. Oct. 24, '64, as Corp'l.
Shick, Francis M.	Lucan	Dec. 29, 1863	"	Discharged Aug. 10, 1864.
Standish, Thomas H.	Mt. Erie	Dec. 3, 1863	"	Mustered out Sept. 8, 1865.
Stout, Abram	Christy	Jan. 4, 1864	"	
Sumner, Henry	"	Dec. 29, 1863	"	" "
Tevis, Lycurgus	Petty's	"	"	" "
Travers, William	Mt. Erie	Dec. 24, 1863	"	Died at Duvall's Bluff, Sept. 21, 1864..........
Turner, Henry C	Christy	Dec. 29, 1863	"	Mustered out Sept. 8, 1865.
Vail, Benjamin F	Bedford	Jan. 1, 1864	"	" "
Walker, Francis M	Mt. Erie	Dec. 24, 1863	"	" "
Wallace, Squire	Johnsonville	Jan. 4, 1864	"	" "
Winchester, D. J	"	Jan. 1, 1864	"	Died at Franklin, Tenn., Apr. 14, 1865.
Winchester, P. W.	"	"	"	Corp'l. Died at Cairo, Jan. 28, 1864
Yocum, Elmore M	Christy	Dec. 29, 1863	"	Mustered out Sept. 8, 1865.
Yohe, Francis M	Mt. Erie	Dec. 24, 1863	"	" "
Yohe, John W	"	"	"	" "
Recruits.				
Ades, Sylvanus	Anderson	Feb. 3, 1865	Feb. 3, 1865	Mustered out Sept. 8, 1865.
Butcher, Lewis	Malom	Mar. 3, 1865	Mar. 3, 1865	" "
Brown, Huston	Martinsville	Feb. 3, 1865	Feb. 3, 1865	" "
Bell, Henry J	Albion	Feb. 3, 1864	Feb. 3, 1864	" "
Cowger, John C	S. West	Feb. 25, 1864	Mar. 3, 1864	" "
Crumbecker, James F	Bedford	Feb. 9, 1864	Feb. 16, 1864	" "
Campbell, Thomas H.	Clark co	Feb. 3, 1865	Feb. 3, 1865	" "
Caldwell, Roland	Oconee	Mar. 15, 1865	Mar. 16, 1865	" "
Campbell, William				" "
Cole, William M	Chicago	Mar. 21, 1865	Mar. 21, 1865	" "
Craig, James	Marion co	Mar. 15, 1865	Mar. 15, 1865	" "
Chafin, John	Chicago	Mar. 21, 1865	Mar. 21, 1865	" "
Donohoe, John	Malom	Mar. 3, 1865	Mar. 3, 1865	" "
Evans, George W	Shelbyville	Mar. 15, 1865	Mar. 15, 1865	" "
Fuson, George P	Embarras	Jan. 5, 1864	Jan. 12, 1864	" "
Griffin, Joseph E.	Washington.	Apr. 5, 1865	Apr. 5, 1865	" "
Higgins, George R.	Hardinsville	Feb. 16, 1864	Feb. 16, 1864	Vet. rec. M. O. Sept. 8, '65.
Hunt, John M	Middleton	Feb. 2, 1864	Feb. 5, 1864	Mustered out Sept. 8, 1865.
Harmon, Jackson	Malom	Mar. 3, 1865	Mar. 3, 1865	" "
Irwin, William H	Johnsonville	Jan. 29, 1864	Jan. 29, 1864	" "
Ivey, Charles	Marion co	Mar. 15, 1865	Mar. 15, 1865	" "
Landis, Jonas	Petty's	Feb. 16, 1865	Feb. 16, 1865	" "
Laws, Elbridge	Parker	Feb. 3, 1865	Feb. 3, 1865	" "
Miller, James	Mt. Erie	Feb. 3, 1864	Feb. 5, 1864	" "
Malcom, John N	Embarras	Jan. 5, 1864	Jan. 12, 1864	" "
North, Charles D	Clay City	Mar. 22, 1864	Mar. 22, 1864	Died, Little R'k., July 7, '64.
Shepley, William	Jerseyville	Jan. 21, 1864	Feb. 22, 1864	M. O. Sept. 8, '65, as Corp'l.
Stine, Michael	Fairfield	Feb. 8, 1864	Feb. 8, 1864	Mustered out Sept. 8, 1865.
Sumner, Alfred M	Marion co	Mar. 15, 1865	Mar. 15, 1865	" "
Stout, Robert C	Alton	Apr. 5, 1865	Apr. 5, 1865	" "
Simms, William H	Marshall	Feb. 3, 1865	Feb. 3, 1865	" "
Smith, Elisha	Malom	Mar. 3, 1865	Mar. 3, 1865	" "
Taylor, William H	Hardinsville	Feb. 16, 1864	Feb. 16, 1864	" "
Terry, Jacob	Embarras	Jan. 5, 1864	Jan. 12, 1864	" "
Thomason, David	Westfield	Feb. 3, 1864	Feb. 3, 1864	" "
Wright, Thomas N	Embarras	Jan. 5, 1864	Jan. 12, 1864	M. O. Sept. 8, '65, as Corp'l.
Watson, Millard F	Chicago	Mar. 21, 1865	Mar. 21, 1865	Mustered out Sept. 8, 1865.
Yocum, Hiel G				" "
Yates, Isaiah	Oconee	Mar. 15, 1865	Mar. 16, 1865	" "

UNASSIGNED RECRUITS.

Name and Rank.	Residence.	Date of rank or enlistment.	Date of muster.	Remarks.
Bratton, William	Jerseyville	Nov. 17, 1863	Dec. 31, 1863	....
Boyd, William	Virginia	Feb. 13, 1865	Feb. 13, 1865	....
Baker, William	Mineral Sprin's	Jan. 31, 1865	Feb. 2, 1865	....
Barlow, Peter C	Barr's Store	Feb. 16, 1865	Feb. 13, 1865	....

Name and Rank.	Residence.	Date of rank or enlistment.	Date of muster.	Remarks.
Carlton, William H...	Glasgow	Sept. 27, 1864	Sept. 27, 1864	Rejected by Board
Clark, Charles	Virginia	Feb. 13, 1865	Feb. 13, 1865	
Carrico, Samuel A	White Hall	Mar. 30, 1865	Mar. 30, 1865	Mustered out June 3, 1865.
Canfield, David L	Marion co	"	"	Mustered out May 11, 1865.
Connell, Edward	Cairo	Feb. 13, 1864	Feb. 13, 1864	
Decker, John H	Albion	Feb. 3, 1864	Feb. 5, 1864	Died, Ca'p Butler, Mar. 6, '64
Dobbins, Vincent	Christy	Feb. 16, 1864	Apr. 5, 1864	
Gates, John W	Hittle	Sept. 28, 1864	Sept. 28, 1864	
Grimm, Napoleon	Richwoods	Oct. 5, 1864	Oct. 6, 1864	Rejected by Board
Hall, Josephus	Calhoun co	Nov. 14, 1863	Dec. 1, 1863	Deserted Dec. 24, 1863
Haner, Augustus	Tazewell co...	Sept. 27, 1864	Sept. 27, 1864	Mustered out May 23, 1865.
Hranitzky, George	Worth	Oct. 21, 1864	Oct. 21, 1864	
Jones, Price M	Barr's Store	Feb. 10, 1865		Mustered out May 21, 1865.
Knight, Joseph	Sandy	Feb. 24, 1865	Feb. 25, 1865	"
Litural, Isaac	Richwoods	Jan. 4, 1864		Deserted Feb. 3, 1864
Lewis, Hark B	Mackinaw	Sept. 28, 1864		
Marsh, Nicholas	N. Western	Sept. 14, 1864	Sept. 14, 1864	
McOlester, Liberty B	Walnut Grove	Feb. 28, 1865	Feb. 28, 1865	Mustered out June 3, 1865.
McDonald, John	Jacksonville	Mar. 31, 1865	Apr. 1, 1865	M. O. to date Sept. 8, 1865.
Matthews, James	Winchester	Nov. 3, 1863	Nov. 3, 1863	
O'Reefe, Patrick	Carrollton	Mar. 15, 1864		Vet. recruit. Rejected
Potter, Charles	"	Jan. 2, 1864	Feb. 2, 1864	
Peters, David	Clear Lake	Sept. 30, 1864	Sept. 30, 1864	
Ramsey, Larkin	Belleview	Mar. 21, 1864	"	Rejected.
Reynolds, Taylor B	"			Died, Ca'p Butler, May 3, '64
Rutherford, George F	Barr's Store	Feb. 15, 1865		Died at Camp Butler
Smith, Riley	Jacksonville	Jan. 4, 1864	Jan. 4, 1864	
Sanders, Simon M	Eastern	Jan. 2, 1864		Deserted Jan. 24, 1864
Spilman, Daniel	Virginia	Feb. 13, 1865	Feb. 13, 1865	
Simons, Daniel A	Dillon	Sept. 27, 1864	Sept. 27, 1864	
Thompson, John	Clear Lake	Sept. 30, 1864	Sept. 30, 1864	
Vogels, Anthony	Carrollton	Jan. 28, 1864	Feb. 22, 1864	
Vaughn, Andrew	Barry	Mar. 8, 1865		Rejected.
Wright, Henry	Woodville	Jan. 2, 1864	May 24, 1864	Mustered out June 8, 1865.
Weatherspoon, Wm. S	Johnsonville	Jan. 29, 1864	Jan. 29, 1864	Died, Ca'p Butler, Feb. 24, '64
Webb, William	Woodville	Oct. 17, 1864	Oct. 18, 1864	Rejected.
Whitten, James M	Walnut Grove	Feb. 28, 1865	Feb. 28, 1865	
Wurman, George	Palatine	Jan. 10, 1865	Jan. 10, 1865	